MW01077031

Alaska and the Yukon

Backroads of
Alaska and the Yukon

LONE
PINE

Joan Donaldson-Yarmey

The Publisher: **Lone Pine Publishing**

206, 10426 – 81 Ave.	202A, 1110 Seymour St.	1901 Raymond Ave. SW, Suite C
Edmonton, AB T6E 1X5	Vancouver, BC V6B 3N3	Renton, WA 98055
Canada	Canada	USA

Canadian Cataloguing in Publication Data

Donaldson-Yarmey, Joan, 1949-
    Backroads of Alaska and the Yukon

    Includes bibliographical references and index
    ISBN 1-55105-217-2

    1. Automobile travel—Alaska—Guidebooks. 2. Automobile travel—Yukon
Territory—Guidebooks. 3. Alaska—Guidebooks. 4. Yukon Territory—Guidebooks.
1. Title.
FC4007.D66 1999   917.19'1043   C99-910321-0
F1091.D66 1999

Editorial Director: Nancy Foulds
Editorial: Volker Bodegom, Lee Craig
Production Manager: Jody Reekie
Layout & Production: Beata Kurpinski, Jau-Ruey Marvin
Book Design: Rob Wiedemann
Cover Design: Rob Wiedemann
Cover Photo: Richard Hartmier, Yukon Dempster Highway at Richardson Mountain
Separations and Film: Elite Lithographers Co. Ltd.

We acknowledge the financial support of the Government of Canada through the Book Publishing Industry Development Program (BPIDP) for our publishing activities.

PC:P6

Canadä

CONTENTS

Dedication

Dedicated to my husband, Metro (Mike Yarmey). Thank you for the fun.

Acknowledgements

The North is such a beautiful place to visit. And the people that one meets here are usually very friendly. However, it is hard to find a northerner born in the North.

Most of the people who work in the service stations and stores in the Yukon come from other parts of Canada. In Alaska, many of the workers in these kinds of businesses come from the lower 48 states to work here during the summer tourist season. A large number of them enjoy the North so much that they stay on after the season ends. As a result of this growing popularity of the North, a resident of Wasilla, Alaska, with whom I talked, stated that he was moving further north because it was becoming too crowded where he lived.

I wish to thank the people of the North with whom I communicated, whether they were native northerners or not, for all the help that they gave me with information, directions and stories.

My editor at Lone Pine Publishing, Volker Bodegom, has done a wonderful job of suggesting the inclusion of extra information, correcting my mistakes and rewriting for clarity. Thank you, Volker.

Introduction

For most people, a visit to the North is a once-in-a-lifetime trip and the planning for it can be intimidating. This book is designed to take you through the Yukon and Alaska (and through parts of northern British Columbia [BC] and into the Northwest Territories [NWT]) with a minimum of fuss and give you as much information as possible to make your trip enjoyable and entertaining.

By following the chapters one after another, you will travel the length of the Alaska Highway, see what the roads of Alaska have to offer, head back into the Yukon to visit its sights and then return to Watson Lake. At Watson Lake you can decide if you want to head southward into British Columbia via the Alaska Highway or via the Cassiar Highway instead. If you average 480 kilometres (300 miles) each day, you should be able to see everything described in this book in one month, or five weeks if you decide to hike the Chilkoot Trail. If you do not have that much time, leave some of the side trips for your next visit—once you see the North, you will definitely plan to return. If you do forego some side trips for now, just remember to reset your odometer as you pass them so that your odometer reading will correspond with the text. Generally, in this book, the odometer is reset after major stops, such as towns, cities and tourist attractions, and sometimes after stopping at pull-outs off the road or after major junctions.

You will be travelling through British Columbia and the Yukon, which generally use the metric system of weights and measures, and through Alaska, which largely uses the imperial system. This book gives both metric and imperial measurements, simplifying the transition.

I cannot possibly mention all of the craft shops, fishing spots, tours, theatres, campgrounds, hiking trails, charters, guides and events—such as fairs and skill demonstrations—in each area. However, most towns have a building where you can pick up pamphlets about the area. These buildings range in size from small cabins to large, multi-roomed structures with slide shows and displays. They may be called 'tourist booth,' 'tourist information centre,' 'visitor information booth' or 'visitor information centre.' To avoid confusion, in this book they are all generally referred to as 'visitor reception centre' or 'visitor centre' for short.

Hiking to falls at Faro.

Many of the places marked on road maps consist of no more than a service station and a lodge, a store, a restaurant and/or a campground. Although not all of them are mentioned in this book, they are spaced at regular intervals (some will warn you how far the next services are), eliminating the need to worry about running out of gas—unless you forget to gas up. Most of these places have displays inside—such as the one about wildlife or the one with thousands of baseball caps—so when you stop to buy gas, take the time to look inside the building. You might find something unusual.

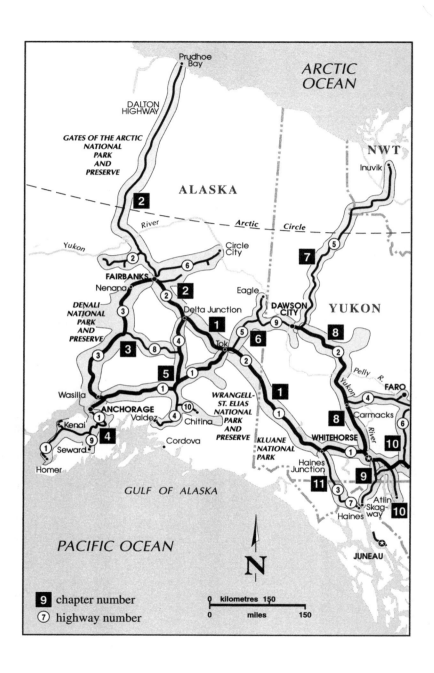

ARCTIC OCEAN

Prudhoe Bay

DALTON HIGHWAY

GATES OF THE ARCTIC NATIONAL PARK AND PRESERVE

NWT

Inuvik

ALASKA

2

River

Arctic *Circle*

Yukon

Circle City

5

7

2

FAIRBANKS

6

Nenana

2

2

Eagle

DAWSON CITY

YUKON

DENALI NATIONAL PARK AND PRESERVE

3

Delta Junction

1

9

8

3

8

4

5

6

Tok

2

Pelly R.

FARO

5

4

Yukon

2

Wasilla

1

1

1

Carmacks

6

ANCHORAGE

Valdez

10

WRANGELL- ST. ELIAS NATIONAL PARK AND PRESERVE

1

8

WHITEHORSE

10

Kenai

4

4

Chitina

KLUANE NATIONAL PARK

River

9

Seward

Cordova

1

Homer

Haines Junction

11

9

GULF OF ALASKA

3

7

Atlin

Skag- way

10

Haines

PACIFIC OCEAN

JUNEAU

N

9 chapter number
⑦ highway number

0   kilometres 150
0   miles   150

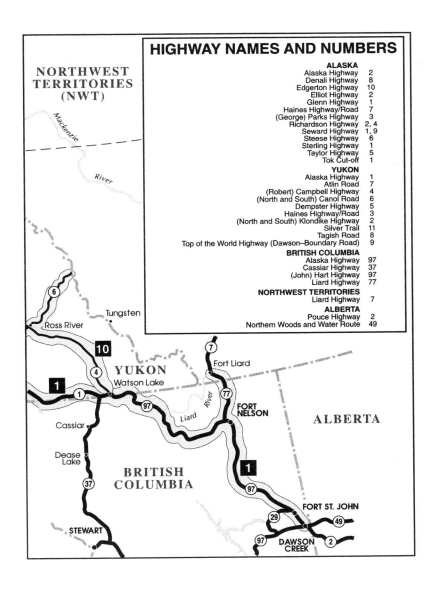

HIGHWAY NAMES AND NUMBERS

ALASKA

Alaska Highway	2
Denali Highway	8
Edgerton Highway	10
Elliot Highway	2
Glenn Highway	1
Haines Highway/Road	7
(George) Parks Highway	3
Richardson Highway	2, 4
Seward Highway	1, 9
Steese Highway	6
Sterling Highway	1
Taylor Highway	5
Tok Cut-off	1

YUKON

Alaska Highway	1
Atlin Road	7
(Robert) Campbell Highway	4
(North and South) Canol Road	6
Dempster Highway	5
Haines Highway/Road	3
(North and South) Klondike Highway	2
Silver Trail	11
Tagish Road	8
Top of the World Highway (Dawson–Boundary Road)	9

BRITISH COLUMBIA

Alaska Highway	97
Cassiar Highway	37
(John) Hart Highway	97
Liard Highway	77

NORTHWEST TERRITORIES

Liard Highway	7

ALBERTA

Pouce Highway	2
Northern Woods and Water Route	49

Old Canadian Imperial Bank of Commerce building in Dawson City.

Sometimes you will have long, scenic drives where the scenery transforms from forest to valleys, to mountains, to rivers, to lakes, to canyons, to hills. It is impossible to describe what is around every curve and up every hill—just be assured that it will be ever-changing.

Many viewpoints and point-of-interest signs give you the history of the area that you are travelling through. Before or after most bridges, a wayside or camping area has been set up. All the pull-outs (called 'turnouts' by the Alaskans), campgrounds, picnic areas, points-of-interest, hiking trails, parks and viewpoints are marked by signs along the highway. Unless otherwise specified, the campgrounds mentioned in this book are government ones. They are usually set beside a river or lake and/or have a hiking trail for you to explore.

On any highway there always seems to be some construction taking place, so you can expect at least one delay on account of road work during your visit. Because of this ongoing construction, which may involve straightening or rerouting the road, the distances given in the text could be off a little bit.

Expect to pay more for groceries and gas in the North and to pay entrance fees at attractions that you wish to visit. Admission to most museums is by donation.

You will be sure to come across animals as you drive along the road. If you encounter large animals while you are in your vehicle, do not get out. Although bears have the biggest reputation of being dangerous, remember that the actions of wild animals of all sizes are unpredictable and that hoofed mammals and smaller animals with sharp teeth can also injure you if they are angry, frightened or hungry.

If you stop to take pictures, park your vehicle off the road as far as possible. Do not encourage animals to come to your vehicle, because they could get run over by another vehicle when they are on the road. And, if they come to your window anyway, do not feed them. Bring binoculars on your trip, for you never know when you will see an animal up a hillside and want to get a better look at it.

When you walk or hike through the bush, always make noise as you walk, so that any bears who might be grazing nearby will notice your approach and have time to leave. If you do come across a bear, back away slowly until you are out of its sight and smelling range. You can return the way you came after it moves on. Visitor reception centres, park offices and ranger stations have more detailed information on how to deal with bears.

Enjoy your visit. The North is like no other place that you have been.

Seafarers' Memorial on Homer Spit.

Helpful Hints

Some out-of-the-way gas stations, grocery stores and gift shops do not take debit cards or credit cards, so make sure that you have some cash with you to pay for your purchases. You can cash in traveller's cheques at larger centres.

Miles Canyon.

If you plan to fish or clam in BC, Yukon, NWT or Alaska, be sure to acquire the correct licence(s). At the place where you get your licence, you can also pick up the current regulations for the area you are in. Regulations for other areas that you might visit are often available at visitor reception centres. Also note that the improper transportation of firearms across the US–Canada border can lead to fines and seizures, so either leave your guns at home or ask about the regulations before you begin your trip.

Make sure that your vehicle has been tuned up and checked for problems before you leave home. Though you will be able to get service and parts in the cities and larger towns, in many smaller places—if there even is a mechanic there—you may have to wait for parts to arrive from elsewhere. Besides a good spare tire, bring along motor oil, belts and wrenches to fit your car.

Put a deflector on the front of your vehicle's hood to help protect the windshield from bugs and flying rocks. Headlight protectors are also a good idea. Take along a tube of Crazy Glue or similar product to put on any rock chips in the glass to prevent cracks from spreading.

On gravel roads in particular, always drive with your lights on. Top up your gas tank before heading out on long gravel roads, not only because of the greater distances between gas stations, but also because of the rougher surfaces, the ups and downs and the frequent slowing down and speeding up, which consume more gas than driving a similar distance on the highway would.

None of the roads described in this book is so remote that would be any longer than a day or so before someone else happens by if you have a vehicle problem, except perhaps in the off-season. If you want to feel safer, or if you decide to take a trip off the beaten track, leave your name and vehicle description, along with information about your planned route and expected return date, with a friend, relative, police officer or store keeper. Include instructions as to what to do if you do not report back by the time that you said you would. (And do be sure to report in when you return!) Do not count on being able to use a cellular phone or even a CB radio to call for help, because mountainous terrain can block the signals from travelling very far (a satellite phone designed for remote use should work, though, but is expensive to operate).

In case you get stranded for several days because of road washouts, vehicle breakdown or other problems, carry extra food, especially canned goods, and some extra drinking water. Blankets or sleeping bags are also a good idea. (If you plan to travel through the North in winter, consult other resources to find out what else you should take.)

Finally, bring along insect repellent, sunscreen and a first aid kit.

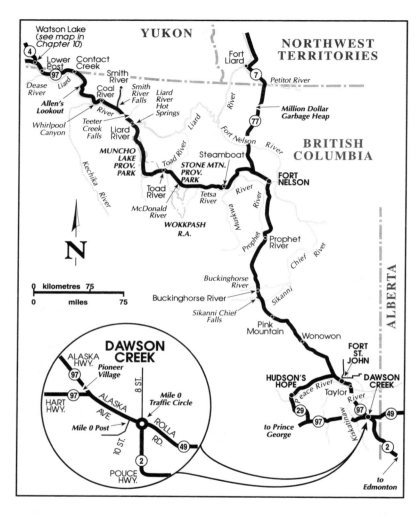

1
The Alaska Highway

The Alaska Highway is one of the most famous highways in the world. Also sometimes called the AlCan Highway (Alaska–Canada), it has a varied and rich history that has lured people from around the world to travel its length to the northern part of North America. As you drive this road and enjoy its ever-changing scenery, you will learn about its history and that of the North. Because you will be so far north, in summer there will be many hours of daylight.

On the 50th anniversary of the building of the highway, North West Highway System (NWHS) signs were put up to mark the original construction camps, airfields, army camps and telegraph stations along it. Some sites are indicated only by a small black-and-white marker, whereas others have a huge NWHS sign and a write-up. These signs are scattered along the highway—although all of them are too numerous to mention in this book, each is worth reading. As you travel the highway and read the signs, you will learn about the difficulties and good times people experienced while building it. There are also other point-of-interest signs that tell about the people, the wildlife and the land of the North.

Expect to take five days to reach Delta Junction.

Dawson Creek to Fort Nelson

Dawson Creek

Dawson Creek is at 'Mile 0' of the Alaska Highway. It is in the Peace River Country in the northeastern part of British Columbia and can be reached by any of three different highways: Highway 97, the John Hart Highway, heads northward from Prince George and becomes the Alaska Highway as it continues north of Dawson Creek; Highway 2 comes from the southeast, through Grande Prairie, Alberta; and Highway 49 comes from the east, also out of Alberta. If you enter Dawson Creek from the west on Highway 97, turn right on Alaska Avenue to go to the Mile 0 Traffic Circle, the true starting point of the Alaska Highway. If you arrive via Highway 2 or Highway 49, you will automatically reach this traffic circle.

Beside the traffic circle is the Northern Alberta Railway (NAR) Park, which contains a 1931 railway station that now houses the Station Museum and a visitor reception centre. At the visitor centre you can get a pamphlet entitled *Alaska Highway Historic Mileposts*, which lists all of the mileposts and gives a bit of their history. While here, you can also book a tour of the Louisiana-Pacific Waferboard plant on the outskirts of town.

The tall grain elevator beside the visitor centre has been renovated to hold the Dawson Creek Art Gallery, which displays works by local artists and travelling collections. The railway car in front is a 1903 model called 'the Blue Goose Caboose.' The Mile 0 Cairn is also in NAR Park. At one time the cairn stood in the centre of

Beginning of Alaska Highway at Dawson Creek.

the traffic circle, however, it was moved to its present site, because tourists would risk their lives dashing across the road to pose beside it.

To see the Mile 0 Post that attests that Dawson Creek is the beginning of the Alaska Highway, from the front of the visitor reception centre, cross Alaska Avenue to 10th Street. Go one block down 10th Street and, in the centre of the Mile Zero Square, you will find the post. The original buildings on the 10th Street block were destroyed when fire ignited 60 cases of dynamite on February 13, 1943.

Blue Goose Caboose in the Northern Alberta Railway Park in Dawson Creek.

The Dawson Creek area was first settled, as an agricultural community, in 1912. In 1930 the town of Dawson Creek was moved here from its original site 3.2 kilometres (2 miles) to the west to become the railhead for the Northern Alberta Railway. The town grew quickly when the US, fearing attacks from the Japanese during the Second World War, decided to construct the Alaska Highway to provide land access to the state.

Work on the 2288-kilometre (1422-mile) 'pioneer road' between Dawson Creek and Delta Junction began in March, 1942, and was completed on November 20 of that same year. During that time, Dawson Creek's population swelled from 518 to over 10,000. More than five thousand train-car loads of materials for construction and equipment for the troops arrived in Dawson Creek during 1942. Today, the industries in and around Dawson Creek include a waferboard (oriented strand board) plant, oil production and tourism.

On your way northward out of Dawson Creek on Alaska Avenue, you come to the junction with the Hart Highway (Highway 97), which goes to Chetwynd and Prince George. Just past that junction is the left turn for the Walter Wright Pioneer Village. In this village you can see a number of old buildings from Dawson Creek, as well as from surrounding communities. The attractions include a general store, antique farm machinery, a tea house and 'Gardens North,' which consists of nine flower-beds and a rose garden. The flowers are best seen in July and August.

The first historic NWHS sign on the highway, on the left after the village, is Historic Milepost 2, which is about US Army Station 2. Then, to your right at

Mile 0 sign in Dawson Creek.

Old building in Walter Wright Pioneer Village in Dawson Creek.

kilometre 2.2 (mile 1.4) from the Walter Wright Pioneer Village, is the Louisana-Pacific Waferboard plant.

As you drive the winding highway through farmland and hills, look to your left at kilometre 18.8 (mile 11.6) from the pioneer village to see a driveway lined with burls.

Farmington and the Kiskatinaw River

At kilometre 21.6 (mile 13.4) from Pioneer Village, a sign says that you are entering Farmington; then you start downhill into a valley. Farmington has a store on the left of the highway with a big stuffed bear (a replica) in front of it.

After Farmington, you come out of the treed valley into open farmland. Then, at kilometre 4.3 (mile 2.7) from the store, turn to the right for the old Kiskatinaw Bridge. You immediately come to a stop sign, where you turn left. You are now driving on an old section of the Alaska Highway that was bypassed during upgrading in 1978.

The pavement here is broken in places, but it is drivable as you go down into the valley of the Kiskatinaw River. At kilometre 4.5 (mile 2.8) from the stop sign, you pass the entrance for Kiskatinaw Provincial Park. Continue ahead to the old bridge, which you reach almost immediately. At a pull-out to the right before the bridge, you can park and take pictures. This white, wooden bridge, built in 1942–43, is 163 metres (534 feet) long and curves to the right at a 9° angle. From the bridge you have a lovely view 30 metres (100 feet) down to the river.

No longer a part of the highway, this bridge is still used by the area's residents. Although the bridge is supposedly two lanes wide, if you see a bus or large truck coming the other way, wait before crossing. After the bridge, the road follows beside the river for a while and, in 5.4 kilometres (3.4 miles) from the bridge, you reach the highway again.

Now go see the new bridge, with its single support system, by turning left on the highway and driving 2.3 kilometres (1.4 miles) back toward Dawson Creek. Park at the near end and walk to the edge of the bank. The one V-shaped support has its bottom sitting on a concrete pillar in the middle of the river.

Old Kiskatinaw Bridge.

Head northward once again and, 15.4 kilometres (9.6 miles) from the bridge, you come to a pull-out and rest area on your right. Here, you can check your brakes and read a sign that describes the descent that you will be making over the next few minutes. As you drive down into the valley, the great views include farmland, the town of Taylor, the Peace River and both the blue bridge and the red-and-white gas pipeline that cross the river.

Taylor

At kilometre 5.2 (mile 3.2) from the pull-out, a sign welcomes you to Taylor. Just past that sign, but before you cross the Peace River Bridge, is another sign that marks the left turn for Peace Island Park, where you can picnic, camp or hike on an island in the river.

On your right, just 0.7 kilometres (0.4 miles) from the highway, you reach the entrance to Peace Island Park. As you follow the road, you can see the island to your right and then you cross a causeway to it. The park

Causeway to Peace Island Park on the Peace River at Taylor.

is open from 7 AM to 11 PM. Dogs are welcome, but must be leashed.

Back at the highway, turn left and cross the bridge over the Peace River. This bridge, like many on this trip, has a metal deck and your steering may be affected. Look to your right, as you cross, to see the red-and-white gas pipeline as it comes out of the river bank, crosses the river and enters the other bank.

During the construction of the highway, two ferries were used to transport workers and vehicles across the river. The crossing was slow and time-consuming. The workers tried three times to build trestles to support a bridge, but each time the pilings were washed out by the river. Finally, a 650-metre (2130-foot) suspension bridge was completed in July 1943—it was one of two such bridges on the highway. It collapsed in 1957 and the current cantilever-and-truss bridge was built in 1960.

As you come off the bridge, you are in the main section of Taylor. Founded in 1912, the town was named after Herbie Taylor, a Hudson's Bay Company trader. Continue along the highway to the visitor reception centre, located in a 1932 pioneer cabin on the left. In its yard there is a large replica of a fur-trade canoe of the type used by

Replica of fur-trade canoe at Taylor.

Alexander Mackenzie on his 8835-kilometre (5490-mile) journey from Montreal, Quebec, to Bella Coola, BC, in the 1790s. He was the first non-Native to cross the North American continent.

World's largest golf ball at Taylor.

On the long weekend in August, Taylor holds an annual World Invitational Class 'A' Championship Gold Panning Competition that attracts professional gold-panners from around the world. Other activities during the weekend include a parade, gold-panning for everyone, claim-staking and bannock baking.

Continue along the highway. Look to your right at the railway crossing to see what is said to be the world's largest golf ball. The giant golf ball is sitting in an open field near the Lone Wolf Golf Club.

After Taylor, you climb out of the Peace River Valley. Take note of the 'Thank You, Come Again' sign as you leave Taylor, because 7.4 kilometres (4.6 miles) from it you reach the left turn for the Honey Place. Drive in. You know you are getting near when bees start hitting your windshield. Bees are constantly flying through the yard, but they are busy and generally ignore you if you leave them alone. Enter the building. Inside, along the right wall, there are three large glass display cases full of working bees. Each case has a clear plastic pipe running from it to a hole in the wall through which the bees come and go on their pollen-gathering expeditions.

You can buy a variety of honey products here. If you would like to sample something unusual, try the flavoured honey sticks, which come in cinnamon, peppermint, strawberry, raspberry, root beer, apple and cherry.

Fort St. John and Charlie Lake

Just 4.1 kilometres (2.5 miles) from the Honey Place, you pass the sign that welcomes you to Fort St. John. Follow the road into town to the traffic lights at 100th Street. Turn right here, go two blocks and turn right again to enter Centennial Park, which contains the city's visitor reception centre and museum and other features of interest. The church here, the Chapel of the Holy Cross, was built in 1934 by Monica Storrs, an Anglican missionary. The one-room trapper's cabin is a replica constructed by the members of the Trapper's Association. Inside are a bed, a little table and a stove. The local oil industry is commemorated here by a pumpjack, a wellhead and a black 46-metre (150-foot) tall oil derrick.

Oil derrick at Fort St. John's Centennial Park.

The Alaska Highway

Construction on the section of the Alaska Highway between Dawson Creek and Delta Junction began on March 8, 1942—less than three months after the bombing of Pearl Harbor. With an agreement that the Canadian section of the Alaska Highway would be turned over to Canada at the end of the Second World War, the Canadian government gave the United States permission to build a road through the northeastern section of British Columbia and the southwestern part of the Yukon.

Thousands of soldiers were sent to the area to begin construction. The road followed Native trails, winter roads and rivers. Where there was nothing to follow, surveyors marked out a route. The routing of the road was designed to follow a line of airfields, 'the Northwest Staging Route,' which ran from Edmonton, Alberta, to Fairbanks, Alaska. Simultaneously, highway construction crews began work in Dawson Creek, Fort Nelson, Whitehorse and Delta Junction (then known as Big Delta). Fort St. John and Whitehorse were the sites of the two largest construction camps.

On September 25, the crews from Whitehorse and Fort Nelson met at Contact Creek and vehicles began travelling that section three days later. On November 20, 1942, the official opening ceremony was held at Soldiers Summit at Kluane Lake, where the crews from Delta Junction and Whitehorse had met on October 29.

This initial construction effort built the pioneer road and the next year it was upgraded to an all-season road by civilian construction crews.

The Canadian part of the highway reverted to Canada in 1946 and was opened to the public in 1948. Despite many twists and curves in the original road, new construction over the years has taken most of them out. For example, in a length of 56 kilometres (35 miles) between Prophet River and Jackfish Creek, 132 curves were removed. The highway is now about 60 kilometres (40 miles) shorter than the first all-season road and about 160 kilometres (100 miles) shorter than the pioneer road pushed through in 1942.

Fort St. John is one of the two oldest non-Native settlements on BC's mainland (in a tie with Hudson's Hope), having been established in 1794, just after Alexander Mackenzie explored the region in 1793 during his trip to the coast. It was originally situated 16 kilometres (10 miles) to the south on the banks of the Peace River, at the mouth of the Moberly River, but it was moved several times before the current location was chosen.

A large oil and gas field was discovered in the area in 1955, and Fort St. John became known as 'the Oil Capital of British Columbia.'

If you wish to get some exercise on a nature trail, turn right when you come out of the park and go 2.7 kilometres (1.7 miles) to East By-pass Road and turn right. Then turn left into the entrance for Northern Lights College and park in the lot. Beside the college is the Fish Creek Community Forest, where there are three self-guided trails, ranging from 30 minutes

Peace River from the Peace River Lookout at Fort St. John.

Charlie Lake.

to 2.5 hours in length. Signs along the trails will help you learn about the insects, birds, animals and plants of the area.

For a view of the Peace River, head back southward on 100th Street past Centennial Park and cross the Alaska Highway at the lights. After you pass businesses and acreages, the road becomes gravel as you work your way down a long hill. In less than 3 kilometres (2 miles), the road curves to your left and you are overlooking the Peace River at Lookout Park.

Back at the set of lights on 100th Street, turn left onto the Alaska Highway. You begin by travelling through an industrial area as you leave town. Then, at kilometre 7 (mile 4.3) from the lights, you enter the community of Charlie Lake, which is spread out along the highway. At kilometre 11.4 (mile 7.1), you come to a junction. To the left, Highway 29 goes to Hudson's Hope and the W.A.C. Bennett Dam. The short road to the right goes to Charlie Lake Provincial Park. There is good fishing for walleye, perch and northern pike on this 16-kilometre (10-mile) long, 3.2-kilometre (2-mile) wide lake. During highway construction, while crossing the lake on pontoon barges, 12 soldiers died.

From the junction, continue along the Alaska Highway and in 13.2 kilometres (8.2 miles) from it you can see a giant statue of a logger on the left at the Clarke Sawmill.

Wonowon, Pink Mountain and Sikanni Chief Falls

Wonowon, formerly 'Blueberry,' is 75.2 kilometres (46.7 miles) from the junction at Charlie Lake. Blueberry was one of many military checkpoints on the Alaska Highway during the Second World War. When the highway was transferred to the Canadian Department of National Defence in 1946, the Royal Canadian Mounted

Police took over staffing the gate. They required that anyone travelling this road carry extra fuel, tire chains, spare parts for their vehicle, tools, food and at least $200. Anyone not having everything on the list was turned back.

In the early 1960s, Blueberry's name was changed to 'Wonowon' a bit of word-play that reflected its location at 'Mile 101' of the highway.

At kilometre 64.5 (mile 40.1) from Wonowon, you reach the settlement of Pink Mountain. It has two service stations, a motel, a grocery store and an RV park. In 24.3 kilometres (15.1 miles) from Pink Mountain, you pass a pull-out for truckers to check their brakes before beginning a steep (nine percent) descent with curves posted at 50 kilometres per hour (30 miles per hour). The Sikanni Chief River and its canyon are to your right as you descend. At kilometre 29.9 (mile 18.6), you reach the bridge over the Sikanni Chief River. Look to your left and you can see pilings in the river, all that is left of the original bridge. Completed in 1943, it was the first permanent bridge on the highway. It was burned by vandals in 1992.

If you want to see Sikanni Chief Falls, watch for the turn-off for the Grassy Gas Field to your left 15.6 kilometres (9.7 miles) from the bridge over the Sikanni Chief River—there is no sign for the falls itself. Turn left onto the gravel oil-field road and in 3.8 kilometres (2.4 miles) you reach a Y. Take the right fork, which does have a sign for the falls, and at kilometre 14.7 (mile 9.1) you come to a three-way branch in the road. Keep to the left

Sikanni Chief Falls.

here and you should see a brown sign for the falls' hiking trail. You arrive at a small parking area with picnic tables in 17 kilometres (10.6 miles) from the highway. The 1.5-kilometre (0.9-mile) hiking trail begins from the parking lot. Much of the trail is downhill, so be sure that you will be able to climb back up. The path is narrow and there are roots underfoot as you walk through the trees.

Soon you come to a sign that points the way back to the parking lot. Just step to your left for a view of the falls. If you want to get closer, follow the path along the ledge to your right. Tread carefully here: part of the trail is along the top of a drop-off. You soon come to a sign cautioning you about the steep cliffs. If you continue, you will arrive at the edge of a cliff, but the trail is quite wide and does lead to a great view of the falls.

Buckinghorse River, Prophet River and Muskwa Heights

From the turn-off for Sikanni Chief Falls, it is 7 kilometres (4.3 miles) to the community of Buckinghorse River, which has a service station, a cafe and a campground.

At kilometre 72.2 (mile 44.8) from Buckinghorse River, you reach Prophet River Provincial Park campground and picnic site, which are on the left. Here, you can walk the first of many self-guided Forest Ecology Tours, called 'Ecotours,' in the

Fort Nelson area. They were established by the Fort Nelson Forest District to give visitors an idea of local landscapes and forest management practices. Pamphlets are available in Fort Nelson, from the forest district office and from the visitor reception centre. Each ecotour is indicated by a sign with a number on it and the word 'site' printed four times around the number. If you miss the ecotours between here and Fort Nelson, many more are along the section of highway between Fort Nelson and Liard River and also along the Liard Highway.

The settlement of Prophet River, at kilometre 88 (mile 54.6), is your last chance to buy fuel until you reach Fort Nelson.

At kilometre 79 (mile 49.1) from Prophet River, you reach Muskwa Heights, a mainly industrial area outside Fort Nelson. Then you begin going downhill into the Muskwa River valley and cross the Muskwa River bridge, which, at 305 metres (1000 feet) above sea level, is the lowest point on the Alaska Highway. When you climb out of the valley, you are in Fort Nelson.

Fort Nelson

The visitor reception centre in Fort Nelson, to your right on Simpson Trail, is in the recreation centre, which also houses the arena. To visit Fort Nelson's community forest, turn onto Simpson Trail and drive five blocks to Mountain View Drive, where you turn left again. Drive past the school to the parking area for the community forest. From here you can hike on two trails, one about 1 kilometre (0.6 miles) long and the other about 2 kilometres (1.2 miles) long.

The Five Sites of Fort Nelson

The first Fort Nelson was established by the North West Company, a rival of the Hudson's Bay Company, in 1805. It was named after Lord Horatio Nelson, the English admiral. The post was moved to a spot south of the original one and in 1813 it was attacked by the Slave people and burned. The eight company employees at the post were killed in the attack.

In 1821, the North West Company merged into the Hudson's Bay Company. In 1865, a third Fort Nelson was built by the company on the banks of the river 1.6 kilometres (1 mile) downstream from the present-day airport. It was erected so that the company could purchase the furs of the area before the Natives could be persuaded to sell them to the newly arriving free traders, who were offering a higher price.

The rising of the Fort Nelson River in the spring of 1890 destroyed this fort and the fourth fort was constructed across the river on higher ground. When the present (fifth) site was established, the fourth fort became known as 'Old Fort Nelson.'

The Fort Nelson Museum is in a log building across the highway from the visitor and recreation centre. In addition to all the displays inside, a number of artifacts are outside the museum. They include an oil derrick, old buildings, old tractors, Model-T cars, road graders, bull dozers and some wooden culverts that were put in during the highway construction and used for 50 years before they were removed in 1992. There is also a 6.7-metre (22-foot) long crankshaft from BC Hydro's Fort

Nelson operations. It was new in 1957 and was in use for 111,722 hours (12 years and nine months) before failure. The museum is open daily from 8:30 AM to 7:30 PM, from May until the end of August.

Fort Nelson Museum.

On Monday, Tuesday, Wednesday and Thursday nights, a 'Welcome Visitor' program runs at the Phoenix Theatre in the Town Square, located one block east of the recreation centre, along the Alaska Highway at 54th Street. Each night a different person gives a talk. You might hear from a resident about past and present times in the area or from a firefighter or from a trapper. If you are staying more than one day, go each night to hear a new talk. Stop in at the visitor centre for more information.

In 1755, the Slave (pronounced 'slay-vee') peoples, now known as the Dene-Dhaa Nation, arrived in the Fort Nelson area from the Great Slave Lake area, with fur traders following in the early 1800s. Until 1922, rivers were the only long-distance routes through this area. In that year, the Godsell Trail was completed from Fort St. John to Fort Nelson. Then, in the 1940s, the Alaska Highway brought much more of the outside world to the area.

Forestry and oil are the main industries in the Fort Nelson area, with agriculture coming in third. The Northwest Energy Plant in Fort Nelson is one of the largest natural gas producers in North America.

Make sure to gas up before you leave Fort Nelson, especially if you are planning to take a side-trip to Fort Liard, because the only services along the Liard Highway are at Fort Liard.

The Liard Highway to Watson Lake

The Liard Highway

At kilometre 28 (mile 17.4) from the Fort Nelson Museum, you reach the junction with the Liard Highway (Highway 77). Turn right here to take a detour off the Alaska Highway to head for the NWT and Fort Liard. Note that there are no services for the next 175 kilometres (110 miles). Highway 77 is a gravel road that is wide enough for two vehicles to pass. The speed limit is 80 kilometres per hour (50 miles per hour).

In 40 kilometres (25 miles) from the Alaska Highway, you begin a downhill descent to the Fort Nelson River, which you cross on a one–lane bridge at kilometre 42.3 (mile 26.3). At 4 metres (13.1 feet) wide and almost 0.5 kilometres (0.3 miles) long, it is believed to be the longest Acrow (or Bailey) bridge in the world. A rest area is after the bridge. On a sign posted here, the local First Nations people have described how they monitor the changes in the river because of the fishing and hunting they do along it.

Look to your left through an opening in the trees at kilometre 97.2 (mile 60.4) to see some long concrete beams almost overgrown with grass. This site is known locally as 'the Million Dollar Garbage Heap.' These concrete beams fell off a truck during the construction of the Petitot River bridge; this accident delayed the completion of the bridge by a year. The beams, which are about 9 metres (30 feet) long, have rusted cables sticking out of the ends.

Fort Nelson River Bridge on the Liard Highway.

At kilometre 36.5 (mile 22.7) from the beams, you reach an 11 percent descent that leads to the Petitot River. This river, called *Meh Cho La* by local Natives, was renamed to honour a Father Petitot of the Oblates of Mary Immaculate, who travelled throughout the North in the mid-1800s teaching the written form of the Dene language. It was at the Petitot River bridge that the ceremonies for the opening of the Liard Highway were held on June 23, 1984. However, instead of cutting the ribbon with scissors, a 1926 Model-T Ford was used; the ribbon was stretched 6 metres (20 feet) along the road before it broke.

Just before the bridge, there is a pull-out; a road from it leads down to a boat and canoe launch.

As you climb above the river on the other side, look to the right to see the river valley. In 3.6 kilometres (2.2 miles) from the bridge, a green sign announces the border between BC and the NWT, where there is a time-zone change. From the border, it is a further 38.2 kilometres (23.7 miles) to Fort Liard.

Fort Liard has a long, warm summer and produces bountiful gardens. It is one of the oldest continually occupied places in the NWT. Although the Slave people live here now, the Small Knife people occupied the area for 9000 years previously.

Stop in at Acho Dene Crafts, on your right at Poplar Road as you come into town. Among the craft items for sale are birch-bark baskets, in a range of sizes, with lovely quill designs on them. Or you might want to purchase moccasins, a change purse or a glasses case, all made of moosehide and also decorated with quills.

BC/NWT border on Liard Highway.

Steamboat and Stone Mountain Provincial Park

Back on the Alaska Highway, as you travel toward Watson Lake, you are driving through the Muskwa Range of the Rocky Mountains. It is 32.5 kilometres (20.2 miles) from the junction with the Liard Highway to Steamboat Creek and the beginning of the climb up Steamboat Mountain. At kilometre 49 (mile 30.4), you reach the settlement of Steamboat, which is marked by a service station and store on the left. As you continue climbing after Steamboat, you can look down on the valley of the Muskwa River.

In 6.8 kilometres (4.2 miles) from Steamboat, you begin descending, and, at about kilometre 15 (mile 9), you can see Indian Head Rock straight ahead.

You then descend into the Tetsa River valley and, at kilometre 39 (mile 24.2), you reach the entrance to Tetsa River Outfitters on your left. A craft shop here sells moccasins and mitts and home-made sourdough bread.

The road is narrow and winding as you follow the Tetsa River. Watch for falling rock and curves posted at 40 kilometres per hour (25 miles per hour). At 13.3 kilometres (8.2 miles) from the outfitters, you cross the Tetsa River Bridge #1. In 1.6 kilometres (1 mile) from the first bridge, you cross the Tetsa River Bridge #2. At kilometre 9.6 (mile 6), you enter Stone Mountain Provincial Park. You reach the community of Summit Lake at kilometre 12 (mile 7.5). Just past the lake itself, you reach Summit Lake Pass, which is the highest point on the Alaska Highway, with an elevation of 1295 metres (4250 feet), and subject to sudden weather changes.

At kilometre 3.7 (mile 2.3) from the pass, look to your right to see erosion pillars up on the hillside. There is a pull-out on the left, across the highway from a 0.5-kilometre (0.3-mile) hiking trail to the pillars. Shortly after the pull-out, you round a curve and have a better view of the pillars on the right. Watch for Stone sheep—a blackish colour phase of white (Dall) sheep—in this area, especially around kilometre 5 (mile 3).

At kilometre 6.2 (mile 3.8), you have a great view of the MacDonald River valley below, with mountains above it. You reach Rocky Mountain Lodge at kilometre 8.4 (mile 5.2) and you start climbing again above the MacDonald River. After following the MacDonald River for a while, you cross it at kilometre 30.8 (mile 19.1). Kilometre 49.7 (mile 30.9) brings you to the community of Toad River.

Toad River and Muncho Lake Provincial Park

Toad River has a lodge, a service station, a cafe, a store and a campground. Walk inside the lodge and look at some of the baseball caps hanging on the walls and from the ceiling. Although more than 5500 are in the collection, some of them are packed away because there isn't enough space to display all of them at the same time. Many of the caps were left here one at a time by visitors who passed through and were inspired to leave theirs, while others have been donated by visitors as cap collections. One such collection came from a man who, with his wife, had planned a trip north. He had decided that he would bring his assortment of caps to leave at

Alluvial Fans

You are in flash-flood country. A flash-flood results when a heavy summer downpour falls on the mainly bare mountainsides. The water washes soil, pebbles, vegetation and even boulders down the ravines between the mountain peaks, to be deposited on the valley floor. Over the centuries, 'alluvial fans' have formed at the bottoms of these ravines, where the water spreads out, slows down and begins to seep into the ground, leaving the solid material behind.

Alluvial fan.

Each time a flash-flood occurs, the streams take a somewhat different route down the mountain, thus distributing this debris, called 'alluvial,' (from a Latin word that means 'wash'), evenly over the ground and building up the fan.

There is a good example of an alluvial fan across the highway from Centennial Falls.

the lodge. Unfortunately, he passed away before they could make the trip, so the widow came on her own with her late husband's 500 caps.

You enter Muncho Lake Provincial Park, 7.1 kilometres (4.4 miles) from Toad River. At kilometre 9.7 (mile 6), look up to see Folded Mountain. The layers of rock look like the mixture for marble cake when you swirl the chocolate and the white batters together. A viewpoint for Folded Mountain is to your left at kilometre 11.2 (mile 7). Folded Mountain is a result of the North American continent pushing westward, catching what was then the continental shelf between it and offshore islands. The flat layers of the shelf buckled upward into the folds that you see on the mountain.

At 8.9 kilometres (5.5 miles) from the viewpoint, watch on your left for Centennial Falls, a long, slim line of water that comes down the hillside to a roadside ditch that empties into the Toad River.

At about kilometre 29 (mile 18), you begin to see the Sawteeth, part of the Sentinel Range, which were formed when huge slabs of dolomite were pushed up during the formation of these mountains.

At kilometre 41.1 (mile 25.5), you come over a hill and beautiful emerald Muncho Lake is in front of you. There are service stations, lodges, cafes and campgrounds beside the highway as it curves along the lakeshore. As with Summit Lake Pass, watch for sudden weather changes in this area, too.

Muncho means 'big lake' in the language of the Tagish First Nation. The lake, which is 12 kilometres (7.5 miles) long, is up to 60 metres (200 feet) deep and reaches a temperature of 10° C (50° F) in summer. Its colour comes from rock particles that

Muncho Lake.

Liard River Bridge.

are ground by glaciers and brought down to the lake by mountain streams. This fine, flourlike glacial silt remains suspended in the water and reflects the blue-green part of the light spectrum for viewers to see.

At kilometre 54.4 (mile 33.8), there is a viewpoint that overlooks Muncho Lake and has some information panels about it. At 15.5 kilometres (9.6 miles) from that viewpoint, a road goes to a natural animal mineral lick. Turn left onto this road and drive 0.2 kilometres (0.1 miles) to the parking area. Take the gravel path that leads from the parking area, and choose the right fork when you come to a Y. The descending path, well used by humans and animals, has been fitted with steps in places. Look down through the trees to your right to see a ridge of erosion pillars. When you reach another Y, take the left fork and you soon arrive at the mineral lick, which is at a fenced area overlooking the Trout River and its valley.

Back on the highway, in 5.7 kilometres (3.5 miles) from the turn-off for the mineral lick, you cross the Trout River. At 10.5 kilometres (6.5 miles), you leave Muncho Lake Provincial Park. You descend into the valley of the Liard River. The name 'Liard' came about because the French Canadian fur traders travelling through this country called the poplars along the river 'liards.' The Liard River is beside you at kilometre 19.4 (mile 12). After a lovely drive through the valley, you reach a bridge that spans the Liard River. This 348-metre (1143-foot) long bridge is now the only suspension bridge on the Alaska Highway.

Essential Minerals

The sediment at this mineral lick is mainly rock flour ground off the mountains by the movement of glaciers centuries ago. This rock flour contains calcium, phosphorus, sulphur, sodium and magnesium—elements essential to the development of teeth, bones, antlers and hair.

During spring and summer, female animals who are nursing their young will come here for the minerals, and so will male animals who are growing antlers. The best time to watch for moose, caribou and Stone sheep around the lick is in the early morning or evening. You may see smaller animals using it, too.

Columns at mineral lick.

Liard River Hot Springs

Just past the Liard River bridge, you enter Liard River Hot Springs Provincial Park and reach the community of Liard River. Downstream from the bridge is the Liard River's Grand Canyon, which can be reached by boat or by helicopter; a third option, a 12.8-kilometre (7.9-mile) path along the river bank, is not recommended by area residents.

The Liard River Hot Springs

The Kaska people, who lived and hunted in the region of the Liard River Hot Springs, used the waters to soothe and heal. The first recorded account of the springs is in the 1835 journal kept by Hudson's Bay Company explorer Robert Campbell. In the 1920s, the area was homesteaded for a few years by a man named John Smith.

During construction of the Alaska Highway, a camp, a sawmill, a hospital and a fuel depot were situated at the nearby crossing of the Liard River. Because of the dust in summer, mud in fall and cold in winter, the workers who lived in the camp spent much of their free time in the hot springs. They built the first boardwalk to the pools but, after the highway was completed, the hot springs were left to nature. In the 1950s, renovations and repairs were made to the site by nearby highway residents. Liard River Hot Springs Provincial Park was dedicated in 1957, and these days up to 150,000 people visit the site every year.

Alpha Pool at Liard Hot Springs.

During the construction of the Alaska Highway, the engineers decided that it would be easier to build if they avoided the Grand Canyon of the Liard and instead followed the Toad River, routed the road beside Muncho Lake and then followed the Trout River to the upper Liard River.

To your right, less than 1 kilometre (0.6 miles) from the bridge, is the Liard River Hot Springs Provincial Park Campground. Signs in the parking area direct you to a boardwalk trail that leads to the two pools. Although the changing rooms and both pool areas are wheelchair accessible, there are no special arrangements for wheelchair users to enter the water. Along the boardwalk through the warm-water swamps and the forest, signs tell you about the plants that grow in the warm climate created by the hot springs, the animals that come to eat them and the small fish that swim in the waters beneath the boardwalk.

Watch for moose: they are frequently seen eating or walking through the bush. Take a deep breath as you stroll and enjoy the warm forest smell. The area was known as 'the Liard Tropical Valley' during the 1940s. Orchids, luxuriant ostrich ferns and cow-parsnips are among the more than 250 plant species that grow here. Many of these plants survive only because of the warmth of the hot springs.

The first pool that you reach is Alpha Pool. There are three different sets of steps into this rectangular pool, which has benches in the middle where you can sit as you enjoy the warm water. Take it slow getting into the pool, because the water temperature averages about 45° C (113° F). On a cool day you can see steam rising off the waters.

When you are done here, follow the signs along the boardwalk toward Beta Pool. On the way, you reach the steps to the hanging gardens, where you can see mosses and wildflowers, some usually not found this far north, growing over a rock-face. Climb up to the second viewpoint to see the gardens from above.

Continue along the boardwalk, at an uphill slant, to Beta Pool. The little streams, flowers and other plants along the way create a setting reminiscent of a rainforest. Beta Pool, smaller than Alpha Pool and round, is 3 metres (10 feet) deep. There are no benches and the temperature is about the same as at Alpha Pool. Look down to see the water bubbling up from the bottom.

Teeter Falls and Smith River Falls

For a relaxing stroll in the forest, and to see the falls on Teeter Creek, watch for a gravel road to your right at 8.1 kilometres (5 miles) from the turn-off for the Liard River Hot Springs. This road goes to a small, circular area just below the highway. Follow the easy, level trail along Teeter Creek through the tall shade trees. You soon reach a bridge over Teeter Creek on which you can stand to take pictures of the small falls. The brown box and numbered stick beside the falls are for measuring the water level.

What you see from the bridge, however, is only a part of the falls. You may want to cross the bridge to the opposite bank and climb the steep trail for a better view of some other cascades of the falls. However, it is a very steep climb on the edge of the cliff, so you do so at your own risk.

Back on the highway, you soon drive over the Teeter Creek culvert and in 19.7 kilometres (12.2 miles) from that culvert you cross a bridge over the Smith River. A

Teeter Creek Footbridge at Teeter Creek Falls.

short distance beyond, at kilometre 20.1 (mile 12.5), there is a one-lane gravel road on your right that leads to Smith River Falls.

At 2 kilometres (1.2 miles) from the highway, you reach a parking area. The trail to the falls begins at the far end of the parking lot. It is a steep descent on steps and then on a path. You get your best view of the falls when you come to an unfenced viewpoint on a cliff.

To reach the river's edge, continue down more steps, into a canyon with black, ochre and grey walls. Here, you can see only the bottom part of the falls. The water roars as it plunges over the rock—the force of the falls creates a mist at the bottom and produces waves that lap up onto the narrow, gravelly beach.

If you have to choose between seeing this waterfall or the one on Teeter Creek, pick this one. It is more spectacular and the walk, though steeper, takes about the same amount of time.

Coal River, Whirlpool Canyon and Contact Creek

The settlement of Coal River is 33.3 kilometres (20.7 miles) from the turn-off for Smith River Falls. Then you cross the mouth of the Coal River. Look to your left to see it flowing into the Liard River. At kilometre 39.3 (mile 24.4), you reach a turn-off to your left for Whirlpool Canyon, known to some people as 'Mountain Portage Rapids.'

Turn off here and park in the campground. Then walk across the huge pile of driftwood and rock to reach the path to the top of the canyon wall. Follow the path along the edge of the canyon with care, because there is no fence. The water sometimes carries logs as it churns and swirls around huge rocks and islands in the middle of the river below.

Smith River Falls.

At kilometre 46.3 (mile 28.8) from the canyon, you can stop in at Allen's Lookout, on the left. During the late 1800s, a band of robbers watched from this vantage point for boats travelling on the river. When they spotted one, they hurried down to their own boat, overtook the other boat and relieved the travellers of their goods. More recently, a cairn dedicated to the surveyors of the Alaska Highway was placed here.

Contact Creek is 27.3 kilometres (17 miles) from the lookout. It is here that soldiers of the 340th Regiment of the United States Army Corps of Engineers, working simultaneously from the southeast and the northwest, met. The creek was named to commemorate the completion of construction on the southern section of the Alaska Highway pioneer road.

Whirlpool Canyon, or Mountain Portage Rapids.

In 1957, the original bridge across Contact Creek was torn down and a second one built. The second bridge was then replaced in 1997.

On the other side of Contact Creek you enter the Yukon. Between here and Morely Lake, near Teslin, the highway crosses the BC–Yukon border a number of times, but it is marked only three times.

You pass Contact Creek Lodge and Iron Creek Lodge and then, at kilometre 47 (mile 29.2) from the border crossing at Contact Creek, you reach the left turn for Lower Post.

Lower Post

Just 1 kilometre (0.6 miles) from the highway, the hamlet of Lower Post, which is in BC, is billed as 'the Home of the Kaska Dena Nation.'

Lower Post, at the

The Evolution of a Name

The name 'Yukon' is derived from the Gwich'in (Loucheux) word *Yu-kun-ah*, which means 'big river.' What we now know as the Yukon was occupied almost entirely by Native peoples until the 1820s, when non-Native explorers began travelling the land. In the 1840s, fur traders set up a few Hudson's Bay Company posts in this region. Prospectors came looking for gold in the 1880s and, in 1896, gold was discovered on Rabbit Creek, later renamed 'Bonanza Creek.' (See sidebar 'The Beginning of the Klondike Gold Rush' on p. 154.)

This discovery quickly resulted in a population explosion, as thousands of men and women and their children arrived, hoping to find their fortunes. Because of this influx of humanity, the area was officially entered into the Confederation of Canada and designated as 'The Yukon Territory' on June 13, 1898.

Eventually, the word 'territory' was dropped and this part of Canada was commonly called 'the Yukon.' Therefore, in this book, 'the Yukon' is used throughout the text, although the author recognizes that many people use the name 'Yukon' by itself, just as 'Alberta' and 'Alaska' do not need the 'the.'

Yukon sign.

junction of the Liard and Dease rivers, was a Native village site that became a stop for miners and trappers travelling the rivers. A Hudson's Bay Company trading post was built here in the 1800s. The settlement had the names 'Sylvester's Lower Post' and 'Liard Post' before becoming 'Lower Post.'

In an effort to make an overland route from Edmonton, Alberta, to the Klondike, the North-West Mounted Police cut a trail that ran through this area, but it was abandoned because it took too long and the country was too rugged. A wagon trail to Watson Lake was constructed and it eventually became part of the original Alaska Highway. During highway construction, the military set up a sawmill here to cut bridge timbers.

From Lower Post, you can drive toward Watson Lake for about 2 kilometres (1.2 miles) along the old pavement that was bypassed by new highway construction in 1985. Park when you reach a berm pushed up to stop traffic. Walk around the

Some Yukon Facts

Although Dawson City was the capital of the Yukon at the time of its joining Confederation, the capital was moved to Whitehorse in 1953. Whitehorse is home to about two-thirds of the Yukon's population of about 33,000.

The highest mountain in Canada, Mount Logan, is in the Yukon. According to Natural Resources Canada, it is 5959 metres (19,550 feet) high. With a base nearly 160 kilometres (100 miles) in diameter, Mount Logan is considered to be the world's largest mountain massif—a huge piece of the earth's crust that has moved upward as a whole.

The Yukon and Porcupine rivers are the two main rivers in the territory. The Yukon River is (according to Heritage Rivers) almost 3200 kilometres (2000 miles) long, making it the fourth longest river on the continent. The waters of Bennett Lake flow into Tagish Lake, which in turn flows into Marsh Lake. The beginning of the Yukon River is at Marsh Lake. It heads northward to Dawson City and then into Alaska. The Porcupine River, with the settlement of Old Crow on its banks, is further north.

The Yukon is warm and sunny in summer and dry and cold in winter.

berm to a bluff from which you can look down on the traffic on the new part of the highway. Return through Lower Post to get onto the highway again.

At kilometre 17.1 (mile 10.6) from the turn-off for Lower Post, a sign at the Yukon border says 'Welcome to Canada's Yukon.'

You reach the Liard Canyon Recreation Site, situated to the left, on the shore of Lucky Lake, 22.7 kilometres (14.1 miles) from the sign at the border. Nearby is the Watson Lake–Lucky Lake Waterslide Park.

Lucky Lake, a 'kettle lake,' was created by a huge piece of glacial ice that was left buried in glacial till as the glaciers around it melted away. When this piece finally melted, too, it left a hole in which the lake formed. Some people say that the lake got its name during highway construction when a 'lady of the evening' set up a tent on its shore. Her visitors liked to say that they were getting a change of luck when they went into her tent, therefore 'Lucky Lake.'

For an easy hike through the trees to the beginning of Liard Canyon, walk into the park from the parking lot. To your right, there is a map of the Liard River Canyon walking trail. It is a 2.2-kilometre (1.4-mile) self-guided trail that descends gradually to the Liard River.

You begin walking past picnic tables on a sandy path between pine trees. The further you go, the wetter the soil. The

Platform at Liard Canyon near Lucky Lake.

pines gradually give way to spruce and poplar. It is a lovely walk among these trees, which are some of the tallest in the Yukon, thanks to the rich soils of the Liard River basin.

When you reach the river, stand on the platform there. To your right there are trees right down to the river bank and to your left is the 400-to-500-million-year-old rock wall that marks the beginning of the Liard River Canyon. The water that flows past you goes to the Mackenzie River and will eventually end up in the Beaufort Sea.

Watson Lake

In 5.8 kilometres (3.6 miles) from Lucky Lake, a sign welcomes you to Watson Lake (incorporated in 1984). Watson Lake, on the 60th parallel, is called 'the Gateway to the Yukon.' The town began as a trading post in Kaska Dena First Nation territory. The official history is that the settlement was named after a trapper and prospector named Frank Watson who homesteaded in the area of the lake with his Kaska Dena wife. Another story states it was named for Bob Watson, who had a store here in the 1930s. Since the Alaska Highway was built, Watson Lake has grown into a major centre that supplies and serves the logging, mining and tourism industries of the region.

Continue up the highway until you come to the visitor reception centre at the junction with Highway 4, the Robert Campbell Highway, which goes past Ross River (see Chapter 10). Turn right to visit 'the Sign Post Forest.' This collection of signs began with one sign put up during the construction of the Alaska Highway. A soldier was given the task of repainting the direction sign on the highway and, being lonely for his home town of Danville, Ohio, he added a sign for it. Other soldiers joined in and the practice was continued by visitors who have been adding home-made signs or ones from their towns as they pass through. There are now long rows of sign-filled posts and the forest is growing every year. If you want to contribute a sign of your own, bring along a hammer and nail to mount it.

Watson Lake Sign Post Forest.

The Yukon Gold Explorer's Passport

To make a person's visit to the Yukon more enjoyable, Tourism Yukon gives out 'Yukon Gold Explorer's Passports,' which can be picked up at visitor reception centres or museums in the Yukon. There are 14 designated sites where you can get your 'passport' stamped.

When you have reached the last site that you plan to visit, fill in the entry form at the back and turn in your passport. It will be stamped, the entry form removed and the booklet given back to you. If you have collected 10 or more stamps, you will immediately receive a poster and your name will be put into the monthly draw to win 31.1 grams (1 troy ounce) of gold. Collecting all 14 stamps means that you are eligible to win 155.5 grams (5 troy ounces) of gold, the winner to be drawn in September. If you win in one of the draws, you will be notified at the address you give.

The program runs from the beginning of June to the beginning of September.

On the same property as the signs, there is some old machinery that was used in the building of the Alaska Highway. One of the pieces is an orange tractor called 'Gertrude.' This 1938 TD 35 International tractor came to the Yukon with her owner, Ed Kerry, in 1942. She worked all over the Yukon for 40 years and was then donated to the Yukon Government by the Kerry family in memory of Ed Kerry.

There is also a model of a Bell P-39 Airacobra plane. More than eight thousand of these planes stopped in at Watson Lake between 1942 and 1954. During the Second World War (when the Russians were on the same side as the Americans), these American P-39s were painted with Russian military insignia and then flown from Great Falls, Montana, to Fairbanks, Alaska, refueling at airfields along the Alaska Highway. Russian pilots then flew them to Nome, Alaska, and across the Bering Sea to Siberia. From there they were sent to the Russian front.

The aurora borealis (northern lights) phenomenon is best seen in winter and, the further north you are, the clearer and brighter they appear. However, most people visit Watson Lake in summer, when there are nearly 24 hours of daylight. To allow summer visitors to see this magnificent light phenomenon, the state-of-the-art Northern Lights Centre, across the Alaska Highway from the visitor centre and one block south, puts on several shows every day between 2 PM and 10 PM, from May into September. Just sit in your chair while the northern lights dance overhead.

Upper Liard to Whitehorse

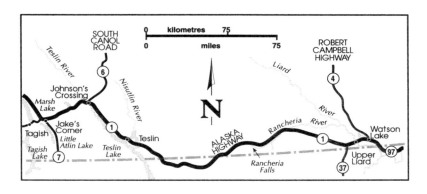

Upper Liard, Rancheria and Swift River

Continuing along the highway, you cross the Upper Liard River bridge 10.1 kilometres (6.3 miles) from the Sign Post Forest in Watson Lake. Across the bridge, to your left, is the hamlet of Upper Liard. To your right is Our Lady of the Yukon Church.

This church was built in 1955 by the priest in charge and members of the local Kaska Dena community. In the yard there is a four-sided building, each side with a mural on it. The murals depict the story of White Calf Woman receiving from Medequdihte—the Creator of the Lakota Sioux and other Native nations—the sacred pipe, which she is to take to her people.

At kilometre 9.8 (mile 6.1) from Upper Liard, you reach the junction with the Cassiar Highway (Highway 37), which heads southward into BC. When you reach kilometre 13 (mile 8.1), for the next 7 kilometres (4.3 miles) watch the hillsides for the long series of names and messages spelled out with rocks.

You cross the Lower Rancheria River at kilometre 71.6 (mile 44.5) and, at kilometre 72.5 (mile 45), a view of the river and canyon is to

Mural at Upper Liard Village.

Early Highway Service

Bus service between Dawson Creek, BC, and Whitehorse, Yukon, began in 1946. The British Yukon Navigation Company (BYN), which owned the buses, built four lodges along the highway to feed the passengers and supply gas to the buses.

Rancheria Lodge, constructed of logs, was one of these original lodges. Over the years, other roadhouses and lodges were built to accommodate the growing number of travellers. They served meals, provided rooms and sold gas; some were open year-round.

However, many of the original lodges have been destroyed by fires caused by faulty wiring or problems with the wood heating. Although new facilities have often been built to replace the ones destroyed, sitting in a large, modern restaurant is not the same as sitting in a piece of history.

your left. Then, at kilometre 93.3 (mile 57.9), you reach George's Gorge. Look to your right to see some of the gorge.

Rancheria Lodge, with a service station, a motel, some cabins, a restaurant and an RV park, is at kilometre 107.5 (mile 66.8).

A turn-off for Rancheria Falls Recreation Site is 12.6 kilometres (7.8 miles) from Rancheria Lodge, but there is no sign along the highway. A map at the parking area shows the 0.5-kilometre (0.3-mile) interpretive trail to the falls and a portage trail to the river. The interpretive trail, which is wheelchair accessible, begins as a path and then you continue on a boardwalk.

You are walking through a spruce forest in the rugged country of the Continental Divide between the watersheds of the Yukon and Mackenzie rivers. The Rancheria River flows east into the Liard River, which drains into the Mackenzie River and ends up at the Beaufort Sea. West of here, water off the mountainsides drains into the Swift River, enters the Yukon River and eventually flows into the Bering Sea.

A platform overlooks the first falls. From here you can take the portage path to the river, where there is a pool good for grayling fishing. Continue along the boardwalk to the second waterfall. Neither of the falls is very high but the walk past the craggy rocks and trees to see the river and canyon walls is worth the time.

As you continue along the highway, you pass Walker's Continental Divide (a service station and restaurant) and then cross the Upper Rancheria River at kilometre 5.9 (mile 3.7) from the turn-off for the falls. At kilometre 7.2 (mile 4.5) to your right, there is a pull-out with a sign about the Continental Divide and a map that shows where the divide runs through the Rocky Mountains and where the highway crosses it.

Four kilometres (2.5 miles) from the sign about the Continental Divide, you cross the

Rancheria Falls #2.

Swift River. You reach the settlement of Swift River, with its service station and lodge, at kilometre 16.5 (mile 10.2).

You dip back into BC at kilometre 17.3 (mile 10.7) and do not get back into the Yukon until kilometre 82.7 (mile 51.4).

Morley River and Teslin

In 2.8 kilometres (1.7 miles) from where you re-enter the Yukon, you pass by the Morley River Lodge, which has a service station, a campground and a coffee shop.

Nisutlin River Bridge at Teslin.

Watch to your left at kilometre 9.7 (mile 6) for a small, white cairn with a white fence around it, erected in memory of Max Richardson, a Corporal with Co. 'F' of the 340th Regiment of the United States Army Corps of Engineers. Although the cairn states that he died October 17, 1942, it does not say where or how.

At kilometre 39.4 (mile 24.5), you round a curve and begin driving along Teslin Lake. Teslin Lake, at about 125 kilometres (78 miles) long and 3 kilometres (2 miles) wide, is aptly named: 'Teslin' is from the Tlingit First Nation word *Tes-lin-too*, meaning 'long, narrow lake.' You soon reach the Nisutlin Bridge, which crosses Nisutlin Bay, an arm of Teslin Lake into which the Nisutlin River drains. With a length of 0.6 kilometres (0.4 miles), the Nisutlin Bridge is the longest water-span bridge on the Alaska Highway. Just before the bridge, there is a pull-out to your right where you can park to take some photographs or launch a boat.

The village of Teslin, home to one of the largest Native populations in the Yukon, is at the other end of the bridge. The Tlingit First Nation was established in the Yukon and Alaska long before the Russians arrived in the late 1700s, looking for furs. A Hudson's Bay Company post was established here on the lakeshore in 1903 to trade with the then-nomadic Tlingit people of the area.

Visit the George Johnston Museum, which is 1 kilometre (0.6 miles) along the highway from the bridge. Its name honours George Johnston, a member of a prominent Native family. In 1928 he bought a car and had it delivered to Teslin by barge. Because there were no roads, Johnston built his own 6-kilometre (4-mile) road, including culverts and bridges with decks made of poles (rather

George Johnston Museum in Teslin.

Legends of the Raven

The raven, now the official bird of the Yukon, has long been the most important animal of the Tlingit people. One Tlingit legend describes how the great being, Raven, who was originally white, became black. On that occasion he was attempting to steal water from a hut. While trying to escape the hut with the water, he got stuck in the smoke hole and the spirits of the smoke hole would not let him go free until the smoke had changed his colour to black.

Another legend tells how, when the world was first created, it was in total darkness, because all of the light was being guarded by one rich man. Raven assumed human form and seduced the daughter of the rich man. A child was born and quickly became the apple of the grandfather's eye. By making requests of his grandfather, the child was able to get the stars put into the previously black sky. One day the child grabbed his grandfather's carefully guarded sunlight, transformed himself into a raven and flew to his father, Raven, bringing light to the world.

than boards). He then operated a taxi along it in summer. He is also known for the photographs that he took of his people and his community from 1910–40.

Go around to the back of the log building that houses the museum to find the entrance. Hundreds of Johnston's photographs and his 1928 Chevrolet are on display in the museum, along with the Yukon's largest display about the Tlingit people, a large homemade lathe and other exhibits.

On the grounds outside the museum you can look at an old wagon, a large boat and several pieces of old machinery and equipment.

If you want to make a 420-kilometre (260-mile) canoe trip downriver to Carmacks, a community at the junction of the Yukon River and the Klondike Highway (Highway 2), begin at Teslin and follow the lakeshore to the Teslin River. There are no portages. The lake and the river are mainly Class I or Class II, with some Class III rapids. Allow about two weeks and provision yourself accordingly.

As you leave Teslin and follow the shore of Teslin Lake some more, in 2.5 kilometres (1.6 miles) from the museum there is a viewpoint that overlooks the lake. A sign here explains that Teslin Lake is part of the Pacific Flyway, a seasonal migration path used by millions of birds annually.

Johnson's Crossing and Jake's Corner

At kilometre 45.5 (mile 28.2) from Teslin, you reach the junction with the Canol Road (see Chapter 10). Just past that junction a bridge spans the Teslin River. This bridge, with a length of 539 metres (1770 feet), is the third longest on the Alaska Highway. Before the highway was constructed, supplies destined for the community of Teslin were brought up the Teslin River by boat. Although the bridge was built high above the water for clearance for the British Yukon Navigation steamers, the steamers ceased operation in 1942, when goods began to arrive by highway instead.

At the other end of the bridge is Johnson's Crossing. The lodge here is one of the original lodges on the Alaska Highway. Stop in to buy cinnamon buns, bread, tarts or meat pies for your lunch. If you feel like fishing, the Teslin River is good for arctic grayling.

Jake's Corner, also known as 'Mile 866 Junction,' consists of a service station and a motel on a hill to the right of the highway, 46 kilometres (28.6 miles) from Johnson's Crossing. In the yard there is a line of old equipment that was used in the building of the Canol Road. Although you can see the equipment as you drive by, for a good look, turn in and park. There are old graders, stationary steam engines with big flywheels, an old bulldozer and army trucks to see, as well as a number of chainsaws hanging on the garage.

Also at Jake's Corner is the junction with Highway 8, where you would turn left off the Alaska Highway if you wanted to go to Tagish or Atlin (see Chapter 10).

You begin to follow Marsh Lake, out of which flows the Yukon River, at kilometre 25 (mile 15.5) from Jake's Corner. There are a number of viewpoints along the lake.

At kilometre 51.2 (mile 31.8), you reach the Yukon River. Look to your right to see the green Marsh Lake Dam. The original wooden dam was built in 1924 by the White Pass and Yukon Railway. The dam was opened as necessary to release some of the water that collected behind it in spring, propelling stern-wheelers downstream from the docks at Whitehorse through the shallow parts of the river above and below Lake Laberge. The fast-flowing water also helped clear old, weakened ice off the lake at spring breakup. The dam was replaced in 1952 and the present one was built in 1975 for the Whitehorse hydroelectric project.

In 11.5 kilometres (7.1 miles) from where you arrived at the Yukon River, you come to the junction with the highway to Carcross and Skagway (Highway 2; see Chapter 9). Although there is a sign that says 'Welcome to Whitehorse' at kilometre 12.3 (mile 7.6), the city centre is still far away.

Yukon Steamboats

Steamboats began plying the Yukon River in 1866. However, the river had many narrow places and a change had to be made to the design of the side-wheelers that were used on the Mississippi. The paddle-wheel was moved from the side of the boat to the back and the boats became stern-wheelers.

Stern-wheelers were usually about 52 metres (170 feet) long and 11 metres (35 feet) wide, with a capacity of approximately 180–230 tonnes (200–250 tons) of supplies and passengers. Whenever possible, each boat also pushed a barge loaded with cargo, thereby doubling its freightage. The steamboats were put into the water as soon as possible after spring breakup and taken out when the river began to ice over.

Even after the Klondike Gold Rush, the steamboats continued to travel between Whitehorse and Dawson City. The *Klondike I* was considered to be 'the Queen of the River.' This stern-wheeler was built in 1929 by the British Columbia Navigation Company, which was a subsidiary of the White Pass and Yukon Railway. She was designed to carry 50 percent more cargo than usual—about 270 tonnes (300 tons). She made the one-and-one-half day downstream trip from Whitehorse to Dawson City and the four-day return trip upstream until 1936, when she ran aground.

In 1937, the remains of the *Klondike I* were used to construct the *Klondike II*, which operated until 1952, when trucks began travelling the newly built road between the two cities. This ship is now on display in Rotary Park in Whitehorse, with the name *SS Klondike*.

Miles Canyon and Whitehorse

Take the turn-off for Miles Canyon at kilometre 23.4 (mile 14.5). Shortly after the turn-off, you reach a Y-intersection. Take the right fork (the left fork would take you past Schwatka Lake, after which you could turn right onto Robert Service Way to go into downtown Whitehorse). Pull into the parking lot almost immediately past the Y. The 1.7-kilometre (1.1-mile) trail to the old site of Canyon City begins at a set of steps and continues across the Robert Lowe footbridge, which spans the Miles Canyon of the Yukon River.

Yukon River at Canyon City.

Once across the river, go straight up the hill to a cross-country ski trail and turn right. Although there are other trails heading in the same direction, including one at the edge of the canyon, all of them eventually reach the black-and-white sign stating that Canyon City is 200 metres (about 660 feet) ahead. At the end of the trail you reach an open area on the bank of the Yukon River.

During the gold rush, many of the people who headed for the Klondike had never handled a boat before and so, when they hit the White Horse Rapids in Miles Canyon, some lost their boats and/or their lives. In the interests of public safety, the Royal Canadian Mounted Police decided that only expert handlers could pilot the boats through the rapids. One of them, writer Jack London, made $3000 in one summer as a boat operator here.

To bypass the rapids, a horse-drawn tramway was soon built to cover the 8 kilometres (5 miles) from Canyon City to where Whitehorse is today. When the White Pass and Yukon Railway reached Whitehorse from Skagway in 1900, it bypassed Canyon City, which died.

The White Horse Rapids, which the Southern Tutchone people called *Kanlin*, meaning 'water flowing through a narrow passage,' were given their name by the Klondikers because the white, foaming water reminded them of the flowing mane of a galloping horse. The rapids no longer exist, having been flooded by the Whitehorse Dam, built in 1953, which formed Schwatka Lake.

Although there are some pines growing here, it is quite open along the shore. As you look out over the river, note that there is a high bank to the left, another one to the right and one across the river. The part of the bank where you are standing is the only one at water level. It is easy to picture the prospectors in their home-made boats putting ashore here below the rapids (when, before the dam, the bank was about 2 metres [7 feet] above the water) to unload their supplies and, in later times, steamboats docking here to let off passengers and freight bound for Dawson City.

You can see evidence of archaeological digs at Canyon City, which had earlier been the site of a Native fishing camp. Among the items that were found here are an

Miles Canyon near Whitehorse.

⌇ Beringia

During the late Wisconsinan ice age (10,000–70,000 years ago), an arid section of the northern hemisphere was not glaciated because of the lack of moisture to support the expansion of the glaciers. The area, called 'Beringia,' after the Bering Strait, which is near the centre of the region, encompassed parts of eastern Siberia, Alaska and the Yukon and ended at the Mackenzie River in the Northwest Territories.

Statue of mammoth outside Beringia at Whitehorse.

The growth of the continental glaciers tied up so much of the earth's water that it led to the sea level dropping by up to 100 metres (350 feet), so that a land bridge formed between northwestern North America and northeastern Asia. It is believed that parts of western Beringia (today's eastern Siberia) were occupied by humans 35,000 years ago. The forming of the Bering Land Bridge allowed people living in Asia to slowly migrate to North America, which anthropologists believe had been previously uninhabited. There is evidence that human history in North America goes back 25,000 years.

Some of the animals that survived for thousands of years in this arid land surrounded by glaciers were the North American horse and camel, the steppe bison, the giant beaver, the mastodon, the woolly mammoth, the giant short-faced bear, the scimitar cat, the American lion and the giant ground sloth.

1854 halfpenny from the Bank of Upper Canada, an 1891 Canadian dime and 1894 American half dollar. A number of rusted cans and pails remain at the site. Please do not disturb them.

Back on the highway, you reach Robert Service Way, 3.1 kilometres (1.9 miles) from the turnoff for Miles Canyon. This road is the first exit off the highway into Whitehorse. However, if you continue on the highway, at kilometre 6.4 (mile 4) you can turn right onto a side road to visit the Beringia Interpretive Centre and the Yukon Transportation Museum, which are side by side.

Inside the interpretive centre there are life-sized replicas of animals who lived in the North during the last ice age. You will see exactly how huge a woolly mammoth was, see a replica of a giant beaver that weighed around 180 kilograms (400 pounds) and learn about the ecology of Beringia—the once-dry area now occupied by the Bering Strait and its surroundings.

The Transportation Museum has displays of unique and varied types of transportation used in the North from the gold rush era, through the building of the Alaska Highway and up to the present.

Drive past the museum on the side road to the T-intersection and ahead of you is what is said to be the world's largest weathervane, a Douglas C-47 (or 'Gooney Bird'). This plane began as a military transport aircraft flying into India and China during the Second World War. When the war ended, it was sold to Grant McConachie, at that time the owner of Canadian Pacific Airlines. It was converted to a DC-3 (on which the C-47 design had been based) and then flew scheduled routes across Canada. Fifteen years later it was relegated to the northern regions. Eventually sold to Connelly-Dawson Airways of Dawson City, it was a bush plane until 1970, when it blew an engine. In 1977 the Yukon Flying Club began restoration. Now, swinging on a pivot, the plane always has its nose pointed into the wind.

At kilometre 2.6 (mile 1.6) from the interpretive centre, turn right when you get to a set of traffic lights at Two Mile Hill Road, the second turn-off for Whitehorse.

To get to the visitor reception centre, continue on Two Mile Hill Road, which becomes Fourth Avenue in downtown Whitehorse, to Hanson Street and turn left. The visitor centre is on your left between Second and First avenues.

World's largest weathervane at the Transportation Museum at Whitehorse.

The city of Whitehorse dates from the Klondike Gold Rush. It developed at the site where 30,000 gold seekers stopped after portaging around the White Horse Rapids in Miles Canyon. The White Pass and Yukon Railway, constructed from 1898 to 1900, replaced the portage, carrying passengers and freight directly from Skagway to Whitehorse. Passengers got off the train at Whitehorse and boarded steamers that hauled them and their supplies to Dawson City, some 640 kilometres (400 miles) to the north. Whitehorse remained a supply point for the area, with the river as the means of transportation until 1942, when the Alaska Highway was constructed. Because of its easy accessibility, Whitehorse took over from Dawson City as the capital of the Yukon on March 31, 1953. When a road was built from Skagway to Whitehorse, it took so much business away from the White Pass and Yukon Railway that it closed down in 1982. However, it reopened as a tourist line in 1988.

The business section of Whitehorse can get crowded, making it hard to find a parking spot. If you wish to do some browsing, it is best to park your vehicle in one place and walk around town.

At the McBride Museum, to the north on First Avenue from the reception centre, is the actual cabin that belonged to Sam McGee (as immortalized in the poetry of Robert Service). From the museum, go two blocks back southward on First Avenue to Elliot Street. Turn right and drive to Third Avenue, where you turn left.

The Old Log Church, built in 1900, is on your right between Elliot and Lambert streets. Services are still held in this church, which was the cathedral of the diocese between 1953 and 1960, even though it became a museum in 1962. Inside, you can examine pioneer artifacts, learn how the Natives were taught to read, see photographs from Whitehorse's past and discover how the lifestyles of the northern Native peoples changed with the coming of the non-Natives and

Sam McGee's Cabin at the McBride Museum in Whitehorse.

SS Klondike at Whitehorse.

the building of the Alaska Highway. From the museum entrance, look at the backs of the buildings on the other side of the street and a parking lot. They have been brightly painted to resemble store and hotel fronts of a bygone day: 'Whitehorse Hotel,' 'Arctic Trading Company' and 'Whitney and Pedlar General Merchandise' are painted on their walls.

To see the *SS Klondike* at the Rotary Peace Park, drive along Second Avenue to Robert Service Way. At this junction, turn left into the park. You can leave your vehicle in the parking lot while you follow the path along the edge of the Yukon River and under a bridge to the *SS Klondike*. This paddle-wheeler, built in 1937, is 64 metres (210 feet) long and 12.5 metres (41 feet) wide. The *SS Klondike* ran from Whitehorse to Dawson City in about one-and-one-half days and used 40 cords of wood. On the return trip upstream, she took 120 cords of wood to make the trip in about four days.

If you like to travel by canoe, kayak or Zodiac, a paddle down the Yukon River from Whitehorse to Dawson is a lovely way to experience a part of the gold-rush adventure. Set aside three weeks for this trip of some 700 kilometres (435 miles). The route leaves Whitehorse, crosses Lake Laberge and then passes Carmacks, which is your last chance to buy additional supplies before Dawson City. Keep right at the Five Fingers Rapids. You will pass old buildings and abandoned villages along your way—all historic sites are legally protected by the Yukon government, so do not disturb anything. You can contact the Yukon Conservation Society (867-667-5678) in Whitehorse for a map and up-to-date information.

Whitehorse is the start or finish (depending on the year) of the annual Yukon Quest International Dog Sled Race held in February (see sidebar on p. 71). As you travel through the Yukon and Alaska, look for the large signs that have been erected at checkpoints along the route of this race.

Whitehorse to Beaver Creek

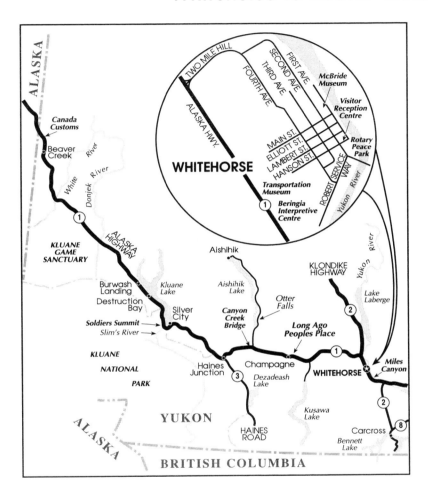

Takhini River, Mendenhall Landing and Champagne

When you are finished touring downtown Whitehorse, take Two Mile Hill Road back to the highway. As you continue up the Alaska Highway, you pass through more of Whitehorse, which is spread out along the road. In 11.6 kilometres (7.2 miles) from the lights at Two Mile Hill, you reach the junction with the Klondike Highway (Highway 2), which goes to Dawson City (see Chapter 8). Continue straight ahead toward Haines Junction.

At kilometre 28.9 (mile 17.9), there is a viewpoint with a sign about the Overland Trail, built between Dawson and Whitehorse in 1902. The trail crossed the Takhini River here and a small settlement was established. Just past the sign you can see the Takhini River to your right. Back on the highway, you eventually cross the Takhini River, at kilometre 43.8 (mile 27.2).

Kilometre 62.9 (mile 39.1) brings you to the site of the Takhini Burn, a forest fire that took place in 1958. You can see for yourself how the northern climate allows plants to grow only very slowly.

At kilometre 64.3 (mile 39.9), you can take a side trip to the left on Kusawa Lake Road, which is gravel. At 2.2 kilometres (1.4 miles) from the highway, you cross the Mendenhall River just upstream from where it flows into the Takhini River. There is a viewpoint here at the former site of Mendenhall Landing. In the early 1900s, freight from Whitehorse was shipped along the Yukon and Takhini rivers to Mendenhall Landing. Here, it was unloaded and put on wagons for the trip north, over the Whitehorse–Kluane wagon road, to the Kluane District mining operations.

Stand with your back to the viewpoint and look upward and slightly to your right to see a small graveyard on a cliff. To visit the site, from which there is a great view of the Takhini and Mendenhall rivers, go 0.3 kilometres (0.2 miles) back toward the highway from the viewpoint and turn left onto the trail. The trail climbs uphill and then goes along the edge of a cliff. Although people have driven along this trail, you might want to leave your vehicle back at the road and walk the 0.7 kilometres (0.4 miles) from the trailhead to the gravesite.

This cemetery is in a lovely spot high above the Mendenhall and Takhini rivers and surrounded by great mountain scenery. Although there are five graves here, two of them, though fenced, are unmarked, and there is no sign to tell you anything about this cemetery. One of the graves has a little log house over it, with a sign on it that is just about gone—although the name is no longer legible, you can read that the person died in 1939. The fourth grave belongs to Cecil L. Guyett, born 1915, died 1993. The last one is for Darrel Richard Smith, born March 5, 1956, died July 16, 1986.

If you want to carry on to Kusawa Lake, where there is a campground, it is 21.8 kilometres (13.5 miles) further down the gravel road. The Takhini River flows out of Kusawa Lake and down to the Yukon River, which eventually empties into the Bering Sea. Beginning canoeists like the Takhini because it offers easy Class I and Class II water. You can put your canoe in at the Kusawa Lake Campground and take it out at the Takhini River Campground, about 10 kilometres (6 miles) toward the highway. If you are a more experienced paddler and want to travel further, you can continue to Mendenhall Landing and pull out there instead.

Back on the highway, you cross the Mendenhall River in 14.5 kilometres (9 miles) from the road to Kusawa Lake. At kilometre 22.5 (mile 14), watch for *Kwaday Dan Kenji* Long Ago Peoples Place to your right—it is marked by a big brown-and-yellow sign along the highway. The Johnson family did a lot of research into the building of a traditional First Nations camp before setting up this site. At the camp you can see a caribou fence (used to herd the animals together during hunting), bone tools, a deadfall trap, a moose-hoof rattle, a house made of brush and many more artifacts that are part of the First Nations' history from before (and after) the non-Natives arrived. You can sip tea and eat bannock or purchase dream-catchers, slippers, jewellery and dolls made by local Natives.

Three kilometres (1.9 miles) from Long Ago Peoples Place, you reach Champagne, a Native village. During its long and varied history, it has been a meeting and trading place on a centuries-old Native trail, a stopover for gold-seekers heading to the Klondike, the site of a trading post, a supply centre on the Whitehorse–Kluane wagon road and the site of a camp during the building of the Alaska Highway.

The young people of the town left after the Second World War to find jobs in larger centres. In the early 1960s, many more people moved west to Haines Junction, but the few who have stayed keep the history of the area alive.

In the village, amongst the historic log buildings, you can see old wagons, old machinery and a horse-drawn mower.

Otter Creek and Canyon Creek

In 11.1 kilometres (6.9 miles) from Champagne, you reach Otter Creek, to the left of the highway, which has a service station and store that offer RV parking. Stop in to see the display of stuffed animals and birds in the store.

Turn right off the highway onto the side road at Otter Creek. A map at the beginning shows how to get to Otter Falls, Aishihik Campground and the Native village of Aishihik. There is also a sign about the Aishihik watershed and there is a write-up about the fish of the area: rainbow trout, lake trout, burbot, northern pike and arctic grayling.

Although the gravel road is in good shape, it has many curves and hills and you have to watch for

Otter Falls in June.

bison and livestock. This drive takes you beside lovely valleys, over streams and creeks and offers you some great mountain scenery. Keep your eyes open for swans flying over adjacent ponds. At kilometre 17.5 (mile 10.9), you cross a wooden bridge and reach a Y. The road to the left is private; go to the right to reach the Otter Falls Day Use Area at kilometre 28.4 (mile 17.6) from the highway.

Otter Falls was featured on the back of the old Canadian five-dollar bill but, since that picture was taken, changes have been made at the falls. In 1975 the Aishihik Power Plant was built. The project diverted the waters flowing from the Aishihik, Sekulmun and Canyon lakes away from the falls to generate power. Because this waterfall was so famous, many public hearings were held, with the

Canyon Creek Bridge.

result that some water is allowed to flow over the falls during the day in summer, when there are visitors there to enjoy the sight. At night and during the winter, the water flow is negligible.

From the falls you can continue about 13 kilometres (8 miles) to the campground or 106 kilometres (66 miles) to the village.

Back on the highway, in 1.4 kilometres (0.9 miles), a rest area is to the right, next to the wooden Canyon Creek Bridge. The original bridge was built in 1904 over what was then Canyon Creek (now the Aishihik River) as a link on the road between Whitehorse and Kluane (also known as 'Silver City'). The bridge was reconstructed in 1942 when the Alaska Highway went through, but was abandoned the next year when the highway route was changed. In 1987 the Yukon government rebuilt the bridge for the enjoyment of tourists—current-day highway traffic does not use it but local traffic does.

As soon as you get back on the highway, you cross the Aishihik River bridge. Just after the bridge, on the left, is the small settlement of Canyon Creek. At kilometre 29.8 (mile 18.5) a sign welcomes you to Haines Junction, 'Gateway to Kluane.'

Our Lady of the Way Church in Haines Junction.

Haines Junction

As you enter Haines Junction, watch to your right for Our Lady of the Way Church, 1.2 kilometres (0.7 miles) from the welcome sign. This church was

Tagish Charlie, who had co-discovered gold on Bonanza Creek in 1896, leading to the Klondike Gold Rush (see sidebar 'The Beginning of the Klondike Gold Rush on p. 154), also found gold on the Fourth of July Creek in 1903. Word got out and, by the end of 1903, two thousand claims had been staked in the Kluane area. Silver City (or Kluane) was established at the mouth of Silver Creek on Kluane Lake.

At the time that the gold rush occurred, the Southern Tutchone residents of the area had a series of trails throughout the region. In 1904 a 233-kilometre (145-mile) wagon road was built from Whitehorse to Silver City, following one of their trails. If conditions were good, the trip would take five to six days.

At first, optimism about gold yields ran high—one hydraulic mining company spent over $300,000 on equipment and buildings. However, the yields were small, so that by 1914 a total of only $40,000 in gold had been taken from the creeks.

Two brothers, Louis and Eugene Jacquot, had set up a trading post where Burwash Landing is today. Freight was brought from Whitehorse along the Whitehorse–Kluane wagon road and then barged down the lake to the post. When the brothers became big-game outfitters in the 1920s, the road was improved to serve the influx of tourists to their camp. The Alaska Highway now follows much of the original wagon road's route.

built in 1954 using an old Quonset hut left by the US Army during the construction of the highway to Haines, Alaska.

Just past that church, turn right onto Kluane Avenue to reach the visitor reception centre. A 15-minute hiking trail leading from the centre through the woods gives you a chance to stretch your legs. Across from the centre, at Cabin Crafts, you can rent canoes and mountain bikes. Beside the shop is the Village Bakery, which is also a coffee house with a deli, ice cream, refreshments, baked goods and sandwiches.

Back on the highway, one block past Kluane Avenue, there is a point of interest on your left. It is a large model of a mountain on which replicas of the different animals in the area have been placed.

Adjacent to the model are an old log building and a record-sized Alaska Highway guest book that you can sign with a felt marker. This guest book was set up in 1992 by the St. Elias Community School, Kluane National Park and the Municipality of Haines Junction. There is a time capsule under the book, intended to be opened in the year 2042.

The routes described in this book will not bring you this way again, so if you want to travel the Haines Road (Highway 3) to Haines, Alaska, you should head there now, because the road begins in Haines Junction (see Chapter 11).

MacIntosh Lodge, Two Summits and Silver City

Heading northwest along the Alaska Highway from Haines Junction, you see the Kluane Ranges of the St. Elias Mountains to your left. They will be beside you as far as the Koidern River. The St. Elias Mountains, which run from Alaska through the

Kluane Lake's Changing Drainage

Kluane Lake and Mountains.

At one time, water flowed out of Kluane Lake by way of Slim's River at the southern end of the lake. However, between three and four hundred years ago, the Kaskawulsh Glacier advanced across the river (where it remains today), cutting off the lake's drainage. The lake level rose about 10 metres (30 feet) before a new drainage formed near the northwestern end. Water that used to go to the Gulf of Alaska now flows via the Yukon River to the Bering Sea.

Yukon and into BC, are the highest mountain range in North America and the second highest coastal range in the world, after the Andes. The peaks of the St. Elias Mountains, many over 5000 metres (16,400 feet) high, are covered by the largest non-polar icefield in the world.

At 10.3 kilometres (6.4 miles) from Haines Junction, you reach MacIntosh Lodge, on the right. Across the highway from MacIntosh Lodge, there is an old log cabin with a huge rock in the yard. The rock marks a grave and, though it is impossible to read the name of the person buried there, you can still discern that the year of birth was 1913 and the year of death was 1989.

At kilometre 19.6 (mile 12.2), you reach a small pull-out to the left at Bear Creek Summit, elevation 1004 metres (3294 feet). Then, 35 kilometres (21.7 miles) from Bear Creek Summit, you reach Boutilier Summit, at an elevation of 1003 metres (3291 feet). You have the beautiful blue-green waters of Kluane Lake ahead as you leave Boutilier Summit.

Take the turn-off to the right for historic Silver City at kilometre 37.7 (mile 23.4) from Bear Creek Summit. Gold was discovered in this area in 1903 and Silver City was established at Silver Creek on Kluane Lake. The settlement's location on the shore of Kluane Lake led some people to call it 'Kluane' instead of 'Silver City.' During the gold rush, the city was the terminus of a road from Whitehorse. Everyone passed through here on their way to the gold-fields. However, the gold yields were small and the freight charges high, so by 1925 there was only one resident left in Silver City. He made his money farming mink and guiding.

Silver City was used as a construction camp during the building of the Alaska Highway, which followed the old wagon road from Whitehorse. Now, the old buildings have been left to nature.

At 3.8 kilometres (2.4 miles) along the side road, you reach the first of many log buildings. Beside one building sit the remains of an old truck: the wooden deck, axle, frame, cab and wheels. The parts are still joined together, but getting very rusty. Although you can see some of the buildings from the road, get out of your vehicle to do some exploring among the trees to discover more such structures.

Old building at Silver City.

Slim's River, Destruction Bay and Burwash Landing

Back on the highway, you begin to follow the shoreline of Kluane Lake, the largest lake in the Yukon. Like most lakes in the mountains, it gets its colour from the suspended glacial silt in its waters. The name *Kluane* means 'big white fish lake' in the Southern Tutchone language.

You reach Slim's River at kilometre 12 (mile 7.5) from the Silver City turn-off. The story of how the river got its name is rather sad: The Natives and fur traders knew not to cross Slim's River because the flats there were like quicksand. However, one prospector new to the area did not know about the danger and tried to take his horse across the flats. They got caught in the slimy mud. Although the prospector was rescued, the horse, named Slim, died.

The visitor reception centre for Sheep Mountain is on your left at kilometre 13.6 (mile 8.4). Stand on the patio and use one of the high-power telescopes to look for sheep on nearby Sheep Mountain.

As you continue along the highway beyond the visitor centre, look up and to your left to see a white cross on Sheep Mountain. It marks the grave of Alexander Clark Fisher, who came here in 1906.

Large gold pan at Burwash Landing.

Kluane National Park Reserve is to the left as you once again drive along the lakeshore. At kilometre 1.7 (mile 1.1), a pull-out is to your left near Soldiers Summit. It was at this summit that the 97th Engineers met up with the 18th Engineers to complete the Alaska Highway pioneer road on November 20, 1942. A moderately steep half-hour climb heads from the parking area to Soldiers Summit. Along the trail there are interpretive signs, pictures of the highway under construction, benches and beautiful views of Kluane Lake.

You reach the settlement of Destruction Bay at kilometre 35.2 (mile 21.9). When you see the service station on your left, turn right at that corner to go to a pebbly beach on the lakeshore. Destruction Bay began as a tent camp during the construction of the Alaska pioneer road and in 1943 was made into a relay station. Relay stations were set up every 160 kilometres (100 miles), so that the drivers of army trucks and road maintenance vehicles travelling the rough road could be relieved and the vehicles inspected and repaired.

As the road improved, these stations were closed and highway maintenance camps set up in their place.

A sign at Destruction Bay explains that the camp here was destroyed by 160-kilometre-per-hour (100-mile-per-hour) winds and that this event led to the place's

Kluane River Valley.

name. Although books on the Alaska Highway state that the storm happened in the 1940s—some say 1942—the sign says that it was in 1952.

Burwash Landing is 15.6 kilometres (9.7 miles) along the highway past Destruction Bay. It was founded by Eugene and Louis Jacquot in 1903, but it was Lachlin Taylor Burwash who gave his name to the settlement. Amongst other enterprises, Mr. Burwash ran the mining recorder's office in Silver City. Burwash Landing was a thriving community, with fresh vegetables and fresh milk, even well before the Alaska Highway went through.

As you come into the village, the Burwash Landing Kluane Museum is to your right. You can recognize it by the giant gold pan, with the picture of a prospector trying his luck on a creek, in its yard. The museum houses artifacts, a gift shop and a visitor reception centre. Also on the grounds are an old cabin with a sod roof and several old wagons and vehicles.

Bridge Construction

In the spring run-off or during a heavy rainfall, the Donjek River, like many mountain rivers, becomes enlarged and fast moving. Huge amounts of ice, rock and debris tumble along in its waters. During the building of the Alaska Highway, this material would sometimes wipe out half-constructed bridges over these waterways. At other times it would cause a change in direction of the river, leaving bridges that spanned dry beds and making new channels to be crossed.

The green Donjek River Bridge, 25 kilometres (15.5 miles) from the Kluane Wilderness Village, is the second one over the river. The first one was upstream and used seven wooden trestles over the approximately 5 kilometres (3 miles) of river flats. Work on the present bridge began in 1948 and, because of flooding, took four years to complete.

Lt. Small's memorial.

Just past the museum, look to your right to see Burl Billy Hill, a small hillside covered with burl crafts. You can visit the workshop here and see the burl products that the owners make. One way that burls can be formed is when damage by insects or a fungus causes the wood of a tree to bulge out.

At 16.5 kilometres (10.2 miles) from Burwash Landing, you cross Burwash Creek and at kilometre 25.7 (mile 16) there is a pull-out to the right that overlooks the Kluane River, which has one of the largest annual gatherings of chum salmon in the Yukon River system. Spawning season for the chum here is from mid-September to mid-November.

There is a memorial to 1st Lt. R.R. Small at kilometre 35.5 (mile 22). Killed in a jeep accident, he was one of five soldiers from the 18th Engineers regiment who died during the highway's construction. Though Small was buried in Whitehorse, this monument was put up here by his men in his honour.

Kluane Wilderness Village, the Koidern River and Beaver Creek

At 37.1 kilometres (23 miles) from Burwash Landing, you reach Kluane Wilderness Village, which claims to the be 'the Burl Capital of Yukon.' There are log cabins, a service station, the 1118th Cafe and a large number of burls here.

A rest area and a platform that overlooks Pickhandle Lake are to your left at 43.5 kilometres (27 miles) from Kluane Wilderness Village. Signs here tell about the landscape, Native life and pond ecology. The valley you are in, the Shakwak Trench, is on a migration route used by thousands of waterfowl each year.

Between here and Beaver Creek there is extensive permafrost, a soil condition that the highway engineers who built the road had never dealt with before. When they scraped off the top layer of soil and opened the permafrost to sunlight, it melted and they were stuck in the middle of a mudbog. During winter the road was good but, come spring, the mud returned. The engineers finally learned to leave the top layer of insulating ground in place and the road improved.

Koidern River Lodge is at kilometre 51.5 (mile 32), just before Koidern River Bridge #2. At kilometre 108.5 (mile 67.4), you are at Beaver Creek, which bills itself as 'the Most Westerly Community in Canada.' Look to your left as you come into the village to see another church in a Quonset hut—Our Lady of Grace Catholic Church, which was built in 1961.

Beaver Creek itself was panned for gold around 1909 but not much else happened here until 1955, when a Canada Customs post was established.

Canada Customs to Delta Junction

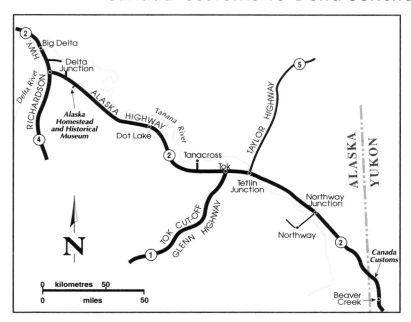

The International Boundary, Northway Junction and Northway

The Canada Customs post is 3 kilometres (1.8 miles) beyond Beaver Creek and the US Customs post is 30 kilometres (18.6 miles) further along the highway. In between the two, a damp 'no-man's land' consists of muskeg, bush and a few tall trees. As you pass through this region, however, watch for the swans swimming or gliding through the air.

The boundary between Canada and the United States, just before the US Customs post, is on the 141st meridian of longitude and is marked by a 6-metre (20-foot) wide cutline. As you cross the border, there is a time-zone change, so set your watch back one hour.

After the US Customs post, you begin the US-maintained portion of the Alaska Highway (Alaska Route 2) and start driving alongside the Tetlin National Wildlife Refuge, established on December 2, 1980. Within its approximately 295,400 hectares (730,000 acres), it has many lakes and two glacial rivers and is the nesting area for a recorded 143 species of birds. Along with other refuges in the state, it provides habitat for wildlife that is safe from industrial activities, although hunting is permitted. Some birds that you might see are sandhill cranes, ducks, loons, bald eagles and osprey. Animals include moose, bears, red foxes, wolves, coyotes and beavers. You can hike, camp and fish in the refuge.

If you want to do a scenic hike to a fish-stocked lake, park at the pull-out on the left at kilometre 28 (mile 17.4) from the border. From here it is a 1.6-kilometre (1-mile) hike to rainbow-stocked Hidden Lake. Just make sure that you have a valid Alaska fishing licence if you plan to drop your line into the water.

As you drive further along the highway, you begin to see sand-hills. The sand here comes from mountainsides that were scraped by glaciers thousands of years ago. The particles were then washed down by streams and rivers and deposited in basins. The wind swept them into sand-dunes and now vegetation is trying to grow on them, in the process stabilizing them.

At kilometre 49.9 (mile 31) from the border, you reach Frontier Surplus, on your left. You can recognize the place by the yellow 1942 GMC truck

Canada/US border.

parked on the hill above the highway. Turn off the highway and drive up the hill to the crowded yard. Go into the building with all the antlers on the front. Inside, you can look over a wide variety of goods, including diamond willow canes, furs, local crafts and T-shirts. Even if you do not wish to purchase anything, come up the hill for the view of the surrounding mountains and a visit with the owner of the business.

You arrive at Northway Junction, 16.1 kilometres (10 miles) past Frontier Surplus. The settlement has a service station, a store, an RV park and a gift shop. At the gift shop you can buy crafts from the Native village of Northway, which is 11.3 kilometres (7 miles) off the highway to the southwest from here.

Some Alaska Facts

Alaska's name comes from the Aleut word for the area, *Alyeska*, 'the Great Land.'

The territory was bought from Russia on behalf of the United States in August, 1867, by William H. Seward, who was then the secretary of state. The acquisition was quickly nicknamed 'Seward's Icebox' and 'Seward's Folly.' The ridicule, however, proved unjustified: gold, copper, coal, timber and, more recently, oil have been some of the main products of the area since its purchase. It became the 49th state of the Union on January 3, 1959, with Juneau as its capital.

The land area of Alaska is 1,518,801 square kilometres (586,412 square miles), which includes 51,748 square kilometres (19,980 square miles) of inland water. Including islands, it has some 53,300 kilometres (33,100 miles) of shoreline. The state has over five thousand glaciers and icefields and 57 active volcanoes.

The south-central area is dominated by the Alaska Range, which includes Mount McKinley, North America's highest mountain (see the sidebar on p. 91). In the north, above the Arctic Circle, stands the Brooks Range. Because Alaska is mainly mountainous country, for many years most travel in the area was on its lakes and rivers.

The name 'Northway' comes from Chief Walter Northway, who had taken claim to the name of a riverboat captain at the end of the nineteenth century. He died in 1993, at what many people believe to be the age of 117.

Northway's airport was built in the 1940s as part of the Northwest Staging Route. This project, set up jointly by the US and Canada, resulted in a chain of airports from Edmonton, Alberta, to Fairbanks, Alaska. Its purpose was to bring in supplies and materials for the defence of the North and for construction projects.

At kilometre 6.6 (mile 4.1) from Northway Junction, you come around a curve and begin driving beside the Tanana River. The Tanana is formed by the joining of the Chisana and Nabesna rivers. It is the largest tributary of the Yukon River, which it enters near the village of Tanana, northwest of Manley Hot Springs (see Chapter 2). You have occasional views of the Tanana River with its mountainous background as you travel toward Tetlin Junction.

Tetlin Junction and Tok

Sixty kilometres (37.3 miles) from Northway Junction you arrive at Tetlin Junction and the turn-off for Chicken, Eagle and Dawson City via the Taylor Highway (Alaska Route 5; see Chapter 6). Tetlin Junction has a cafe and a service station.

Continuing toward Tok, you cross the Tanana River 2.4 kilometres (1.5 miles) past Tetlin Junction and begin driving through parts of the Tok (or Porcupine) Burn, which occurred in 1990. The fire destroyed 39,397 hectares (97,352 acres) of forest. The Tok River State Recreation Site—where you can camp, hike or launch a boat—is to your right at kilometre 12.1 (mile 7.5) and then you cross the Tok River.

After driving through more of the Tok Burn, you reach the edge of the town of Tok at kilometre 17.7 (mile 11) from Tetlin Junction. Tok, which is pronounced to rhyme with 'poke,' means 'peaceful crossing' in the language of the Athabascan peoples.

At the junction of the Alaska Highway with the Glenn Highway (Alaska Route 1, also known here as 'the Tok Cut-off'), go to the large log building with the red roof on the right. The largest free-standing log structure in Alaska, it was constructed by the community. Numbers on the logs tell how big each tree was and how old it was when cut for this building.

This building contains Tok's visitor reception centre, which offers pamphlets, displays and write-ups on the animals in the area and sells souvenirs and gifts.

The log building also houses the Tok field office of the Bureau of Land Management (BLM). The BLM looks after 36 million hectares (90 million acres) of public land in Alaska. Because one of the BLM's responsibilities is the recreational use of public lands, the office has brochures on trails that you might want to hike and rivers that you might want to canoe.

In one corner of the BLM office there is a stuffed bear that was illegally shot from an airplane on the Alaska Peninsula in 1986. The hunter was tracked down and taken to court, where he was fined $20,000. The already-stuffed bear was taken from him and set up here.

At Burnt Paw, kitty-corner from the visitor centre, you can watch dog-sled demonstrations in the evening, every day except Sunday. You can see how the dogs are hooked up to a sled, which is on wheels for summer, and even buy a ticket for a dog-sled ride around the parking lot.

Tanacross, Dot Lake and Delta Junction

As you head out of Tok, look to your left at kilometre 4.7 (mile 2.9) to see what is said to be the world's largest mukluk (traditional northern Native footwear) hanging at the entrance to Mukluk Land, a campground and museum with gold-panning, golf and many more activities.

Along the highway from Tok, a bicycle path is to your right. It follows the highway as far as the junction with the road to Tanacross, which you reach 23.4 kilometres (14.5 miles) from the visitor reception centre in Tok.

To visit the small Native village of Tanacross, or to launch a boat in the Tanana River or picnic beside it, turn right onto the road to Tanacross and drive 1 kilometre (0.6 miles) to a T-intersection. To go to the village itself, at the site where the Eagle Trail (from Valdez to Eagle) crossed the Tanana River, turn left here. Go right instead if you want to follow the river to the picnic site and boat launch. As you drive, there are two runways that belong to the small airport on your right.

Back on the highway, you cross Cathedral Creek three times between kilometre 20.3 (mile 12.6) and kilometre 21.6 (mile 13.4). By and by you enter the community of Dot Lake, reaching the Dot Lake School at kilometre 58 (mile 36) and the Dot Lake Lodge shortly thereafter.

Although there are no trappings of civilization along the highway for a while, a pull-out with a pay phone is to your left at kilometre 86.9 (mile 54), in case you have vehicle problems.

At kilometre 108.8 (mile 67.6), you cross the channels of the Gerstle River on the Black Veterans Recognition Bridge. (Two of the regiments that took part in the construction of the Alaska Highway, the 93rd and the 97th, were completely composed of soldiers of African descent.) Then you enter an area that was burned in 1994. Watch for caribou, sheep and bison from here to Delta Junction.

The local bison herd began as 23 animals transplanted from Montana in 1928. Today, about 375 bison roam through the approximately 36,400-hectare (90,000-acre) bison sanctuary, which is to your left. Over 1200 hectares (3000 acres) of grassland in the sanctuary gives the animals a place to graze during fall and winter, helping to stop them from ruining farmers' crops in the area.

In 17.8 kilometres (11.1 miles) from the bridge, you reach Sawmill Creek Road, on your right. At the beginning of the road there is a map that shows how the farms of the Delta Barley Fields agricultural project are laid out. The best time to drive down this road to see the fields is in August, when they are ready to be harvested.

On the left, at kilometre 13 (mile 8.1) from Sawmill Creek Road, is Cherokee Lodge, which has a cafe. In front of the lodge there is a large wagon with huge tires. Three of these wagons were brought to Alaska during US Army manoeuvres in 1961 to see how they would perform in the bush in winter. The army found out that they were okay in snow where the vegetation was low. In the bush, however, the trees would not bend to allow the wagons to pass over. Instead, the trunks would break and the snags would pierce the tires. The wagons were deemed unfit for service and abandoned.

Dorshorst Road is to your left at kilometre 18.5 (mile 11.5). Go 1.6 kilometres (1 mile) down this gravel road to the Alaska Homestead and Historical Museum. Just before the parking lot at the end of the road, a working sawmill is on the left. In the parking lot you can look over some old equipment: bulldozers, a wagon, a boiler, sleighs for hauling logs in winter and an old truck. To see inside the museum itself, which is open from 9 AM to 7 PM, you must join a guided walking tour.

At 8.1 kilometres (5 miles) from Dorshorst Road, you pass the welcome sign for Delta Junction and then you reach the visitor reception centre at kilometre 10.6 (mile 6.6). At the visitor centre a post says 'End of Alaska Highway.' However, there is a controversy over where the Alaska Highway really ends. On the one hand, Delta Junction claims to be the terminus because it was the endpoint of the 1942 highway construction project. On the other hand, Fairbanks claims to be the terminus because it was the destination that the Alaska Highway was built to reach. Fairbanks supporters maintain that the portion of the Richardson Highway between Delta Junction and Fairbanks (also Alaska Route 2), already in place well before 1942, is in practice a part of the Alaska Highway.

At the visitor centre you can pick up a certificate stating that you have travelled the Alaska Highway. Upstairs in the same building there is a museum that contains artifacts from the area's history and from the building of the highway. Outside there are information panels that show the types of crops—such as onions and potatoes—grown in the area and the harvesting of them. In front of the visitor centre there is a 'pig,' a device that was once used to clean the Trans-Alaska Oil Pipeline.

Delta Junction grew from a camp that was established in 1919 during the building of the Richardson Highway from Valdez to the gold-fields near Fairbanks. Its name was first 'Buffalo Center,' because of the 'buffalo' (bison) moved here in the 1920s, but it was later changed to 'Big Delta' to reflect the Delta River. The settlement then became known as 'Delta Junction' after the Alaska Highway was built. Agriculture in this area has been encouraged by the government since the late 1970s, resulting in over 45,530 hectares (112,500 acres) being planted in grains or vegetables. There are also dairy, beef, pig and bison farms and greenhouses as well.

As mentioned above, although Delta Junction is the end of the Alaska Highway, this road continues to Fairbanks as the Richardson Highway (see Chapter 2).

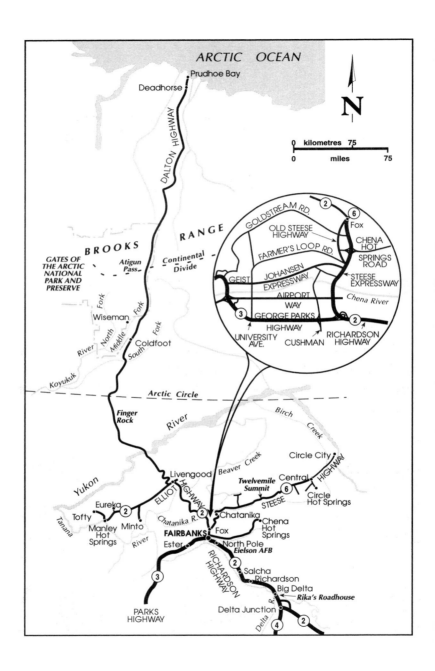

ARCTIC OCEAN

Prudhoe Bay

Deadhorse

N

kilometres 75

miles 75

DALTON HIGHWAY

BROOKS RANGE

GATES OF
THE ARCTIC
NATIONAL
PARK AND
PRESERVE

Atigun
Pass

Continental
Divide

Wiseman

North Fork

Middle Fork

South Fork

Koyukuk River

Coldfoot

Arctic Circle

Finger
Rock

River

Birch Creek

GOLDSTREAM RD.

OLD STEESE
HIGHWAY

FARMER'S LOOP RD.

JOHANSEN
EXPRESSWAY

GEIST

AIRPORT
WAY

GEORGE PARKS
HIGHWAY

UNIVERSITY
AVE.

CUSHMAN

Fox

CHENA
HOT
SPRINGS
ROAD

STEESE
EXPRESSWAY

Chena River

RICHARDSON
HIGHWAY

Circle City

Livengood

Beaver Creek

Twelvemile
Summit

Central

Circle
Hot Springs

Yukon

Eureka

Tofty

Manley
Hot
Springs

Minto

Tanana

River

ELLIOT HIGHWAY

Chatanika R.

Chatanika

STEESE

CIRCLE HIGHWAY

FAIRBANKS

Fox

Ester

North Pole

Chena
Hot
Springs

Eielson AFB

Salcha

Richardson

Big Delta

Rika's Roadhouse

RICHARDSON
HIGHWAY

Delta Junction

Delta R.

PARKS
HIGHWAY

2
Delta Junction to Prudhoe Bay

North Pole, the Arctic Circle and the Arctic Ocean are just some of the places that you visit in this chapter. A few of the activities covered in this chapter include exploring a gold dredge, panning for gold and relaxing in a hot spring.

This chapter will take you to the most northerly point in North America that is accessible by road. You will learn about the history of mining for gold in the area and maybe take some gold home with you. And you will drive beside the Trans-Alaska Oil Pipeline almost to its beginning at Prudhoe Bay.

Delta Junction to Fairbanks

Rika's Roadhouse

You have the Delta River to your left as you leave Delta Junction northbound on the Richardson Highway (Alaska Route 2). You pass Jack Warren Road and then the Tanana Loop Road, both of which go through farmland. August is the best time to see the fields.

Rika's Road, which goes to Big Delta State Historic Park, is to your right at kilometre 14.3 (mile 8.9). The park is on the site of a stopover on the old road from Valdez to Fairbanks. A roadhouse was built here in the early 1900s to serve travellers using the government ferry to cross the Tanana River. (Only northbound travellers were charged for the ferry service.) In 1923 Rika Wallen, who had been working for the owner and was owed back wages, either bought the roadhouse or took it over as payment. She operated it until the late 1940s, when she closed it down.

Rika's Roadhouse at Big Delta State Historic Park.

In the early 1950s, truck drivers, angry at the road toll on the bridge that had replaced the ferry, built a warehouse on Rika's property. They stored their freight in the warehouse until they could sneak it across at night. When the toll was dropped, the structure became Rika's. Intending to convert it into a new roadhouse, she put it on a concrete foundation, painted it pink and moved into it. On December 24, 1965, the place burned and Rika, then age 89, suffered frostbite while waiting for neighbours to come to her rescue. She moved into the old ferry operator's cabin, which had been built in 1929, and lived there until her death in 1969.

There is a pamphlet with a map that you can pick up at the entrance to the park. Follow the self-guiding trail to visit Rika's Roadhouse (carefully restored), a smithy, a barn, a museum and a number of other buildings. You can camp in the campground if you wish, and look at the buildings at your leisure.

Back at the highway, the Tanana Trading Post is across from Rika's Road. Watch for an ongoing 'garage sale' at the post.

Just down the highway you can see the Trans-Alaska Oil Pipeline to your right and then you cross the Big Delta Bridge over the Tanana River. As you follow the Tanana River downstream, you can occasionally see the pipeline. Look to your left to enjoy the view of the canyon wall and the mountains.

Salcha

Salcha River Lodge is to your right, 75.4 kilometres (46.8 miles) from Rika's Road, and then you cross the Salcha River at 1.8 kilometres (1.1 miles) from the lodge. As you drive through Salcha, watch for the school sign at kilometre 5 (mile 3.1) so that you know to watch for children at play, because the school itself is hidden by trees. You continue through the community, passing a gas station and store, the Salcha Store and Service, at kilometre 9.9 (mile 6.2).

The Knotty Shop is to your left at kilometre 16.3 (mile 10.1). Watch for the moose, elk, sheep and giant mosquitoes made out of burls in the front yard. Inside the shop there are all sorts of burl souvenirs, plus Native crafts such as moccasins and jewellery. Go into the back area to see a wildlife exhibition of stuffed animals and birds. For a bite to eat, stop in at the lunch counter, which is made of a length of log with burls and is supplied with burl stools.

In Alaska the soil where spruce trees are found with burls on them often has a naturally occurring level of arsenic in it. Arsenic apparently causes a cell blockage in the tree's cambium layer. To compensate, the tree grows new cells in the outer layer. These, too, are impeded and more cells are grown around them, thus forming a burl.

Knotty Shop.

North Pole

As you continue north on the Richardson Highway, you come to the entrance to Eielson Air Force Base at kilometre 14 (mile 8.7) from the Knotty Shop. You can book a tour of the base (Fridays only) by phoning the public affairs office at 907-377-2116. Then watch for Laurence Road, which goes to the Chena Lakes Recreation Site. It is a popular place for swimming, fishing, canoeing, sailing, sunbathing and picnicking, and you can count on it being crowded. The many lakes at the 810-hectare (2000-acre) site were created by the US Army Corps of Engineers as part of a water-control project after the Chena River flooded in 1967. The engineers also constructed a dam on Moose Creek, a levee and a spillway into the Tanana River.

In 26.4 kilometres (16.4 miles) from the Knotty Shop, you reach Mission Road and the settlement of North Pole, Alaska. Turn right on Mission to find North Pole's visitor reception centre, on the right at Mistletoe Drive, just off the highway. It is in a very short log building with a sod roof.

From the visitor centre go back along Mission Road to cross the highway and you find yourself on 5th Avenue. Santa Claus House is one block down St. Nicholas Drive—the first turn to your right. Here you can sit on Santa Claus's knee, buy some

Santa Claus House at North Pole.

Christmas decorations, or arrange for a letter 'from Santa Claus' to be sent to a child in December. (Similar letters can be arranged for at the visitor reception centre.)

To see the actual 'North Pole,' return to 5th Avenue and turn right. Go 0.5 kilometres (0.5 miles) down the avenue, which has striped candy canes along it, until you see a park to your right. In front of that park is the red-and-white striped 'North Pole.' Continue down 5th Avenue to reach the business section of the village.

The story of North Pole, Alaska, began in 1949 when Con Miller, a resident of Fairbanks, found a Santa Claus suit. He began wearing it on his visits to the interior of the state, where the children loved it. He moved about 19 kilometres (12 miles) southeast of Fairbanks and set up a trading post and called it 'Santa Claus House.' In the 1950s the residents of the area hoped to attract a toy manufacturer and so established the town of North Pole. No manufacturer came, but the town thrived anyway and has named a number of its streets and avenues in the Christmas tradition.

Fairbanks

Once you are back on the Richardson Highway, 1.1 kilometres (0.7 miles) from 5th Avenue, you come to Badger Road. (Turning right onto Santa Claus Lane from 5th Avenue or continuing past the Santa Claus House on St. Nicholas Drive would also take you to the highway; if you crossed the highway at this junction, you would be on Badger Road.) If you want to bypass Fairbanks and head straight for Chena Hot Springs, turn right onto Badger Road. Follow it until you reach Nordale Road and turn right again. In 16.1 kilometres (10 miles) from Badger Road, turn right onto Chena Hot Springs Road (see p. 66).

If you stay on the highway, you reach the welcome sign for Fairbanks at 20.5 kilometres (12.7 miles) from 5th Avenue in North Pole. When you reach Airport Way, at 21.8 kilometres (13.5 miles), you are at the end of the Richardson Highway, though the road continues as the Steese Expressway. To reach the Fairbanks' visitor reception centre, turn left on Airport Way, go two blocks and turn right on Cushman, which is a one-way street. Drive down to 1st Avenue (just before the bridge across the Chena River) and turn right. The visitor centre is on your left.

To get to Alaskaland theme park, return to Airport Way and turn right. Drive to Peger Street and turn right, and then right again to reach the parking lot. Admission to the Alaskaland grounds is free, but you do pay for the entertainment here. Alaskaland has a large play area for children, miniature golf, museums and a train that offers rides around the park. There are many historic buildings here that now have craft shops, fast-food outlets and galleries in them. Some of the buildings have plaques on them that describe their history. One reads: 'Wold Family Home from 1946 to 1969. Joanne, one of the daughters, is known for her writing talents, *This Old House* and *Gold City Girl.*'

Two other things to do at Alaskaland are to visit the steamer *SS Nenana*, which plied the waters of Alaska

Alaskaland at Fairbanks.

from 1933 to 1952, and to see the gold-mining exhibit. Stay for the Salmon Bake at 5 PM each day.

In August of 1901, E.T. Barnette and his wife, Isabelle, were headed up the Tanana River to establish a trading post near present-day Tanacross. The Barnettes and their supplies were aboard the *Lavelle Young*, captained by Charles Adams. When the *Lavelle Young* could not navigate the rapids on the Tanana River, the captain turned up the Chena River, where the ship ran aground on a sand bar. The only way to get off the bar was to lighten the load. Adams did this by dumping the Barnettes' supplies on the river bank, near where the visitor reception centre is today.

Well, E.T. Barnette set up shop where the supplies had been unloaded and his first customer was Felix Pedro, a prospector in the area. The Barnettes decided to stay, which was fortunate for them, because three months later Pedro found gold nearby in what was later named Pedro Creek (see p. 68) and the Fairbanks gold rush was on.

In 1923 the Alaska Railroad connected Fairbanks to Anchorage and Seward, and gold dredges began digging up the permafrost and riverbeds in the search for gold. The gold rush died down, but in 1942 the Alaska Highway brought further building to this community. The construction of the Trans-Alaska Oil Pipeline in 1968 kept Fairbanks going and it is now the second-largest city in the state.

Train at Alaskaland.

Fairbanks to Circle

Chena Hot Springs Road

To head northward to Chena Hot Springs, take Airport Way back to the junction with the Steese Expressway and turn left onto the expressway. After 7.8 kilometres (4.8 miles), turn right onto Chena Hot Springs Road, which is paved.

After driving past acreages, you reach Skip's Cache, a service station and grocery store with a greenhouse, on your left at kilometre 17 (mile 10.6) from the turn-off. Tacks' General Store and Greenhouse Cafe, in two buildings, is at kilometre 38.5 (mile 23.9).

At kilometre 42.6 (mile 26.5) you enter the Chena River Recreation Area, which extends for the next 40 kilometres (25 miles). It is the largest recreation area in Alaska, covering about 102,800 hectares (254,000 acres); only three state parks are larger: Denali, Kachemak Bay and Chugach. As you drive, you pass picnic areas, campgrounds, hiking trails and places where you can launch a canoe and paddle downstream to Fairbanks. Small lakes throughout the area are stocked with grayling.

Although there are no private residences within the recreation area, at kilometre 81 (mile 50.3) you pass Angel Creek Lodge, an official checkpoint on the Yukon Quest (see sidebar on p. 71).

You leave the Chena River Recreation Area at kilometre 83 (mile 51.6) and reach the end of the pavement at kilometre 92.4 (mile 57.4). After you drive under a wooden archway and cross a short one-lane wooden bridge, you reach the parking area for the Chena Hot Springs Resort. You can rent a cabin, take a trail ride, soak in the indoor pool or the outdoor hot tub, or wander through the yard and look at the old vehicles.

Old car in yard of Chena Hot Springs.

Though local Natives already knew of these hot springs, according to the resort operators, the first non-Natives to visit them were Robert and Thomas Swan. In search of relief for Robert's rheumatism, they set out to follow up a US Geological Survey field team's 1904 report of steam along the upper Chena River and found the hot springs over one month later. Another account says that Felix Pedro found them in 1903. A resort had already formed around the hot springs by 1911. The first road to the resort was constructed in 1967, but it was destroyed by a flood that same year. It was rebuilt and then paved in 1983.

The Trans-Alaska Oil Pipeline and Gold Dredge No. 8

Back on the Steese Expressway, watch for the Trans-Alaska Oil Pipeline to your right as you drive north. In 5.5 kilometres (3.4 miles) from Chena Hot Springs Road there is a pull-out to your right where you can read about the pipeline and see it up close. From this pull-out, Prudhoe Bay (the source of the oil) is 724 pipeline kilometres (450 miles) to the north and Valdez (where the oil is loaded into tankers; see Chapter 5) is 563 pipeline kilometres (350 miles) to the south.

Next to the pipeline there are two different types of 'pigs' on display. One is used to scrape the wax off the inside walls of the pipeline, which improves the flow of the oil. The other checks the oil temperature and speed of flow and monitors changes in the pipe wall.

If you want to see Gold Dredge No. 8, turn left onto Goldstream Road 1.7 kilometres (1.1 miles) from the pipeline pull-out. Turn

The Trans-Alaska Oil Pipeline

The 1288-kilometre (800-mile) long, 122-centimetre (48-inch) diameter Trans-Alaska Oil Pipeline took from April 29, 1974, to June 20, 1977, to build. It stretches from Prudhoe Bay, through the Brooks, Alaska and Chugach mountains and crosses 34 major rivers and 800 other rivers and streams on its way to Valdez.

Slightly less than half of the pipeline is below ground, some of it by up to 4.9 metres (16 feet). Most of the section above ground is along the Dalton Highway, because of the permafrost in this part of the state. Because the temperature of the oil is maintained at 63° C (145° F) to keep it flowing easily, unless the pipeline was extremely well insulated, the heat would melt the permafrost, causing heaves in the pipeline. The above-ground part of the line zig-zags to allow for expansion and contraction—the ambient temperature varies from –62° C to 35° C (–80° F to 95° F).

The first tanker loaded with North Slope oil left Valdez on August 1, 1977.

Alaska Pipeline.

left again onto the Old Steese Highway and in just 1 kilometre (0.6 miles) you reach the parking lot for the dredge. Besides the dredge itself, there are a number of old buildings that were in use when the dredge was in operation, including several theatres, the dredgemaster's house, a bathhouse and others. You can go on a tour of the equipment house, the offices and the dredge itself.

This steel-hulled dredge, built in 1928 and operated until 1959, became a national historic site in 1984 and a national historical mechanical engineering landmark in 1986. It has five decks, is five storeys high and has a length of 76 metres (250 feet).

Gold Dredge No. 8.

Return to the Steese Expressway and turn left. In 2.4 kilometres (1.5 miles) the expressway becomes the Steese Highway and forks to the right (as Alaska Route 6) to go to the communities of Central and Circle. Straight ahead, the Elliot Highway (Alaska Route 2) continues on to Manley Hot Springs (see page 76). Turn left off the highway here to visit the hamlet of Fox.

Fox and Central

Fox was established in 1905 as a camp for miners working in the Goldstream Valley. That silver-coloured building to your right as you turn into Fox is the his-

Panning for gold on Pedro Creek.

toric Fox Roadhouse. It was clad in metal siding in the mid-1980s to preserve it. Across the road from it is the Howling Dog Saloon, which claims to be the most northerly rock-and-roll bar in the world.

Return to the highway junction and continue on the Steese Highway toward Central. The highway travels through mounds of tailings (gravel) left by the gold dredges years ago. These piles, some of them with trees growing on them, are beside the road for much of the drive.

Watch for the turn to the right into the pull-out beside Felix Pedro's Discovery Claim on Pedro Creek at kilometre 8.5 (mile 5.3) from the junction of the Steese and Elliot highways (there is no sign). The public is allowed to pan for gold here and you can see where people have dug into the banks and tailings to look for gold.

Across the highway from the creek there is a monument to Felix Pedro, the first person to discover gold (the latter part of 1901) in the Fairbanks area. His real name was Felice Pedroni and he was born in Italy. He died in Fairbanks eight years to the day after his gold discovery.

Back on the highway, you begin climbing and in 6 kilometres (3.7 miles) from the monument you reach Cleary's Summit, with an elevation of 681 metres (2233 feet). There is a parking area to the right and you have a great view of the Chatanika Valley below.

You then head down into the valley and in 17.4 kilometres (10.8 miles) from the summit, you reach the turn-off for the old Fairbanks Exploration Company Gold Camp at Chatanika. A metal archway is at the entrance and a large gold pan is to the left on the ground. To the right there is a bucket from a gold dredge. The parking lot and the buildings of the camp are up the driveway.

The camp was established in 1925 to accommodate the crew working Gold Dredge No. 3 on the Chatanika River. The site, open 365 days per year, offers gold-panning, hiking, canoeing, boat trips and fishing in summer. In winter you can enjoy dog-sled rides, sledding and cross-country skiing.

The town of Chatanika, built near the dredge, had a post office, a school, a railroad station, a bank and a jail with a marshal. The town moved up the valley with the dredge and, when the dredge quit working in 1957, the town died.

Just up the highway past the turn-off for the gold camp, you pass the Chatanika Lodge, which is to your right. Look to your left over the piles of tailings to see the top of Gold Dredge No. 3, the second largest dredge that worked in the area. Constructed on Cleary Creek during the winter of 1927–28, it yielded 10 million dollars worth of gold in its lifetime. The dredge is on private land, so anyone going for a closer look would be trespassing.

At 2.7 kilometres

Dredging for Gold

The earliest miners in the Fairbanks area dug as far as they could in the topsoil with their picks and shovels and left when the accessible gold was gone. It was later discovered that the gold was most abundant under 24–30 metres (80–100 feet) of muddy soil, permafrost and gravel.

After the railroad was built from Seward to Fairbanks in 1923, the US Smelting, Refining and Mining Company acquired the gold claims around Fairbanks. A subsidiary of that company, the Fairbanks Exploration Company, built the Davidson Ditch (see sidebar on p. 70), set up a power plant in Fairbanks, and operated three dredges between Chatanika and Ester.

To reach the deeper gold, the surface layer of dirt and gravel was hosed off by shooting pressurized water from hydraulic cannons. The permafrost was allowed to thaw and then sprayed again. As the workers went deeper, they would heat the frozen soil before washing it out. The water for the dredging projects was brought by the Davidson Ditch.

When the miners got down to the better-paying gravel, they set up giant dredges. The dredges, which floated on water provided by the Davidson Ditch, scooped the gravel up with buckets attached to a circular conveyer. The gravel was dumped onto a screen inside the dredge and then sluiced. The gold fell through the screens and was collected, while the gravel, called 'tailings,' was pushed out the back.

By the late 1950s or the early 1960s (depending on the site), the gold was exhausted and the dredges were left where they stood. By some accounts, over 100 million dollars worth of the yellow metal had been found.

(1.6 miles) from the gold camp, you reach the Poker Flat Research Range, said to be 'the world's largest land-based rocket range,' which is owned and operated by the University of Alaska's Geophysical Institute. The gate to the site is marked by a tall, thin, red-and-white rocket. University researchers and their colleagues from other institutions use the facility to study the aurora borealis and other atmospheric phenomena for scientific and military purposes.

Look to your right at kilometre 4.8 (mile 3) to see the Imaging Riometer Antennae Array, which is used to study radio waves coming through the aurora borealis. A drawing on a sign along the highway shows how some of the naturally occurring radio noise coming through the atmosphere is absorbed by ionized particles—the particles that are responsible for the aurora borealis. The drawing also shows how the reduced noise intensity is detected and analyzed by a collection of equipment called an 'imaging riometer,' (where 'rio' stands for 'Relative Ionospheric Opacity'). This facility, part of the Poker Flat Research Range, was dedicated on September 29, 1995. If you look through the fence you can see the antennae array grid of the imaging riometer in a field near the highway.

Kilometre 13 (mile 8.1) brings you to 'Weltown; Population: 4,' on your right. You can visit the store, buy gifts or stay in one of several cabins.

Once the pavement ends, 11.8 kilometres (7.3 miles) from Weltown, you are on a good gravel road with frequent steep climbs and descents. The scenery is pretty and there are a number of campgrounds and recreation sites along this stretch of road. After you cross Long Creek at kilometre 14.6 (mile 9.1), you can stock up on provisions at the Long Creek General Store, on your left.

Turn left onto the US Creek Access Road for the White Mountains National Recreation Area at kilometre 32.8 (mile 20.4). Ahead you can see part of the pipe (a historic site) belonging to the Davidson Ditch. You can follow the road

Poker Flat Research Range.

until you are on top of the pipe where it enters the hillside. If you continue down this road for about 11 kilometres (7 miles), you arrive at Nome Creek in the White Mountains National Recreation Area, where you can try your luck panning for gold again.

The buildings on the left at 35.7 kilometres (22 miles) from the Davidson Ditch historic site are the Montana Creek Station of the State of Alaska Department of Transport. The road then climbs to Twelvemile Summit, which you reach at kilometre 44.1 (mile 27.4), on the divide between the drainages of the Yukon and Tanana rivers.

The Davidson Ditch

The 145-kilometre (90-mile) long Davidson Ditch, actually part ditch and part pipe, was built in 1925 by the Fairbanks Exploration Company to transport water to float its gold dredges. The ditch part was 1.2 metres (4 feet) deep, 3.6 metres (12 feet) wide and 134 kilometres (83 miles) long. The pipeline part was 1.2 metres (4 feet) in diameter and 11 kilometres (7 miles) long. The Davidson Ditch could carry about 212,360 litres (56,100 US gallons) per minute.

When the company quit using dredges, the Davidson Ditch was used to supply water to generate power until a flood destroyed about 300 metres (1000 feet) of pipe in 1967. As you drive toward Central, you will sometimes be able to see the pipeline on your left, sometimes on your right.

Twelvemile Summit was named by some early miners because of its distance, about 19 kilometres, from mining claims on Birch Creek. On a clear day you can have a great view of the valley way below you from the pull-out on your right. However, because of the 972-metre (3190-foot) elevation of the summit, on an overcast day you will be in clouds and mist. Even if it is cloudy and cold here or on Eagle Summit up ahead, do not let that stop you from continuing your trip, because it is usually warm and sunny around Central and Circle even when these summits are overcast.

Davidson Ditch.

As you drive toward Eagle Summit, keep a watchful eye on the alpine tundra slopes because between late July and mid-September you may see caribou. The area between the summits is also an active mining area where bulldozers and backhoes are used to dig out the river banks and dump trucks to haul the gravel to their huge sluice boxes.

You reach Eagle Summit 33.2 kilometres (20.6 miles) from Twelvemile Summit. With an elevation of 1123 metres (3685 feet), the highway here is above the treeline in a landscape of rock and alpine meadows. This summit is part of the Yukon Quest route (see sidebar, below).

If you want to climb to the actual top of Eagle Summit, there is a short road to a parking lot on your left. From there it is a 1.3-kilometre (0.8-mile) hike to the top. It is usually very windy here, so dress accordingly and you may prefer not to do this hike if it is cold and cloudy.

As you continue toward Central, you cross a number of creeks on this road. One is Mammoth Creek, at 14 kilometres (8.7 miles) from Eagle Summit. It takes its name from the race of huge woolly creatures that wandered these parts 25,000 years ago—some mammoth remains were unearthed by strip mining in the area.

Central, formerly known as 'Central House,' is at kilometre 33.4 (mile 20.8). You pass the elementary school, a

The Yukon Quest

The first run of the 1600-kilometre (1000-mile) Yukon Quest International Dog Sled Race was held in 1984, with 26 mushers (sled drivers) vying for $50,000 in prizes. The race, held every year since, takes place in February and runs between Whitehorse and Fairbanks. It changes direction each year. Teams come from countries such as Germany, Switzerland, Scotland, Finland, France and Japan to compete.

There are only seven checkpoints (another race, the Iditarod, has 20) along the trail, with a stopover in Dawson City, the official halfway mark. This 36-hour rest period gives the mushers a chance to get some sleep while veterinarians check the dogs.

The race follows the Yukon River for much of the way and climbs three summits, with temperatures that vary from above freezing to –40° C (–40° F) or lower. Each musher starts with 14 dogs. Although it usually takes about 12 days to complete the run, the record is 10 days, 16 hours.

Each checkpoint on the Yukon Quest has a large sign set up for visitors to see.

Nozzle for hydraulic gold mining at Central Museum.

market and several old and new log cabins as you come into the village. The Circle District Museum serves as the visitor reception centre. Look in the yard to see a nozzle from a hydraulic cannon that was used to hose the soil and gravel off the bedrock. Past the museum, turn right to go to Circle Hot Springs.

Circle Hot Springs and Circle

You pass Cemetery Road and cross Deadwood and Ketchem creeks before reaching Circle Hot Springs in 12.1 kilometres (7.5 miles) from Central. The four-storey hotel, built in 1930, is in excellent condition and the 1930s interior decor has been kept as original as possible. Two bedrooms on the main floor are open for you to look at and you can see an old poker table in the lobby.

The hot springs, which were used by the Athabascan peoples, were visited by the first non-Native, a prospector named William Greats, in 1893. The spring water begins at 59° C (139° F) but, by the time it gets to the Olympic-sized outdoor pool, it has cooled to 38° C (100° F).

Back at the Steese Highway, turn right to go to Circle. You cross a one-lane bridge over Crooked Creek and to your right is the remains of the Central House Roadhouse. The first roadhouse here was constructed in 1894 and it operated until it burned down in 1926. It was rebuilt in that year but now the elements have taken their toll and the old log building is collapsing.

At 32.6 kilometres (20.3 miles) from the turn-off for Circle Hot Springs, you need to slow down as you begin an 18-kilometre (11-mile) section of curvy road. At kilometre 53.8 (mile 33.4), you reach the hamlet of Circle. As you drive through it, you see the post office and a church to your right and pass an aircraft-crossing sign and several old log buildings. The road ends at the Yukon River.

Gold was discovered in Birch Creek (which you crossed about 24 kilometres [15 miles] from town) in 1893 and a supply town was established here on the bank of the Yukon to supply the miners. The miners named their new community 'Circle City' because they thought that it was on the Arctic Circle, but in reality the settlement is 80 kilometres (50 miles) south of that latitude. Until the Klondike Gold Rush beckoned miners to the Dawson City area, Circle was the largest town on the Yukon River.

In 1909, following the decline of gold-mining in the vicinity, after which most of the people left Circle City, the Rasmussen family built a house and began farming. They grew vegetables, milked cows for milk, cream and butter, and raised chickens for meat and eggs. Across from the Yukon Trading Post, the Rasmussen house still stands.

Hotel at Circle Hot Springs.

Buildings at Circle Hot Springs.

Along the Yukon River here there is a camping area and also some picnic tables and a boat launch. People from around the world have come here to spend a few days panning the river. Try it yourself—you might find a few small nuggets.

Having reached the end of the Steese Highway, return to the community of Fox, where the Elliot Highway branches off.

Beginning of Elliot Highway to Prudhoe Bay

Beginning of Elliot Highway to Livengood

Turn off the Steese Highway onto the Elliot Highway (a continuation of Alaska Route 2). This highway was named for Malcolm Elliot, who was president of the Alaska Road Commission between 1927 and 1932.

On your left, 0.5 kilometres (0.3 miles) from the beginning of the Elliot Highway, there is a roof-covered spout that dispenses spring water. This spring water from the hillside is free of bacteria and is excellent for drinking. You can take as much as you wish—just push the button.

On your left at kilometre 0.9 (mile 0.6) is the turn-off for the Little El Dorado Gold Mine, situated on one of the area's original gold-fields. Here you can ride a train to a working gold mine, pan for gold or take a walking tour of the old buildings.

If you need gas—there are no service stations for the next 189 kilometres (117 miles)—the Hilltop Service Station is to your left at kilometre 8.6 (mile 5.3). Kilometre 14.2 (mile 8.8) brings you to 'Olnes City; Population 1.' Olnes is a former railway stop on the Tanana Valley Railroad, which began as a mining railroad around 1904 and was absorbed in 1917 by what became the Alaska Railroad. The Elliot Highway originated in 1906 as a wagon road from Fox to Olnes. By 1915 a sled road continued on to Livengood.

You cross the Chatanika River at kilometre 16.9 (mile 10.5). Watch out for the sharp curves that begin at around kilometre 36 (mile 22). Just past the sign at kilometre 43.6 (mile 27.1) that announces that you are entering the Livengood–Tolovana Mining District, the pavement ends. You are now travelling on old chip seal in such poor condition that it is broken up in places.

Look ahead and to your left around kilometre 51 (mile 32) to see the silver of the Trans-Alaska Oil Pipeline amid the greens and browns of trees and rocks. This sighting is the first of many that you will have of the pipeline. On a hill to your left at kilometre 66.4 (mile 41.3), there is a sign for Pump Station 7. This pump station, one of many along the pipeline, helps maintain the flow of the oil, which travels at about 10 kilometres per hour (6 miles per hour). It takes 66 hours and 11 minutes for the oil to get from Prudhoe Bay to this station and another 61 hours and 41 minutes for it to travel the rest of the way to Valdez.

'Welcome to Joy, Alaska,' reads the sign at kilometre 77.3 (mile 48). Joy was named after Joy Griffin who, with her husband and two children, homesteaded here in the 1960s and 1970s. She wrote about her experiences in the book *Home Sweet Homestead: Sketches of Pioneer Life in Interior Alaska*. The Arctic Circle Trading Post (Wildwood General Store) is to the right just after the sign. You can get snack foods, books, jewellery and crafts here, as well as T-shirts and sweatshirts that state that you have crossed the Arctic Circle. However, the Arctic Circle is actually still over 100 kilometres (60 miles) due north of here.

At kilometre 29.7 (mile 18.5) from Joy you cross Livengood Creek. Then turn right at kilometre 30.7 (mile 19.1) to go to Livengood, where you can see some old log cabins but where there are no services. In 2.8 kilometres (1.7 miles), when you reach a T-intersection where there are log cabins among the trees, turn left to enter Livengood.

Livengood began as a gold town in 1914 and remained vibrant until 1920. Miners came to the area again in the 1930s and 1940s, but nothing came of their efforts. In the 1970s Livengood was a construction camp during the building of the Dalton Highway and the oil pipeline. It is now a ghost town. Although the town's name suggests that its residents had found the ideal place to live, the settlement was actually named after Jay Livengood who, along with Nathaniel Hudson, discovered gold in the area.

Back on the Elliot Highway, in 3.5 kilometres (2.2 miles) you reach a junction. Here, where the Dalton Highway (see p. 77) continues straight ahead, go left to stay on the Elliot Highway and continue to Manley Hot Springs.

Manley Hot Springs

Past the Dalton Highway junction, the Elliot Highway is surfaced in gravel and it is winding, so you will have to travel slowly. As you drive, keep watching for views of Mount McKinley to your left.

At kilometre 38.6 (mile 24) you reach Ptarmigan Pass, which is the highest point on the Elliot Highway. Look for Mount McKinley from here. Minto Road is to the left at kilometre 60.3 (mile 37.5). The Native village of New Minto is 17.7 kilometres (11 miles) down this side road. Old Minto was further south, on the Tanana River, but frequent flooding forced the residents to move to their present site on the Tolovana River in 1969. Most of the Native peoples here fish and hunt for a living, while some make crafts for sale.

You drive through a burn area and reach Eureka Junction 33 kilometres (20.5 miles) from the Minto Road. The road to the right, which leads to the Eureka mining area, is not maintained. At kilometre 64.3 (mile 40), again on the right, you reach Tofty Road. If you turn onto it, you will find that it immediately splits: the right branch goes to another mining area and the left one to the now-closed (since 1997) Manley Hot Springs Resort.

Turn left 1.6 kilometres (1 mile) past Tofty Road and cross Manley Hot Springs Slough to enter the village of Manley Hot Springs. Originally, the area was known as 'the Baker Creek Hot Springs,' because of nearby Baker Creek. In the early 1900s, wagon and sled roads connected the mining towns of Tofty, Eureka and Baker Creek Hot Springs. Baker Creek Hot Springs, with a population of 101, provided services for the miners of the area and had a resort hotel.

Over time, 'Baker Creek Hot Springs' was shortened to 'Hot Springs' and stayed that way for many years. Then, in 1957, because the postmaster was tired of the residents' mail being first sent to Hot Springs, Arkansas, the name was changed to 'Manley Hot Springs,' in honour of miner Frank Manley, who had built the Hot Springs Resort Hotel half a century earlier. By the time that the Elliot Highway (as a summer road) was completed to Manley Hot Springs in 1959, the neighbouring towns had disappeared.

If you are looking for a place to stay, consider the Manley Roadhouse, 'serving Alaska since 1906,' which has a prehistoric display inside. Other choices include renting a cabin, staying at the campground on the Manley Hot Springs Slough or setting off to do some wilderness camping in the area. There is lots to do in Manley Hot Springs, even though it currently has a population of only about one hundred. For example, you can visit the village artisans, fish for pike or take a boat charter on the Tanana River. Ask at the roadhouse for information, even if you plan to stay elsewhere. Inquire about the Greenhouse if you would like to pick up some tomatoes and grapes (in season) or have a soak in a hot tub.

If you want to see the Tanana River, follow the Elliot Highway to its end 4.8 kilometres (3 miles) past the village. Then, as you head back toward Fairbanks, you can take a side trip northward, almost to the Arctic Ocean, on the Dalton Highway.

Yukon River.

The Dalton Highway

Built in 1974 to accommodate traffic hauling supplies for the building of the Trans-Alaska Oil Pipeline, the Dalton Highway was first known as 'the North Slope Haul Road.' It was subsequently renamed after James W. Dalton, an engineer who was involved in oil exploration in the area. In places, foam insulation under the roadbed prevents the permafrost from thawing. It is the only road in the US that crosses the Arctic Circle.

This very rough packed-gravel road can be slippery when wet and very dusty when dry. There are no shoulders and there are often no guardrails at drop-offs. Downhills are steep, meaning lots of wear and tear on your brakes. Although the speed limit is 80 kilometres per hour (50 miles per hour), you will spend more time travelling at 65–70 kilometres per hour (40–45 miles per hour). If you have a bigger vehicle, such as a motorhome, or are pulling a trailer, you will be down to 55–65 kilometres per hour (35–40 miles per hour) most of the time.

Watch for large trucks on the road. Pull over and slow down or stop when you meet one to avoid a flying rock hitting your windshield. Also pull over when one is coming up behind you to allow it to pass. Some hills have limited visibility, so keep to the right when climbing them.

Originally exclusively for pipeline traffic, the highway was opened to the public as far as the Yukon River Bridge in 1978. In 1982 the public was permitted to travel as far as Disaster Creek—about 160 kilometres (100 miles) north of the Arctic Circle. Now the highway is open all the way to Deadhorse, which is just short of the Arctic Ocean.

All types of vehicles, from little cars to motorhomes, are seen on this road. You even have to watch for bicyclists. Some people who have travelled the Dalton loved the experience, while others were disappointed that they went. Your own reaction

Yukon River Bridge on Dalton Highway.

will depend on what you expect. If you know ahead of time that it will take you three days, possibly four, to make the 1332-kilometre (828-mile) round-trip and that you will be going slowly, then you will be more likely to enjoy it if you do go. Just remember that you will not be able to drive up to the Arctic Ocean and camp on its shore, because the last section of road through the oilfields is still closed to the public. (However, you can see the ocean by taking an organized one-hour tour from Deadhorse.)

The lovely scenery does make up for the slow going along this road, which has many pull-outs, viewpoints, creeks, rivers and pipeline-viewing points along the way. You can call the Alaska Department of Transportation at 907-456-7623 to ask about current road conditions.

At kilometre 87.7 (mile 54.5) from the Elliot Highway you can see the Yukon River below you as you approach Yukon River Crossing, which is at kilometre 91.7 (mile 57). The Yukon River Bridge—also known as the Edward L. Patton Bridge, named after the president of the Alyeska Pipeline Service Company during the bridge's construction—was completed on October 11, 1975. It is 698 metres (2290 feet) long and has a six percent grade because the north bank of the river is lower than the south one. The oil pipeline is attached to the right (east) side of the bridge.

To the left, after the bridge, there is a very large parking area with a restaurant, a service station, a visitor reception centre and access to the Yukon River. Down at the river you can join Yukon River Tours for a boat tour to an Athabascan fish camp. Beside the visitor centre there is a platform with interpretive signs about the Dalton Highway, the history of the Yukon River, the life cycle of the salmon and the life of Edward Patton. On your return leg of this drive remember to stop in at the restaurant here to ask for a certificate that states that you have been to the Arctic Circle.

At 6.9 kilometres (4.3 miles) from the visitor centre, keep a watch for airplanes crossing the highway—you may be asked to stop as a plane takes off from a runway beside the highway. Past the plane crossing, you go across a bridge over the oil pipeline and pass the runway, which is to your right.

After the first 60 kilometres (40 miles) of the highway, during which you drove through a landscape mainly forested in black spruce and willow, with a few poplar trees, the trees are replaced by tundra with lots of small flowers. To your right at kilometre 67.7 (mile 42.1), in the middle of the tundra near the summit of Finger Mountain, like a pointing finger, is 12-metre (40-foot) high Finger Rock.

This 'tor'—an outcropping of boulders or heavily jointed rock on otherwise smooth terrain—is one of a number in this area. They originated 110 million years ago, when magma bubbled up through the bedrock and hardened into granite. Over the millennia, water froze in the cracks between the bedrock and the granite, so that the surrounding bedrock broke away. Even though the granite itself is slowly breaking down, the bedrock has weathered much more quickly, leaving the granite exposed as tors.

Tor on Dalton Highway.

Finger Rock and the other tors have a long history as landmarks for Native peoples. More recently, explorers, fur traders and even early bush pilots used them to guide their travels as well.

Just after Finger Rock there is a parking lot beside one huge tor. From here you can follow a self-guided path to the top. Signs along the path explain about the birds, animals and plants of the tundra.

The line of tors ends at about kilometre 71 (mile 44) and then you reach the Old Man Lodge and Circle Gift Shop, to your left at kilometre 75.8 (mile 47.1). At the gift shop you can get sweatshirts stating that you have crossed the Arctic Circle. The proprietors operate a cafe and bed-and-breakfast as well.

You actually reach the Arctic Circle at kilometre 94 (mile 58.4). The parking lot, campground and picnic area are to the right. Interpretive signs here tell about the ever-changing climate and how the animals, birds and plants survive here in the cold of winter and heat of summer. Note that the further north you travel above the Arctic Circle, the more summer days there are without a sunset—and the more winter days without a sunrise.

Between here and Atigun Pass you first cross the Jim River three times and then you pass viewpoints overlooking the South Fork Koyukuk River. You cross it and then cross the Middle Fork Koyukuk River four times. These rivers are good for chum, king salmon, burbot, pike, grayling, Dolly Varden and whitefish, but be sure to check the current fishing regulations.

Coldfoot (as two words on some signs) is 96.5 kilometres (60 miles) above the Arctic Circle. The amenities include a visitor reception centre, a service station, a campground, a store, motels, a gift shop, a 24-hour restaurant and a dump station (the most northerly one on this highway). These services are the last ones before Deadhorse.

Coldfoot developed at the site of an old mining camp that was set up when gold was discovered on Tramway Bar on the Koyukuk River. The settlement was first called 'Slate Creek,' after the creek on which it sat. The story goes that its name was changed after prospectors travelling up the Koyukuk River in 1900 made it as far as Slate Creek and then got cold feet because of winter and headed back home.

Many people come to Coldfoot to begin their visit to the Gates of the Arctic

Arctic Circle sign on Dalton Highway.

National Park, which is accessible only by foot. Stop in at the visitor reception centre for more information about this park and the Arctic.

Seven kilometres (4.3 miles) from Coldfoot is Marion Creek campground, which has well water. As you drive, there are many viewpoints, bridges, sites of former pipeline construction camps and pipeline pump stations along the highway. A few of these sites have outhouses.

At kilometre 22 (mile 13.7) there is a left turn for Wiseman, a historic mining town with about 25 permanent residents. The Wiseman Trading Company building, constructed in 1910, houses a general store and a gift shop.

You enter the Brooks Range and, at about kilometre 86 (mile 53) from the Wiseman turn-off, you begin climbing to Atigun Pass, which you reach at kilometre 90.3 (mile 56.1). At about 1450 metres (4800 feet) above sea level, Atigun Pass is the highest highway pass in Alaska and the northernmost highway pass in the world. During the steep descent from the top, you cross the Atigun River for the first time at kilometre 13 (mile 8.1) and again at kilometre 42 (mile 26.1).

You continue to cross rivers, see more of the pipeline and enjoy great views of the mountains and tundra until you reach Deadhorse, at the end of the public highway, at kilometre 272 (mile 169) from Atigun Pass.

There are hotels, service stations, a general store and repair shops at Deadhorse. Information on tours of the oilfields and the Arctic Ocean are available at the Arctic Caribou Inn and at the Prudhoe Bay Hotel. In addition, you can camp overnight at the Tesoro service station but there are limited facilities.

Even in the middle of summer you can expect the weather to be cool and windy, so dress accordingly. From here, head back to Fairbanks, remembering to purchase any last-minute mementos of the far north along the way.

Passing through Fairbanks and Ester Dome

Once you return to the Steese Highway, you soon pass Chena Hot Springs Road. Then, if you don't need to stock up on groceries, turn right onto the Johansen Expressway at the second set of traffic lights. When you cross University Avenue, the expressway becomes Geist Road. Continue on Geist Road to the George Parks Highway (Alaska Route 3) and turn right.

(If you want to do some grocery shopping first, stay on the Steese Expressway past the Johansen Expressway and take Airport Way toward downtown. To continue sightseeing, go back to Airport Way, head west past Alaskaland and turn right onto the George Parks Highway.)

For a lovely view, and maybe a glimpse of Mount McKinley, watch for Sheep Creek Road on your right shortly past Geist Road. Turn here and follow it to Ester Dome Road, which is gravel, where you turn left. When you reach a Y-junction, 1 kilometre (0.6 miles) from Sheep Creek Road, take the right fork. At kilometre 6.2 (mile 3.8) from Sheep Creek Road you come to Ester Dome, a wide open area, with communication towers straight ahead. Walk along the pathway that goes into the bush to your left. On a clear

View from Ester Dome in Fairbanks.

day you can see Mount McKinley, which is about 270 kilometres (170 miles) to the southwest. Even if the mountain has clouds around it, you might still be able to see the summit above them. If you are visiting Fairbanks in winter, come to Ester Dome just as the sun is rising, because Mount McKinley with a pink tinge to it makes a lovely photograph.

For additional views, drive along the road toward the communication towers. In 0.8 kilometres (0.5 miles), you arrive at a T-intersection, (to the right is blocked by a fence). Because the turn-around up ahead is tight, leave your trailer or motorhome here. Turn left and in 0.5 kilometres (0.3 miles) you reach the edge of the hilltop. From here you have an excellent view of the Tanana River, its valley and the mountains beyond.

On your way back down, watch for Henderson Road North, on the right at about 1.8 kilometres (1.1 miles) from the T. Turn onto it—it is a narrow one-lane road through tall trees. On the right, at kilometre 2.5 (mile 1.6) from the T, you pass Ryan Lode Mine, which is closed to the public, but just past the mine there is a view of the valley to the right. The road improves and, at kilometre 3.9 (mile 2.4), you reach pavement.

At kilometre 5.8 (mile 3.6) from the T-intersection, you reach Goldhill Road. Turn right onto it and you soon arrive at the George Parks Highway again. From here, you can continue toward Anchorage (see Chapter 3).

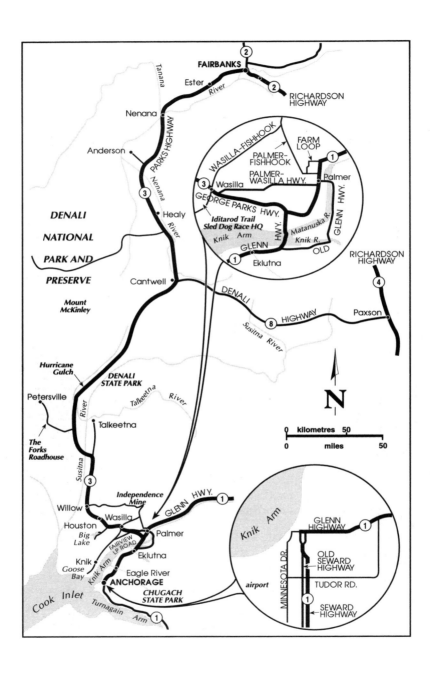

3
Ester to Anchorage

Visiting a historic saloon, seeing Mount McKinley (the highest mountain in North America), driving to a historic gold-mine site and learning about the Iditarod Trail Sled Dog Race are some of the highlights on this route. You can lay a bet on when the ice will break up on the Nenana River, take a tour through Denali National Park or hike to a waterfall—all on the route between Ester and Anchorage.

Ester to Denali National Park

Ester

Travelling westward from Fairbanks on the George Parks Highway (Alaska Route 3), at kilometre 1.2 (mile 0.7) from Goldhill Road (see end of Chapter 2), you reach the Old Nenana Highway. Turn right onto it, go 0.5 kilometres (0.3 miles) and

turn right again onto Village Road. Follow it a short distance to a T-intersection. Turn left here and drive into the parking lot by the big hotel with 'Ester Gold Camp' printed in large letters on its front. The lot serves the hotel, the Malemute Saloon, the Pig and Poke Gift Shop and the visitor reception centre.

All the buildings here are historic, some dating back to the early 1900s. Each one has a plaque on it that describes its history. From 1900 to 1914,

Malemute Saloon at Ester Gold Camp.

Ester served the miners in the area. The Fairbanks Exploration Company began dredging the creeks for gold and in 1936 it set up the Ester Gold Camp for its workers. In 1987, Ester Gold Camp, with its 11 historic buildings, was named to the National Register of Historic Places.

The visitor reception centre is in the old assay office, circa 1906, which was used by the superintendent of the Fairbanks Exploration Company. The false fronts and porches were added in 1958, using historic materials from a bunkhouse that once stood near the mess hall (now the hotel and restaurant). At the visitor centre you can register for camping or purchase tickets for the 9 PM show in the Malemute Saloon.

Sawdust covers the floor inside the Malemute Saloon, the tables have initials and dates carved into them and mining equipment hangs on the walls and from the ceiling. Robert Service's poem, 'The Shooting of Dan McGrew,' was set in the Malemute Saloon. The bar, from the Royal Alexandra Hotel in Dawson City, was built around 1900. If you order peanuts while in the saloon, make sure that you throw the shells on the floor, because there is a fine for leaving them on the table.

Gift Shop at Ester Gold Camp.

The Pig and Poke Gift Shop is in a former blacksmith shop that was built in Ester around 1906. The hotel was built as a bunkhouse in Fox in 1934 and moved here in the winter of 1936–37. If you want to take a shower, ask at the hotel about the bathhouses behind the building.

Back on the George Parks Highway, at kilometre 10 (mile 6.2) from the Old Nenana Highway, there is a pull-out to your left for a monument dedicated to George

George Parks Monument.

Alexander Parks, after whom this highway is named. Kilometre 39.7 (mile 24.7) brings you to a viewpoint from which you can see Mount McKinley if the weather is clear.

You cross the Tanana River at kilometre 31.5 (mile 19.5) from the viewpoint and reach the community of Nenana 1 kilometre (0.6 miles) later.

Nenana

Nenana, located just east of the confluence of the Tanana and Nenana rivers, gets its name from a Native word that means 'a good place to camp between the rivers.' In 1902 a trading post was established here and, when the Alaska Railroad was being built in 1916, Nenana became a construction camp. The last spike of the Alaska Railroad was driven here on July 15, 1923, when Nenana was one of the state's largest towns. (In summer this railroad still offers daily 12-hour trips between Fairbanks and Anchorage.) Today, though relatively small, Nenana is the home port for a fleet of tugs and barges that haul supplies, freight and gas to villages along the Tanana and Yukon rivers.

Nenana is perhaps best known for the annual Nenana Ice Classic, which the city has been holding since 1917, when railroad workers began guessing when the ice on the Tanana River would break up. A black-and-white struc-

Tripod in Nenana.

ture of local logs, which is traditionally called 'the tripod' (although it has more than three legs) is frozen into the ice of the river in the tripod-raising ceremony in early March. As breakup approaches, a wire is tied from the tripod to a mechanism that controls a clock in a tower on the shore. Residents, visitors and other people (by mail, e-mail and phone) have all year to bet on the exact minute that the ice will break up, as indicated by the stopping of the clock when the structure on the ice

Taku Chief in Nenana.

moves more than 30 metres (100 feet). Everyone who has bet correctly shares in the jackpot, which can get into the hundreds of thousands of dollars.

The visitor reception centre is to your left as you come into the village. In its yard you can see a black-and-white metal replica of the Ice Classic tripod and the restored Taku Chief, the last commercial wooden tugboat to work the Nenana and Yukon rivers; though it is on display, it is not meant for climbing on.

The Tripod Gift Shop, which has a wooden Ice Classic tripod beside it, is across 'A' Street from the visitor centre. This tripod was recovered as it went down the river on May 6, 1977, during that year's Ice Classic. You can pick up an entry form for next year's classic at the gift shop. Note that, since the contest began, the ice has broken up anywhere between April 20 (a record set in 1940) and May 20 (as was recorded in 1964).

Drive down 'A' Street until you come to a T-intersection at Front Street. Straight ahead is the State of Alaska Railroad Museum, located in the railway depot, which is on the National Register of Historic Places. Beside the museum there is a monument to the Alaska Railroad's last spike, driven by former US President Warren G. Harding during his first visit to the state, thus completing the tracks from Seward to Fairbanks.

Turn right onto Front Street. In one block you reach St. Marks Mission on the right. Built upriver from the town in 1905, it was moved in the 1930s when the river bank it was on began to erode. Across Front Street from the church is the Watchman's Building, in which officials are stationed to watch over the tripod and clock around breakup during the Nenana Ice Classic. There is another tripod beside this building—no matter where you drive in this town, you will see various sizes of the famous tripod.

Railroad bridge in Nenana.

Continue down Front Street. Just before you reach the railroad bridge ahead, you can turn left to go to the beach. From this beach you have a good view of the railroad bridge. With a length of 213 metres (700 feet), it is the second-longest single-span railroad bridge in the US. It was at the north end of this bridge that President Harding drove the last spike.

Anderson and Healy

Continue south on the highway for 34.3 kilometres (21.3 miles) from Nenana; then turn right at the turn-off for Anderson and the Clear Air Force Base. In 1.8 kilometres (1.1 miles), turn right again to go to Anderson. (The Clear Air Force Base, straight ahead, is closed to the public.)

Drive 6.2 kilometres (3.9 miles) down the road to the small town of Anderson, which consists mainly of a store and a few houses. There is a large campground on the Nenana River here. At the annual Bluegrass Festival, held on the last weekend in July, you can listen to music, look at crafts and sample different foods.

Return to the highway. At kilometre 12.1 (mile 7.5) from the road to Anderson, you cross the Nenana River, which flows 53 metres (174 feet) below you in its canyon. You can occasionally see the river and the Nenana Valley to your left as you drive south. Look to your left at kilometre 55 (mile 34.2), just before you drive into Healy, to see a 1.8-million-kilogram (4-million-pound) walking dragline working in the coal fields.

A few settlers founded Healy in 1904. Coal mining began in 1918. When the Alaska Railroad was built, a station was constructed at Healy. During the Second World War, the demand for coal increased so much that soldiers were sent to work in the mines. Although a number of mining companies operated over the years, the Usibelli Coal Mine, established in 1943, is the only commercial coal mine in Alaska today. Some of the coal that the dragline digs up is currently shipped to Korea and some of it is used in a power plant that supplies the Tanana Valley and Fairbanks with electricity.

Healy has many services located along the highway and a sign gives a long list of bed-and-breakfast operators in the area.

You cross Bison Gulch at 8.5 kilometres (5.3 miles) from Healy and then you cross the Nenana River for a second time at kilometre 9.4 (mile 5.8). As you do so, look to your left to see the canyon formed by the river. You then begin working your way down into the canyon. At kilometre 12 (mile 7.5) there is a wall beside you, so watch for rocks on the road. From kilometre 14.6 to kilometre 15.9 (mile 9.1 to mile 9.9), you are in the canyon itself, with the river beside you and walls on both sides. Notice the reds, greys, ochres and tans of the rock here. On leaving the canyon, you pass a long row of tourist accommodations where you need to watch for people walking on the highway.

Kilometre 17.5 (mile 10.9) brings you to the third bridge over the Nenana River and then, at kilometre 18 (mile 11.2), a sign notifies you that you are driving alongside Denali National Park and Preserve, which is on your right.

Denali National Park and Preserve

Turn right into the park 0.5 kilometres (0.3 miles) from the sign. Riley Creek campground is to your left and, in 1.1 kilometres (0.6 miles), turn right to park at the visitor reception centre, where you can get a map of the park, register for camping and pick up backcountry permits.

To protect the wildlife of the park and safeguard the wilderness as much as possible, private motor vehicles are permitted only on the 23.5 kilometres (14.6 miles)

Denali National Park

This park was established in 1917 under the name 'Mount McKinley National Park,' even though at the time the mountain was not entirely inside the park boundaries. Charles Sheldon, a naturalist who had travelled through the area in 1906 and the person behind the idea of the park, had wanted the name to be Denali, a Native word meaning 'the Great One.' It was not until 1980, when the park was enlarged, that its name was finally changed to 'Denali National Park and Preserve.' It now covers more than 2.4 million hectares (6 million acres).

Denali National Park sign at entrance to park.

More than 600 species of flowering plants, plus fungi, lichens and mosses can be found within the park. It is inhabited by 159 species of birds and about 37 species of mammals. The boreal forest, made up mainly of black spruce, extends from sea level to about 700 metres (2300 feet) within the park. Above the black spruce is the taiga (Russian for 'land of twigs'), whose larger vegetation consists mostly of shaggy, bushy specimens of dwarf willow, spruce, aspen and birch. Above the taiga, at over 760 metres (2500 feet), is the tundra (from a Lapp word meaning 'vast, rolling, treeless plain'). Higher still, the tundra gives way to glaciers.

of road between the entrance and the Savage River. You have a choice of three campgrounds that you can drive to in your vehicle.

To go further into the park, you can go on foot, by bicycle or by bus. There are two kinds of bus service offered within the park (both operated by Denali Park Resorts): a sightseeing service with tours of three lengths (the longest, to Wonder Lake, takes 11 hours for the round-trip) and a shuttle-bus service that provides transportation to and from campsites and trailheads. (Buses run by private food and lodging operations at Wonder Lake also use the park road.)

Bus tickets of both kinds are available at the visitor centre, but it is best to reserve ahead. To reserve shuttle-bus tickets, call 1-800-622-7275 (PARK) or, from Anchorage, 272-7275. To reserve sightseeing tickets, call 1-800-276-7234 or, from Anchorage, 276-7234; within two days of departure, call the Denali Park Hotel at 907-683-2215.

Immediately after turning back onto the George Parks Highway, you cross Riley Creek. At kilometre 9.7 (mile 6) from the park road, you leave Denali National Park behind and come to your fourth crossing of the Nenana River. Kilometre 34.7 (mile 21.6) brings you to the final crossing of the river. You reach the junction with the Denali Highway (Alaska Route 8) at kilometre 44.3 (mile 27.5).

Turn left here if you want to take a side trip on the Denali Highway, which ends at Paxson (see Chapter 5), a community on the Richardson Highway (Alaska Route 4) about 200 kilometres (125 miles) due south of Delta Junction. The Denali Highway is paved for the first 4.5 kilometres (2.8 miles) and is gravel for most of the remaining 208 kilometres (129 miles). Do not expect to go any faster than about 50–65 kilometres per hour (30–40 miles per hour). The Denali Highway does not have any really steep climbs, although it does cross the second highest pass in Alaska, MacLaren Pass, at an elevation of 1245 metres (4086 feet).

Work on the Denali Highway began in 1940 and was completed in 1957. Until 1971, when the George Parks Highway was built between Fairbanks and Anchorage, the Denali Highway was the only road into Mount McKinley National Park, as it was then called. People from Fairbanks had to travel about 530 kilometres (330 miles) to get to the park and those in Anchorage had an approximately 685-kilometre (425-mile) trip.

Cantwell to Wasilla

Cantwell and Denali State Park

To visit the site where the village of Cantwell developed, as a stop on the Alaska Railroad, turn off the George Parks Highway onto the road opposite the terminus of the Denali Highway. A bar and a coffee shop are still located at this original site, although most of the local services are now along the highway. The town was named after John C. Cantwell, an army lieutenant who surveyed the area in the 1880s. The Nenana River also used to be named after him.

Alaska Veterans' Memorial.

Continuing on the George Parks Highway, look for the Igloo Lodge to your left at kilometre 34.3 (mile 21.3) from the junction for Cantwell and the Denali Highway. It is a hotel built and painted to resemble an igloo; little windows mark where the rooms are.

Hurricane Gulch is at kilometre 58.5 (mile 36.4). Just before the bridge, a parking area to the right provides access to trails that allow you to walk beside the gulch, although the gulch itself is hard to see because your view is blocked by trees.

In 8.6 kilometres (5.3 miles) from the bridge you enter Denali State Park. This park was established in 1970 and expanded to 131,220 hectares (324,240 acres) in 1976.

As you cross Little Coal Creek, at kilometre 17.5 (mile 10.9), you can have another long look down. Kilometre 43.2 (mile 26.8) brings you to the left turn for the Alaska Veterans' Memorial in Denali State Park. There is

Looking for Mt. McKinley from viewpoint.

a picnic area beneath the trees and there are benches to sit on. Signs inform you about several topics: one tells about the Second World War and the threat of a Japanese attack; another explains that the deadliest enemy during the war was the weather—the wind, fog, snow and ice—that damaged equipment and caused the death of soldiers; a third recounts how New England's whaling industry (which hunted whales in the Bering Sea) helped finance the northern forces during the American Civil War; and another describes the battle between 16,000 American soldiers and 2650 Japanese soldiers (on higher ground) who fought on the island of Attu for 19 days in May of 1943.

The viewpoint on the right, 19.5 kilometres (12.1 miles) from the memorial, is said to be the best place from which to see Mount McKinley. Panels show a drawing of Mount McKinley without clouds and provide a write-up on Denali State Park and on the area around you. At kilometre 24.5 (mile 15.2) you leave Denali State Park.

At kilometre 51.5 (mile 32) you cross Trapper Creek and reach Trapper Creek Trading Post.

Trapper Creek, The Forks and Petersville

On the right, 1 kilometre (0.6 miles) from the trading post, take the turn-off that goes to Trapper Creek and Petersville. The road, though narrow, is paved to begin with. There are a number of bed-and-breakfast operations, campgrounds and

Historic buildings in Talkeetna.

cabin rentals between the highway and Petersville. Watch for moose as you drive. If you are here between October 15 and June 1, be advised that there is no road maintenance. During winter, area residents travel by snowmobile or dog sled.

You pass a greenhouse and some farms and acreages. After you pass Trapper Creek Elementary School on your left at kilometre 4.2 (mile 2.6), you drive through the settlement of Trapper Creek. Then the road turns to hard-packed gravel with rough spots, holes and dips. You come to the small settlement of Moose Creek, 11.2 kilometres (7 miles) from the highway.

At kilometre 27.5 (mile 17.1) you pass the road to the Peter's Creek subdivision, sometimes referred to as 'Petersville.'

At the 30-kilometre (18.6-mile) point, you arrive at The Forks Roadhouse, which consists of the original log building and a newer addition. Note the parking area for dog teams—winter, when dog mushers and skidooers come through here, is the big season, so the place may be quiet in summer.

The roadhouse offers a bar, a pool table, a restaurant/cafe and lodging—in rooms, cabins or a campground. The interior decor includes pictures of the previous owners, bear-skin rugs and a wall-mounted collection of dollar bills to which you are welcome to add yours.

On a clear day you can get a good look at Mount McKinley if you drive past the roadhouse to the first hill and look northward.

The Forks Roadhouse is on the way to the former mining town of Petersville. The 34 kilometres (21 miles) of road from here to Petersville, used by miners and trappers in the area, is not maintained; only drive it if you have a four-wheel–drive vehicle.

Mount McKinley

Long before it was renamed after President William McKinley in 1897, the highest mountain in North America was Denali, meaning 'the Great One,' to the Athabaskan peoples of Interior Alaska. The mountain has two peaks: the South Peak is 6194 metres (20,320 feet) high and the North Peak 5934 metres (19,470 feet) high. The North Peak, which was previously believed to be the highest, was the first one to be tackled by mountain climbers. The north face of the mountain rises at a 60° angle to around 6100 metres (20,000 feet), making it the highest vertical rise in the world.

Although Mount McKinley is the dominant feature of Denali National Park, only about one in four visitors that come to the area each year actually get to see it. Because of its height, the mountain creates its own weather, which is usually cloudy and cold. Winds of 160 kilometres per hour (100 miles per hour) have occasionally been measured on its slopes.

Your chances of seeing the entire mountain are best on an August morning, before the clouds begin to gather.

Talkeetna

It is 26.5 kilometres (16.5 miles) from Petersville Road to the junction with Talkeetna Spur Road. Turn left onto it. Just as you turn, there is a visitor reception centre to your right with a large stuffed replica of a bear next to it.

Mary's Fiddlehead Fern Farm is to the right at kilometre 1.5 (mile 0.9). You can recognize it in summer by the ferns growing in the front yard. Drop in to visit with Mary Carey, one of Alaska's most famous women. She has had a very interesting life as a journalist and writer, both in the lower 48 states and in Alaska. Mary has written 12 books about her life and you can purchase autographed copies of any of them directly from her. One of these books, *Alaska—Not For a Woman*, is about her move to Talkeetna, Alaska in 1962, and her life as a teacher, reporter and homesteader in the Talkeetna area. Mary's McKinley View Lodge on the Parks Highway is the site of her homestead.

In her shop, along with crafts made by local people, you can buy fresh, frozen or pickled ferns. She picks the ferns when they are still in the rolled-up stage and pickles or freezes them. To some people they taste like asparagus.

At 19.4 kilometres (12.1 miles) from Mary's shop, there is a viewpoint on your left. A drawing on a sign identifies the mountains, rivers and glaciers around you. Look for Mount McKinley from here. Just past the viewpoint is the village of Talkeetna. In the local Tanaina language, *Talkeetna* means 'where the rivers meet' (or, according to other sources, 'river of plenty'), which is appropriate because the village

Juneau, the capital of Alaska since 1906, is accessible only by ferry or plane and, because its airport is often covered in fog, landing and taking-off can sometimes be a problem. In the early 1970s, motivated by exasperation at the situation, a committee was formed to begin the long and extensive search to find a more approachable site for a capital. The committee considered Fairbanks. However, that choice was rejected because the people of Anchorage disliked the idea of Fairbanks as the capital, so the committee looked at Anchorage. This choice was also discarded, because most of the state disliked the idea. Finally, the settlement of Willow was chosen.

In 1976 the people of Alaska voted to move the capital to Willow. Immediately, the price of lots increased and speculators gathered. Almost as quickly, the residents of the state, worried about the high costs involved in moving the capital, began to wonder if it was such a good idea after all. The plan faltered and, after another vote in 1982, all funding for the idea stopped.

Willow is now a small village.

is at the confluence of the Susitna, Chulitna and Talkeetna rivers.

In 1896 a gold rush on the Susitna River brought prospectors to the area. The settlement of Talkeetna was established as a riverboat station in 1910 to serve the miners. The population increased during the building of the Alaska Railroad, but decreased with the advent of the First World War. Talkeetna continued as a supply centre and became the jumping-off point for mountain-climbers who wanted to scale Mount McKinley.

Today, more than one thousand climbers come here between the end of April and the end of June each year, to be flown to the Kahiltna Glacier, where they begin their climb of the mountain. If you are thinking of climbing Mount McKinley yourself, note that the National Park Service has instituted a preregistration and special-use fee program, with the intention of reducing the number of ill-prepared climbers who get lost, injured or killed on the mountain.

As you come into Talkeetna, you arrive at a T-intersection. Ahead is the Village Park. The visitor reception centre is to the right in the Three German Bachelors' Cabin. Downtown, which includes most of the businesses and the historic section, is to the left. Instead of driving, find a place to park. Then pick up a *Take a Walk Through Our History* pamphlet at the visitor centre and tour the village on foot. Most of the sights are along Main Street as you head the short distance toward the Susitna River, where it ends, or along one of the three side streets running southward off Main Street. Some businesses are in old buildings and others are in new buildings that blend in with the old ones.

As you stroll through the village, you can visit a museum, see a number of historic buildings (such as the Fairview Inn), peruse gift shops and check the companies that offer 11 charters for rafting, fishing, glacier sightseeing and visiting Mount McKinley.

Miners Last Stand Museum of Hatcher Pass in Willow.

Hatcher Pass and Willow

As you continue down the highway, 43.5 kilometres (27 miles) from the Talkeetna Spur Road you reach Hatcher Pass Road, a four-wheel–drive route over Hatcher Pass to the Independence Mine Historical State Park. Usually the road does not open to summer travellers until sometime in July, because of snow at the pass. It is much easier to visit the Independence Mine from Wasilla. (See 'Wasilla and the Independence Mine' on p. 95).

Three kilometres (1.9 miles) from Hatcher Pass Road you arrive at the village of Willow (see sidebar, p. 92), which has its businesses spread out along the highway. Watch for the Miners Last Stand Museum, which is adjacent to Newman's Hilltop Service Station. Also known as the Historical Museum of Hatcher Pass Mining, it is housed in 'the Willow Jail.' When you enter this old-style jail, you may be locked into a cell. If the 'old man' is there, ask him how you can escape. Also ask him to tell you some stories about the area. The museum is open daily, 10 AM–8 PM, from June 1 until mid-September.

Houston and Big Lake

You reach the city limits of Houston, 12.9 kilometres (8 miles) from Willow, even though you do not enter Houston proper until kilometre 18.3 (mile 11.4). Houston bills itself as the largest second-class city in the Matanuska-Susitna Borough. It was incorporated on June 6, 1966, and covers an area of 58.3 square kilometres (22.5 square miles).

Most of the businesses are along the highway. Watch for the turn-off on the right for the city-operated Little Susitna River Campground. It has over 80 sites and you can also picnic, boat and canoe on the river from here.

One-half kilometre (0.3 miles) past the road to the campground, you cross the Little Susitna River. In late May and early June you can fish this river for king salmon, also called chinook. If you are here in late July or August, try for silver salmon. The coho are best from mid-August to the beginning of September. Rainbow trout can be caught before June or from the beginning of September to freeze-up. Before you fish, be sure that you have a valid Alaska fishing licence and do consult a current copy of the regulations.

Turn right onto Big Lake Road at kilometre 7.8 (mile 4.8) from the Little Susitna River to head for Big Lake, a resort area. On the left, just after you turn off, there is a big sign with a map that gives you an idea of the attractions at Big Lake—for instance, Fish Creek Park, the salmon observation deck, the day-use area, the recreation site, the campground and the boat launch.

After travelling 1.2 kilometres (0.7 miles) along the road to Big Lake, you see part of the Big Lake Burn. It resulted from the Miller's Reach wildfire, which raged through the Big Lake and Houston areas in June of 1996. Firefighters built a firebreak 60 metres (200 feet) wide to battle this inferno, which created its own wind as it burned over 15,170 hectares (37,500 acres) of land, destroying over 350 homes.

On your right, at kilometre 5.4 (mile 3.4), is Beaver Lake Road. The salmon observatory deck and fish hatchery are 1.3 kilometres (0.8 miles) down that road.

Continuing on the road to Big Lake, you reach a Y-junction. A left turn here will take you to the Big Lake Mall, various businesses and the Big Lake South State Recreation Site at kilometre 3 (mile 1.9), and then the road continues into a rural area. A right at the Y will get you to the Big Lake North Recreation Site in 2.6 kilometres (1.6 miles).

Wasilla and the Independence Mine

Both sides of the highway are lined with businesses as you approach Wasilla. To visit the Museum of Alaska Transportation and Industry (MATI), turn right onto Nueser Drive 8.6 kilometres (5.3 miles) from the Big Lake Road. Just 0.5 kilometres (0.3 miles) from the highway you arrive at the 6-hectare (15-acre) site, where you can see vehicles from times past—includ-ing planes, firetrucks, boats, trains, trac-tors, helicopters—and industrial equip-ment from Alaska's history. A number of events—such as demonstrations of steam engines and displays of antique machin-ery—are planned to occur here through-out summer.

Old Wasilla Townsite.

At kilometre 2.5 (mile 1.6) from Nueser Drive, you reach Wasilla's city lim-its. Turn left off the George Parks Highway onto Main Street and drive one block to the Dorothy G. Page Museum, which is on the right. The late Dorothy Page was the per-son who conceived of the Iditarod Trail Sled Dog Race as a project to mark Alaska's Centennial Year in 1967 (see 'The Iditarod Trail' on p. 98.) The museum also houses a visitor reception centre, where you can ask about the road conditions on the route to the Independence Mine or Hatcher Pass and pick up pamphlets about hikes in the area.

Behind the museum is 'the Old Wasilla Townsite,' which has a bunkhouse, a smokehouse, a schoolhouse, a cache and a steam bath.

The city of Wasilla, named after Chief Wasilla of the Dena'ina Athabascan peo-ples, was established as a supply centre for the mines in the area when Anchorage evolved as a seaport and the Alaska Railroad was built through here on its way to Fairbanks. (Knik, which had been the area's supply centre since the 1880s, disap-peared—except for the one building that became the Knik Museum.) The Miller's Reach fire almost reached Wasilla—it came close enough that the residents were considering evacuating the town. The fire did get as far as Knik and all the artifacts in the Knik Museum were temporarily moved to Wasilla.

Continue on Main Street past the museum for two blocks to the Y. To go toward the Independence Mine and Hatcher Pass in the Talkeetna Mountains, take the left fork, Wasilla–Fishhook Road. Follow this winding, paved road through the first stop sign and then turn left onto Palmer–Fishhook Road when you reach the second stop sign at kilometre 17.1 (mile 10.6) from the museum. (Palmer, described in Chapter 5, is on the road to the right.)

The beginning of this road is also paved. At kilometre 2.5 (mile 1.6) you cross the Little Susitna River and the road turns to gravel. Then, until kilometre 4.2

Independence Mine building.

(mile 2.6), as you drive alongside the river through the Little Susitna River Canyon, there is a high rock wall on each side of you.

At kilometre 4.5 (mile 2.8) you enter a 4.7-kilometre (2.9-mile) stretch of river that is open to recreational gold mining. Stop at the pull-out here and try your luck.

Keep watch for a sign at kilometre 5.1 (mile 3.2) that says whether Hatcher Pass and the road to the Independence Mine are open. As you slowly climb, you can see glimpses of the river to your right.

At the end of the recreational gold-panning section, you reach the Motherlode Lodge at kilometre 9.2 (mile 5.7). As well as having rooms to rent, the lodge has a restaurant and a gift shop and offers gold-panning. This lodge opened in 1946 as the Little Susitna Roadhouse, in a 3.7 x 3.7-metre (12 x 12-foot) building. The size of the roadhouse was doubled in 1947 and the upstairs was added in 1949. No more additions were made until 1985, when the two wings were built on.

After the Motherlode, the road makes a Y. To the right is the trailhead for the Gold Mint Trail, which follows the Little Susitna River almost to the Mint Glacier. Go left to continue to the Independence Mine. As you leave the river behind, you pass several viewpoints that overlook the Little Susitna River Valley. At kilometre 12.8 (mile 8), from the beginning of Palmer-Fishhook Road, you pass Archangel Road to your right. It leads to a trailhead to the Archangel Valley (pamphlets available at the visitor centre in Wasilla). You pass a sign for Independence Mine Historical State Park at kilometre 16.5 (mile 10.3).

To your right, just past the sign, is the Hatcher Pass Lodge. Across from the lodge is the road (recommended for four-wheel–drive vehicles only) to Hatcher Pass, which you reach in 2.6 kilometres (1.6 miles). The road then follows Willow Creek and continues to the George Parks Highway.

Continue straight ahead to the minesite, which is open from 11 AM to 7 PM when the road is passable. The parking area, where you pay to enter the site, is at kilometre 18 (mile 11.2). You can then walk through the minesite and read the signs on the buildings that explain their original uses, or you can take a guided tour led by one of the park staff. Some of the structures have already been

Old safe inside Assay Office at Independence Mine.

restored—for instance, the bunkhouse, which was built in 1940, and the assay office—whereas others are leaning or falling apart as they await repair.

Although mining in the area began in the first decade of the 1900s, the buildings standing today at the Independence Mine Historical State Park are from the time when the Alaska Pacific Consolidated Mining Company mined here, between 1937 and when mining activity wound down during the 1950s. The old buildings and 110 hectares (271 acres) of land were left to the state in 1980 and the historic park was created that same year.

When this hard-rock mine was in operation, the miners would drill holes in promising rockfaces and put in explosives. At the end of their shift, they would set off the explosives. The next day, when the fumes and dust had subsided, the crew on duty gathered up the rock fragments and hauled them out for crushing and assaying. In their search for gold, the miners dug a whole network of tunnels under Granite Mountain.

As you return toward Wasilla, you have great views of the Little Susitna Valley.

Knik to Anchorage

Knik

From the George Parks Highway and Main Street in Wasilla, go across the highway to head toward Knik on the Knik–Goose Bay Road. In 3.4 kilometres (2.1 miles), turn right into the parking lot at the Iditarod Trail Sled Dog Race Headquarters. Inside the large log building there are souvenirs from the Iditarod Trail Sled Dog Race, pictures of past winners, newspaper reports on the races and some of the prizes.

Iditarod Headquarters.

Continue on the Knik–Goose Bay Road and in 3 kilometres (1.9 miles) from the race headquarters you pass a service station with a store at the junction with Fairview Loop Road. Then, for a side trip, turn right onto another side road at kilometre 13 (mile 8.1). After another 2.3 kilometres (1.4 miles) on this side road, turn right again and follow the road to the end to arrive at the Knik Knack Mud Shack. There are old wagons, pieces of machinery and an old ambulance in the yard. Inside the 'shack' there is a wide selection of ceramic supplies, equipment and products, including greenware, glazes, wheels, designer stencils and finished gift items.

Back on the Knik–Goose Bay Road, you can see Knik Inlet as you travel toward the Knik Museum. In 5.1 kilometres (3.1 miles) from the turn-off for the ceramics place, you reach Knik Lake and at kilometre 5.5 (mile 3.4) you arrive at the Knik Museum and Dog Mushers' Hall of Fame on your right. Inside this building, circa 1910, there are mushers' portraits, pieces of dog-mushing equipment, write-ups

The Iditarod Trail

The Iditarod Trail was originally a mail- and supply-route that began in Seward and ran to mining towns in Interior Alaska and then northward to the settlements of Iditarod and Nome. On the return trips from these towns, the mushers brought back gold. In January of 1925, a relay of heroic mushers used the Iditarod Trail to transport three hundred thousand units of serum to Nome to quell a diphtheria outbreak. With the coming of bush planes and snowmobiles, however, the trail was abandoned.

In 1967 the trail was revived to celebrate the hundredth anniversary of the purchase of Alaska from Russia. That year, the first Iditarod Trail Sled Dog Race covered only about 43 kilometres (27 miles). The same length race was held again in 1969, but in 1973 it was extended from Anchorage to Nome, increasing its length by about 37 times. The winner took 20 days to reach the finish line.

These days the ceremonial start of the 1688-kilometre (1049-mile) race is held in Anchorage, with the teams going only as far as Eagle River the first day. The teams are trucked to Wasilla and the race begins in earnest the following morning. After Knik, the course heads northwest through villages that cannot be reached by road. When the mushers get to the ghost town of Ophir, during odd-numbered years they take the southern route to Kaltag, going through Iditarod, Shageluk, Anvik and Grayling. During even years, they pass through Cripple, Ruby, Galena and Nulato to reach Kaltag; from Kaltag they head southwest to Unalakleet and follow the shore of Norton Sound to Nome.

About 60 men and women compete each year. The competitors have come from as many as 15 different countries and have ranged from teenagers to octogenarians.

about Iditarod Trail history and memorabilia of Knik when it was the centre of trade for the gold-fields and coal mines of the area between 1897 and 1916. The museum, the only building in Knik left from that era, is on the National Register of Historic Places. The museum is open Wednesday to Sunday, from noon to 6 PM.

Although the road continues beyond Knik for another 5.4 kilometres (3.3 miles) to Goose Bay, there is not much to see. Drive back to the service station with the store and turn right onto Fairview Loop Road to bypass Wasilla and return to the George Parks Highway by a quieter, scenic route. This paved, 18-kilometre (11-mile) road winds through woods, acreages and farms. Watch for the sharp left curve at kilometre 3 (mile 1.8).

Once back at the George Parks Highway, turn right onto it and immediately cross Wasilla Creek. In 3.4 kilometres (2.1 miles), the visitor reception centre for the Matanuska–Susitna area is on your left.

One kilometre (0.6 miles) from the visitor centre you reach the Glenn Highway (Alaska Route 1). Turn right to go to Anchorage (a left turn would take you to Palmer, Glennallen and Tok [see Chapter 5]). This divided highway takes you through a flat area with few trees and with mountains in the background. Watch for the purple irises all along this road in June. You cross the Matanuska River and its flats at kilometre 5.6 (mile 3.5) from the junction and then you cross the Knik River for the first time at kilometre 6.7 (mile 4.1) and then again at kilometre 7.2 (mile 4.4). Between the two bridges there is an access road that goes down to the Knik River.

St. Nicholas Russian Orthodox Church in Eklutna.

Thunderbird Falls.

At kilometre 14.8 (mile 9.2) an exit to the right leads to the village of Eklutna. The cabin of the late Dena'ina Chief Mike Alex (1908–77) is to your right as you come into the village. To your left is the Eklutna Village Historic Park, which features the Heritage House and the St. Nicholas Russian Orthodox Church, which was built circa 1830–40. Between 8 AM and 8 PM daily, half-hour tours are offered of the church, which was restored in the 1970s. In the yard there are gravesites covered by spirit houses. At the village you can learn about the heritage and traditions of the Athabascan peoples, who have lived at this location for the past 350 years.

To get to Thunderbird Falls, which is on Peter's Creek, when you come out of Eklutna, take the overpass to cross over the highway and then turn right at the T-intersection. Drive past the turn-off for Eklutna Lake. You cross the Eklutna River in 0.8 kilometres (0.5 miles) from the T-intersection. Turn left into the parking lot for the falls.

The hiking trail climbs for a ways from the parking lot. Some of the trail is among tall, shady trees and some of it is beside a cliff where signs warn you to stay away from the edge because of erosion. In about 0.8 kilometres (0.5 miles) there is a platform where you can take a look down into the canyon to the river way below.

When you reach the place where the Creek Trail goes steeply down to your left, go straight ahead on the Falls Trail, which continues on a walkway built out from the bank. After that walkway you reach the falls lookout and the falls, which are partially hidden by trees.

Continuing along the highway, you reach the exit for Eagle River 20.1 kilometres (12.5 miles) from the Eklutna exit. If you want to go to the visitor reception centre for Chugach State Park, take this exit and then, once you have crossed the

A General History of the Anchorage Area

Having discovered the Alaskan mainland in 1741, with the help of Danish-born Vitus Bering, the Russians began to come regularly in the late 1700s to trade for furs. They had been settling in the area that we now call Alaska for almost a century when the US bought the land in 1867. In the 1800s, when gold was found at Crow Creek (near Girdwood, to the southwest of present-day Anchorage; see Chapter 4) and then in the Matanuska and Susitna valleys, Anchorage was a crossroads for prospectors travelling between the two gold-fields.

Even as late as the early 1900s, the area where Anchorage is now was still mostly bush. It was not until 1915 that the town truly had its beginnings, as a construction camp for the Alaska Railroad, which originated in Seward. During the Second World War, army and air-force bases were constructed near the town, which by this time had a population of three thousand.

On March 27, 1964, much of Anchorage was destroyed by an earthquake that registered 9.2 (out of 10) on the Richter scale. (Originally thought to have been 8.5, the intensity of the quake was recalculated in 1977.) The citizens rebuilt and, in the following decades, oil and gas developments brought rapid expansion to the city. Anchorage, now the centre of commerce for Alaska, has a population of over one-quarter million people.

highway, take the first right, onto Eagle River Road. From here it is 17.7 kilometres (11 miles) to the visitor centre, from which radiate many hiking trails, ranging in length from 0.8 kilometres (0.5 miles) to 40 kilometres (25 miles).

From Eagle River, head toward Anchorage. To bypass Anchorage, turn left onto Muldoon Road at 14.4 kilometres (8.9 miles) from the Eagle River exit. Muldoon curves right and becomes Tudor. Continue on Tudor to the new Seward Highway (Alaska Route 1) and turn left. You are now on your way to Seward and Homer (see Chapter 4).

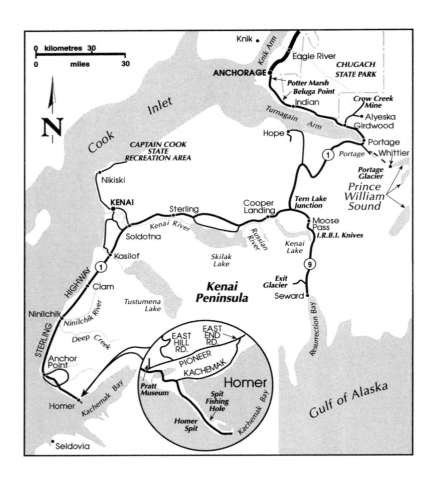

4
Potter Marsh to Seward and Homer

This trip begins south of Anchorage and takes you around Turnagain Arm to the Kenai Peninsula, which includes going down to Seward on the Seward Highway and then along Cook Inlet on the Sterling Highway to Homer. Most of the Kenai Peninsula is within the boundaries of the Kenai National Wildlife Refuge, the Kenai Fjords National Park or the Chugach National Forest. Much of this route is along narrow, curving highways. If you are going slower than regular traffic—especially if you are holding up more than five vehicles—use the pull-outs provided so that the people behind you can pass.

Potter Marsh to Portage Glacier

Potter Marsh

As you head southward from Anchorage on the Seward Highway (Alaska Route 1), watch for the sign that marks the exit for the Old Seward Highway. Stay on the Seward Highway and 1.2 kilometres (0.7 miles) past that sign you arrive at Potter Marsh, which was formed when a small creek was dammed during railroad construction. Turn left off the highway here and drive into the parking area for the Potter Point Wildlife Viewing Area.

Potter Marsh boardwalk.

A long boardwalk, suitable for wheelchairs, goes from the parking area, across the marsh toward the highway, and then runs between the edge of the marsh and the highway. Interpretive signs along the boardwalk tell you about the surrounding mountains, the vegetation of the marsh, and the birds, fish and animals that inhabit this wetland.

Back on the Seward Highway, you drive with the marsh on your left for 3.6 kilometres (2.2 miles) until you reach Potter Valley Road. On your right, just past that road, is the entrance to Chugach State Park's Potter Historic Site. At this site is the Potter Section House, in which workers on the Alaska Railroad once lived. It now houses the park's visitor reception centre. In the yard you can see old equipment that was once used by the railroad, such as a 2.7-metre (9-foot) rotary snowplough, crew accommodation car and a section car. On each piece of equipment a write-up describes how it was operated.

The 'Goat Lookers'

From the Seward Highway, as it runs alongside Turnagain Arm, you may be able to see Dall sheep scaling the high rock walls—they sometimes even come down to eat grass along the roadside. Many people who see them get so excited that in their haste to take a picture, they abandon their vehicles right on the narrow roadway, possibly even leaving the doors open.

This carelessness can cause major traffic problems and so a police officer sometimes patrols this road to ask visitors to return to their vehicles and move them to a pull-out.

If you see any sheep and want to get a better look, be sure to drive to a pull-out, park and walk back. Otherwise, you will be termed a 'goat looker' by truck drivers on the highway.

After the historic site you follow the north shore of Turnagain Arm. If the tide is out, you can see huge mud-flats stretching out into the arm. There are pull-outs along both sides of the highway for you to get a good look at the flats. Do not, however, actually walk out onto these mud-flats— or those of Cook Inlet—because some people have gotten stuck in the mud and could not be pulled out before they drowned in the rising tide.

Turnagain Arm was called 'Return' by the Russians. When Captain James Cook explored the area looking for the Northwest Passage in 1778, he named it 'Turnagain River' because when he reached its end he had to turn around again. Upon surveying the area in 1794 and finding the waterway to be an extension of Cook Inlet, Captain George Vancouver renamed it 'Turnagain Arm.'

In 5.7 kilometres (3.5 miles) from the historic site, you reach a pull-out for Chugach State Park's McHugh Creek site to your left. You can walk up the hillside to the picnic area or look at the falls beside the road.

At kilometre 12 (mile 7.5) you reach the large parking lot for Beluga Point on your right. You can use the telescopes provided to see the whales better. Beluga whales, the only all-white whales, are best seen in late May and late August, when they follow salmon into the arm.

At kilometre 13.8 (mile 8.6) there is a trailhead for the Old Johnson Trail, which has been used by Native peoples, fur trappers, miners and missionaries over the centuries.

Falls Creek Trail is to your left at kilometre 15.6 (mile 9.7). Look to your left as you pass it to see the falls beside the road. Look to your left again at kilometre 16.9 (mile 10.5) to see a cave with a waterfall.

Beluga Whales

The Russians called belugas 'white ones' because of their all-white colour. The whalers nicknamed them 'canaries of the sea' because they create different sounds by changing the shapes of their heads.

Belugas are among the smallest of the whales. They can survive in cold northern waters because of the 20 centimetres (8 inches) of blubber under their thick skin. Belugas find food by echolocation—emitting a high-frequency sound wave that bounces off any object and returns. They can dive as deep as 40 metres (130 feet) in search of salmon and eulachon (also called 'ooligan,' 'candlefish' or 'sea-run smelt'), which are their main food supply.

McHugh Creek Falls.

Indian, Girdwood and Crow Creek Mine

Indian Valley Mine National Historic Site is to your left at kilometre 18.4 (mile 11.4). This mine was one of only two underground mines that operated in Alaska between 1920 and 1939. A small museum recounts the mine's history.

You drive past a restaurant, a gift shop and a motel and then cross Indian Creek at kilometre 20.1 (mile 12.5). The Indian Creek Wayside, which has telescopes and information panels about avalanches, mud-flats and tidal bores, is just past the creek. Across Turnagain Arm from here are the former sites of the city of Sunrise and the present-day hamlet of Hope.

Old building at Crow Creek Mine Site.

At kilometre 21 (mile 13) from Indian Creek take the left turn to go to Girdwood and the Alyeska Resort. There is a service station with a cafe on the corner.

At the beginning of the road to Girdwood, known as 'the Alyeska Highway,' there is a visitor reception centre at the Glacier Ranger Station of the Chugach National Forest. It is open Monday to Friday, from 8 AM to 5 PM.

On the left, just past the ranger station, is the Candle Factory. The Candle Factory makes hand-crafted candles in the shapes of moose, bears, puffins, eagles, seals and walruses. The candles are made by filling silicone molds with a hot mixture of paraffin, Alaska crude, seal-oil byproduct and stearic acid, which then cools and hardens in the desired shapes. The factory is open daily from 10 AM to 7 PM.

Turn left onto Crow Creek Road at kilometre 3 (mile 1.9) from the beginning of the Alyeska Highway for a side trip to the Crow Creek Mine. It is part of the old Iditarod Trail but is not used for the present-day race. At 3.7 kilometres (2.3 miles) from the junction you enter the Chugach National Forest, which encompasses Prince William Sound and part of the Kenai Peninsula within its approximately 2.3 million hectares (5.6 million acres). At kilometre 5 (mile 3.1) from the junction, there is a Y in this rough road. Take the right fork to visit the Crow Creek Mine, 0.5 kilometres (0.3 miles) along the road. A gold strike was made here in 1897. Eight restored buildings sit on the 22-hectare (54-acre) minesite. While here, you can pan for gold, take a tour and/or camp.

Go back to the Y in the road and, to see the scenery or to go hiking, take the other fork to go to the Crow Pass. As the road climbs you can see glaciers and snow-covered mountains around you. In 3 kilometres (1.9 miles) from the Y, you reach a sign that says 'National Forest; Crow Pass.' Go to the right (the road straight ahead is private property) and in 1.5 kilometres (0.9 miles) from the sign you reach the trailhead and parking area for the Crow Pass Trail. It is a 4.8-kilometre (3-mile) uphill climb to the pass. The Crow Pass Trail is also called 'the Historic Iditarod Trail' because it is part of the Old Iditarod dog-sled route used in the early 1900s. It is 36.2 kilometres (22.5 miles) long and ends at the Chugach visitor reception centre in Eagle River, northeast of Anchorage.

You just get back onto the Alyeska Highway and continue driving up it when you come to Hightower Road, which goes left into Girdwood, a resort town whose businesses cater to skiers in winter and to hikers, rafters and travellers in summer. Continue on the Alyeska Highway and you cross Glacier Creek immediately after Hightower Road. At kilometre 1 (mile 0.6) from Hightower Road you reach Alyeska Resort, which offers lodging in chalets and bed-and-breakfasts and a tram ride to the top of Mount Alyeska, good for the view in summer or for skiing in winter.

Return to the Seward Highway. As you head southward, look to your left at kilometre 0.7 (mile 0.4) from the Alyeska Highway for an excellent view of the three glaciers on the mountains surrounding Crow Pass. Note that the only service station between Girdwood and Seward is in Hope.

The Tidal Bore

Turnagain Arm is second only to the Bay of Fundy (between Nova Scotia and New Brunswick on Canada's east coast) when it comes to having the highest tidal bore (or bore tide) in the world.

A tidal bore is a fast-moving, large and forceful wave that is created when a rising tide enters a shallow, narrow inlet. The tidal bore here occurs when the waters of Cook Inlet are forced into narrower, shallower Turnagain Arm. The wave forms just after low tide and moves up the inlet, attaining speeds of up to 16 kilometres per hour (10 miles per hour).

To see the tidal bore at its highest, consult an Anchorage-area tidetable and add two hours and 15 minutes to the time given for low tide. Then arrange to be along Turnagain Arm between Beluga Point and the junction with the Alyeska Highway at that time.

Watch for a series of undulating swells coming across the channel. Although they are often only 0.6–1 metres (2–3 feet) high, if you are lucky you might see them foaming up to a height of 1.8 metres (6 feet) when conditions are right. Because of the arm's shape and location, its water level can have a daily change in height of more than 10 metres (33 feet).

Portage

As you continue southeast, the dead trees to your right were killed when the 1964 earthquake that hit the area submerged them in salt water. Watch for bald eagles sitting on their limbs. At kilometre 15.2 (mile 9.4) from the Alyeska Highway, you cross the Twentymile River.

Then you approach Portage, which was at first a construction town for the railroad, then for the highway. When the earthquake hit in 1964, the banks of Turnagain Arm, where Portage used to stand, dropped between 1.8 and 3.7 metres (6 and 12 feet). Salt water flooded the area and the residents of Portage were forced to move. On your right along the highway are old buildings left from the former village.

At kilometre 15.9 (mile 9.9), just before you actually pass the buildings of today's Portage, you reach the first of two turn-offs for a large parking area. The train that stops here on its way from Anchorage provides the only land connection to Whittier, which is located to the east on Prince William Sound, from Portage

The Train to Whittier

The part of the Alaska Railroad that goes to Whittier, including two tunnels, was built between 1941 and 1943 to make a new access route from the ocean to the military bases in Anchorage and Fairbanks. Seward, also on the ocean and already connected by train, was considered too vulnerable to Japanese attack. When the Cold War began, Whittier became a permanent base and remained one until 1960.

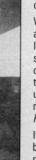

Boarding the train to Whittier.

When Whittier became a civilian town, varying levels of passenger train service were provided over the years. The track to Whittier was even used in scenes from a movie—the 1986 film *Runaway Train.*

If you are reading this book before the train is relegated to cargo only, you can buy a ticket for the 35-minute trip at the building in the middle of the parking lot at Portage, which also houses a gift shop and a visitor reception centre. The train departs Portage several times per day from early May until late September. Be sure to catch an early train if you plan to take a cruise on Prince William Sound. (Although vehicles as big as tour buses can be accommodated on the train, leave your vehicle in the parking lot unless you plan to catch a ferry from Whittier, because you can walk the main part of the small town in an hour.)

For the best view of the lovely scenery—mountains, lakes, marshes and rivers—sit on the right side of the train.

The ride through the first tunnel, which is 1497 metres (4910 feet) long, takes about 2.5 minutes. The second tunnel is 3990 metres (13,090 feet) long and you are in it for just over six minutes. Then look to your left to see an oil tank farm that was used by the US Army but is now shut down. When you see a marina out of the left windows, start watching to your right for a waterfall. Then you enter Whittier (see p. 110).

Lake, prior to the opening of a road that is scheduled for 2000. From Portage, resume driving on the Seward Highway. The entrance to Big Game Alaska Wildlife Park on your right at 1.5 kilometres (0.9 miles) from the railroad parking lot. Walk or drive through this park and see wild animals in a park-like setting on the other side of a tall fence. Immediately past the park, the Portage Glacier Road goes off to the left.

Five Glaciers

Head along Portage Glacier Road into the Chugach Valley of the Chugach National Forest. You pass ponds and campgrounds and in 3.7 kilometres (2.3 miles) you reach a pull-out. From the pull-out, take the very short trail to the creek and look up at the mountain on the other side to see the Explorer Glacier. This hanging glacier was named for the Explorer Group of the Boy Scouts because they used to practise ice-climbing on it.

The Explorer Glacier is one of the glaciers left from the time when the whole Portage Valley was covered in ice some 20,000 years ago. It was once joined to the Portage Glacier but when that glacier melted back, Explorer was left 'hanging' above the valley.

Look to your right after the pull-out to see the Explorer Glacier as you drive. At kilometre 6.8 (mile 4.2) from the highway, you pass a campground below the Middle Glacier.

You reach a Y-intersection at kilometre 8.4 (mile 5.2). The left fork leads to the Begich-Boggs Visitor Center and Whittier (see p. 110). Take the right fork to reach the trailhead for the Byron Glacier hiking trail in 1.3 kilometres (0.8 miles).

On a clear day you can see lovely scenery from this trail. If it is overcast, you could be walking through mist, so wear warm clothing. Though the trail, which follows a creek to your left, is fairly level, it is in places covered in gravel and big rocks and is sometimes muddy.

In about 15 minutes you reach a sign that notifies you that the trail is not maintained after this point and cautions you about going onto the Byron Glacier. You can see the glacier and take pictures from the sign or you can continue on, at your own risk, to the glacier.

As you continue along the road, you reach Portage Lake, less than 1 kilometre (0.6 miles) from the trailhead. From here you can take a charter across the lake to the remaining part of the Portage Glacier, which is hidden behind a point of land. Portage Lake was formed when the Portage Glacier, which used to join onto the Burns Glacier, began melting back in 1914. Note the huge icebergs that have broken off the Portage Glacier and floated down the lake. Some are white and some are blackened with rock flour.

Return to the Y in the road

The Ice Worms

The elusive ice worm, a tiny annelid known as *Mesenchytraeus solifugus*, is black, about 2.5 centimetres (1 inch) long and as big around as a sewing needle. Ice worms live in the crevices between the ice crystals and come out on cool nights to eat microscopic bits of algae and pollen that the wind blows onto the glacial ice.

Ice worms are quite particular about the temperatures that they like. On warm summer days, they burrow down into the insulating ice to escape the heat and direct sun. In winter they stay below the surface and hibernate to avoid the extreme cold.

Fortunately for those who like a chunk of glacial ice to cool their beverage of choice on a hot day, ice worms, which are found on glaciers everywhere, are not known to be toxic.

and take the other fork to visit the Begich-Boggs Visitor Center, which is on the shore of Portage Lake. Outside the visitor centre there are telescopes that you can use to get a closer look at the icebergs in the lake and at the Burns Glacier across the water.

Inside, this popular visitor centre has a glassed-in viewing area that looks onto the lake, a room that gives information about glaciers and a relief map of the surrounding icefields.

When the Tanaina and Chugach peoples travelled between Prince William Sound and Cook Inlet, they crossed the Portage and Burns glaciers. When the Russians arrived, they, too, followed this route. Miners on their way to the gold-fields around Hope arrived at what is now Whittier and portaged their supplies and boats over the glacial pass to the shores of Turnagain Arm, hence the Portage Glacier's name.

To the left of the visitor centre there is a road that goes along the lakeshore. This road, after it is completed in 2000, will go to Whittier, via the second of the two railway tunnels mentioned in the sidebar 'The Train to Whittier' (see p. 108).

Whittier

Whittier's small boat harbour.

The former military base of Whittier is now a popular embarkation point for cruises on Prince William Sound and a port of call on the Alaska Marine Highway ferry system. Whittier's visitor reception centre is beside the railroad tracks in a railway car. Here, you can pick up a walking map of the town.

The brown 14-storey building next to the train station is Begich Towers (originally the Hodge Building). Built in 1954 for housing military personnel and their families, its name honours Congressman Nick Begich, who was killed in a plane accident while campaigning for re-election. Although the tower was damaged in the 1964 earthquake, it has been restored and turned into condominiums, which now house most of the town's residents.

Across from the visitor centre there is a harbour for small boats. At the adjacent square, shops offer coffee, ice cream and food, and sell tickets for charters. You can stroll along the boardwalk past the shops and watch the cruise ships depart and return.

Turnagain Pass to Seward

Turnagain Pass and Hope

In 6.1 kilometres (3.8 miles) from the Portage Glacier Road, the Seward Highway pulls away from Turnagain Arm and you enter Alaska's Kenai Peninsula, which covers 41,582 square kilometres (16,056 square miles). Before the Russians arrived, the Kenai residents had this land to themselves. Then, in the 1790s, the Russians built a shipyard near where Seward is today, a fort at Kenai and a stockade near Kasilof. However, no more development occurred until gold was discovered near present-day Hope.

At kilometre 17.1 (mile 10.6) you reach Turnagain Pass, at an elevation of 301 metres (988 feet). Kilometre 36.2 (mile 22.5) brings you to a high, curved bridge; look to your left to see the

Byron Glacier.

gorge made by Canyon Creek. Just past the bridge, turn right onto the Hope Highway to visit the hamlet of Hope, which is 27 kilometres (16.8 miles) from the Seward Highway. This winding, paved road with no shoulder has a number of pull-outs on the right that offer beautiful views of Turnagain Arm. At one of the pull-outs you can look down at Sixmile Creek and its valley. The site of Sunrise, formerly a gold-mining settlement, is at its mouth. The 20-odd residents now living at the Sunrise site use boats for transportation because their settlement has no road access.

At the sign for Hope, turn right onto the Hope Loop Road to enter the hamlet of Hope, which currently has a population of just over two hundred. Drop in at the Sunrise Historical Society's Historical and Mining Museum, to your left on this road. If it is a chilly morning, you can enjoy the warmth and smell of a fire in the wood stove here. Be sure to look at the pictures of Hope and Sunrise taken during the gold rush.

Mudflat on Turnagain Arm.

The cities of Hope and Sunrise were quickly set up in 1895 when word got out that Alexander King had struck gold on nearby Resurrection Creek in 1890. In 1896, three thousand miners arrived in the hopes of staking claims. Four years later, however, the rush was over and Sunrise had disappeared but Hope remained as a small hamlet.

The Hope Highway continues beyond the first exit for Hope and past a second one before it crosses Resurrection Creek and heads uphill above Turnagain Arm. One kilometre (0.6 miles) after the second exit, the highway ends at the Chugach National Forest's Porcupine Campground.

Summit Lakes and Moose Pass

Back on the Seward Highway, at 13.9 kilometres (8.6 miles) from the Hope Highway, you drive past Lower Summit Lake, followed by Summit Lodge and Upper Summit Lake. Drive past the first exit for Homer, at kilometre 30.4 (mile 18.9), and also the second, Tern Lake Junction, 1 kilometre (0.6 miles) from the first exit, to continue toward Seward. Although you are still on the Seward Highway, it is Alaska Route 9 here.

At kilometre 39 (mile 24.2) there is a pull-out to the right with a sign that says 'trail to stream' on it. In August you can see spawning salmon from the platform that overlooks the stream at the end of the trail. However, it is a nice five-minute walk anytime during summer or fall.

Trail Lakes Hatchery on Moose Creek is to your left at kilometre 39.2 (mile 24.4). The facility is open daily from 8 AM to 5 PM and offers tours at 10 AM, from June 1 to September 15. Then, at kilometre 43 (mile 26.7), you drive into the town of Moose Pass, which is spread out along the highway. Its amenities include a

Sign at Moose Pass waterwheel and grindstone.

lodge, a museum and a gift shop. At kilometre 44 (mile 27.3), just before you reach Estes Brothers Grocery, look to your right to see a working water-wheel. At the wheel there is a sign that says 'Moose Pass is a peaceful little town. If you have an ax to grind, do it here.'

Sure enough, the water-wheel turns a grinder on which you can sharpen axes, knives and scissors.

From the water-wheel in Moose Pass, it is 10 kilometres (6.2 miles) to where you can see the beautiful light turquoise waters of Kenai Lake to your right. Though it is illegal to fish for salmon in this lake or its tributaries, you can try for Dolly Varden or lake trout.

The huge knife in front of an old log building to your left at kilometre 14.9 (mile 9.3) marks I.R.B.I. (I'd Rather Be Independent) Knives. The knives, hand-crafted in various shapes and sizes, come with handles of caribou or moose antler, Dall sheep horn or wood.

This family-run business, now operated by the son and daughter-in-law of the man who started making knives here years ago, is open every day from 10 AM to 5 PM.

The Exit Glacier and Seward

At the building occupied by Seward Building Supply and True Value Hardware, 26 kilometres (16.2 miles) from I.R.B.I. Knives, turn right onto Exit Glacier Road. In 12 kilometres (7.5 miles) you reach a sign for the Exit Glacier Area of Kenai Fjords National Park, the only part of the park that is accessible by road. After coming around a curve, you can see the Exit Glacier ahead of you.

Although thousands of years ago the Exit Glacier stretched almost to Seward, it is now only about 5 kilometres (3 miles) long. It begins at the northern end of the Harding Icefield, which is roughly 80 kilometres (50 miles) long and 50 kilometres (30 miles) wide.

At kilometre 14 (mile 8.7) you reach a parking lot for glacier visitors. The map at the parking lot shows three trails: the Glacier Trail, the Overlook Trail and the Harding Icefield Trail. All three trails begin as one from the parking lot, first as asphalt, then gravel. In a few minutes you reach the parting of the trails.

The Glacier Trail goes close to the toe of the glacier, but visitors are not permitted to go right up to it, because of the danger of falling ice chunks. If you take this trail, be prepared to walk on boards that have been laid over streams created by the melting ice.

From the toe you can take a trail to the right of the glacier that will hook up with the Overlook Trail, which goes part-way up the glacier. As you walk beside the glacier, you can see little rivulets of water running out of the crevasses and down beside the ice.

The 7.2-kilometre (4.5-mile) Harding Icefield Trail, which may still have snow

Exit Glacier.

on its upper parts, climbs to about 915 metres (3000 feet). Allow most of a day if you choose to do this rough, steep hike.

As you continue toward Seward after Exit Glacier Road, you cross the Resurrection River. In a further 1.1 kilometres (0.7 miles), you reach the city limits of Seward, which bills itself as 'the Fun Capital of All America.' You cross the Resurrection River twice more before you reach downtown Seward.

In 1793, Russian fur trader and explorer Alexander Baranof (later to become governor of Russian America) established a shipyard on Resurrection Bay (where he had sheltered from a storm the year before on the Russian Sunday of the Resurrection). The first ship, the *Phoenix*, was launched from the shipyard in 1794. However, it was not until ice-free Resurrection Bay was made the terminus of the Alaska Central Railway in 1903 that the town now known as Seward was established. Seward, incorporated in 1912, was named after US Secretary of State William H. Seward, who instigated the purchase of Alaska from the Russians in 1867.

On the right where the Seward Highway curves left and becomes Third Avenue, there is a lagoon. Next to the lagoon there is a memorial to Benny Benson, who designed the state flag in 1927, when he was just 13 years old.

Benny Benson Memorial at Seward.

The Origins of the Iditarod Trail

Before the building in 1903 of the Alaska Central Railroad (which became the Alaska Northern and was later incorporated into the Alaska Railroad), a number of trails led inland from Resurrection Bay to the gold-fields of Nome. In 1908, a more direct dog-sled route was surveyed; by 1911, almost 1600 kilometres (1000 miles) of it were marked. Originally the Rainly Pass/Kaltag Trail, it was renamed for the Iditarod gold-mining district, which was its main destination.

Do not underestimate the carrying capacity of these dog teams! By way of example, one shipment of gold from Iditarod to Seward in 1915 involved 46 dogs pulling sleds laden with a total of 1.4 tonnes (1.5 tons) of the yellow metal.

By the mid-1920s, the railroad had been routed as far as Fairbanks. Bush planes began to take over other routes and dog sleds were completely abandoned. Today, the trail is used mainly by hikers.

Although the annual Iditarod Sled Dog Race (see 'The Iditarod Trail' on p. 98) uses only part of the trail, from Anchorage to Nome, the Iditarod Trail's official beginning is in Seward. (However, some sources place the actual beginning of the dog-sled trail about 80 kilometres [50 miles] north of Seward, at what was once the northern terminus of the Alaska Central Railroad.)

As you continue on Third Avenue, the visitor reception centre is to your right between Madison and Jefferson streets. Follow Third Avenue to Railway Avenue and turn left. Go one block to Fourth Avenue and in a small park on the right corner there is a dog sled that marks the original beginning of the Iditarod Trail.

Be sure to visit the Alaska SeaLife Center next to the park. Partially funded by the settlement from the Exxon Valdez Oil Spill in 1989, the facility opened in May 1998. Its mission is to research Alaska's marine environment, to rehabilitate sick and injured marine mammals and birds and to educate the public on how this environment should be protected. Habitats for numerous marine creatures have been re-created within the facility so that you can get a close look at them, both ashore and through underwater viewing windows. You can watch puffins diving in a pool for food and see Steller sea lions lounging on rock slabs.

If you are here on the Fourth of July, you can watch the Mount Marathon Race (register ahead of time if you want to participate). This race is the oldest in Alaska, having begun in 1915 with just five runners. Now over eight hundred men, women and children participate in the 4.8-kilometre (3-mile) looped race that climbs and then descends around 900 metres (3000 feet).

Tern Lake Junction to Kenai

Tern Lake and Cooper Landing

Drive back along the Seward Highway to the Tern Lake Junction and turn toward Homer on the Sterling Highway (Alaska Route 1). After the junction there is a pull-out to your left that has a platform overlooking Tern Lake. Signs here tell about the lake and the waterfowl that it supports, including the nesting arctic terns for which the lake is named. To help you identify tracks in the area, there are life-sized replicas of prints made by bear, beaver, moose, goat and sheep.

Starting at about kilometre 13 (mile 8) from the junction, you begin driving through the settlement of Cooper Landing, which stretches out along the highway for quite a distance. Throughout this resort area on the shores of Kenai Lake there are campgrounds, service stations, restaurants, outfitters, rafting businesses, fishing charters and other businesses to serve visitors.

At kilometre 25.6 (mile 15.9) from Tern Lake you reach the Russian River Campground. It is a popular place during red (sockeye) salmon fishing season—arrive early if you want to camp here. During fishing season on the Russian and Kenai rivers, you can park at the campground for a fee but, because most people leave their vehicles along the road, watch for parked vehicles and people walking on the highway.

Path through the Kenaitze Indian Interpretive Site.

You can fish the Kenai and Russian rivers for king salmon, red salmon, pinks, silvers and rainbow trout. The best bait is salmon roe, bounced slowly on the bottom. You have to go deep to catch these fish, so expect to lose a lot of hooks to snags before getting your fish.

In 0.4 kilometres (0.2 miles) from the campground entrance, you cross the Kenai River. Stop in at the Kenaitze Indian Tribe Interpretive Site, *Hchan'iyut*, which means 'Beginnings,' at kilometre 1.6 (mile 1) from the campground. The Kenaitze people fished on the Kenai River, which they called *Kahtnu*, for hundreds of years before non-Natives came to the area. The river also provided them with a means of transportation to their seasonal camps and for visiting and trading with other tribes.

There is parking to your left. Go over to the pamphlet box and pick up a copy of *Walk in the Footprints of Time*. As you walk the 335-metre (1100-foot) long trail between the highway and the river, watch for rocks with numbers on them. Then find each spot's number in the guide to read about it.

Fishing Runs on the Kenai River

Four different species of salmon return to the Kenai River in summer to spawn. Three of these, the kings, the silvers and the reds, have two separate runs.

The king (or chinook) salmon's first run begins in mid-May. Fishing opens June 1 and is at its best in mid-June. The second (or late) run of kings arrives at the beginning of July, with the peak fishing time in the latter half of the month. The largest king taken so far from the Kenai River, weighing in at 44.1 kilograms (97 pounds, 4 ounces), was caught in 1985.

The early run of the silver (coho) salmon starts in late July and lasts until early September. The late run is from early September to late October. The red or sockeye salmon arrive in late May, but you are not permitted to catch them until mid-June. The late arrivals come in early July and the run is over by early August. Pink salmon come only during even-numbered years. Other fish that you might want to try for on the Kenai are rainbow trout and Dolly Varden, both here year-round.

Courtesy is an important part of fishing here, because popular places along the banks of the Kenai and Russian rivers are crowded with anglers during the fish runs. Elsewhere on the Kenai Peninsula, the Kasilof, Ninilchik and Anchor rivers and Deep Creek also have runs of king, silver, red and pink salmon. Because changes occur from time to time, be sure to consult a current copy of the fishing regulations before trying for salmon or any of these other fish.

You reach the Russian River Ferry 1.9 kilometres (1.2 miles) from the interpretive site. This privately owned ferry takes fishers across the Kenai River to fish on the far bank or at the junction of the Russian and Kenai rivers.

The Skilak Wildlife Recreation Center is to the right at kilometre 7.7 (mile 4.8). On the left, just past it, is Skilak Loop Road, along which there are many campgrounds, lakes and hiking trails. The road arrives back at the Sterling Highway, about 28 kilometres (17 miles) along the highway to the west of here.

Sterling and Soldotna

The community of Sterling, also known as 'Naptown,' is 44 kilometres (27.3 miles) from the Skilak Wildlife Recreation Area. Its charters, guides, outdoor adventures, gifts shops, fishing and RV parks are spread out along the highway most of the way to the city of Soldotna, which you reach in about 15 kilometres (9 miles).

Soldotna was established in 1947 during the building of the Sterling Highway. Many of its first homesteaders were veterans from the Second World War. Watch for the Kenai Spur Highway, on your right at a set of traffic lights. Before turning here to go to the city of Kenai, continue along the Sterling Highway until you come to Soldotna's visitor reception centre, on your right after you cross the Kenai River. A boardwalk from the centre leads back to a place on the Kenai River where you can enjoy the view or try some fishing.

Just past the visitor centre, turn right onto Kalifornsky Beach Road and then right again onto Centennial Park Road. The Soldotna Historical Society Museum is a short distance down this road. On the grounds there are many buildings from the city's early history. Inside, there are photographs and displays depicting the early settlers in the area, plus stuffed and mounted wildlife against a scenic background. The museum is open from 10 AM to 4 PM Tuesday to Friday and from noon to 4 PM on Saturday and Sunday.

Kenai

Return to the Kenai Spur Highway and turn onto it. You reach Kenai, an old whaling town, 16 kilometres (9.9 miles) from the lights. There are residences and businesses along the road as you come into Kenai, which is proud of its 1992 designation as an 'All-America City.' Every year the non-partisan National Civic League, sponsored by the Allstate Foundation, selects 10 US communities as recipients of its All-America City Award based on their 'collaborative, grassroots efforts to improve their quality of life.'

The visitor reception centre is at the corner of Kenai Spur Road and Main Street. Turn left onto Main Street and then right to park at the visitor centre, where you can pick up a guide for a walking tour of the city and its historic buildings.

Kenai, the second oldest permanent settlement in Alaska, sits above Cook Inlet at the mouth of the Kenai River. Its growth over the past two centuries has been slow but steady. There was a village of the Dena'ina Athabascan Native peoples here when the first of the Russian fur traders arrived in 1741 and called the residents 'the Kenai People.' In 1791 the Russians set up a trading post, their second permanent settlement in Alaska. Then, in 1869, the US Army built Fort Kenay here, but it was abandoned soon after. Following the initial Cook Inlet Gold Rush of 1895–98, the Alaska Railroad constructed a track to the area. Oil exploration began in the mid-1950s and, in 1957, oil was found north of Kenai, near the Swanson River. In 1979, natural gas was discovered south of Kenai.

From the visitor centre, turn right off Main Street onto Overland Avenue and continue to Mission Avenue, where you turn right to get to the Holy Assumption of the Virgin Mary Russian Orthodox Church, built in 1896. It is the second oldest Russian Orthodox

Holy Assumption of the Virgin Mary Russian Orthodox Church in Kenai.

church in Alaska (the oldest is on Kodiak Island). You can recognize it by its white walls and onion-shaped blue domes. West of the church is the St. Nicholas Memorial Chapel. Constructed in 1906, it sits over the grave of Kenai's first priest, Father Egumen Nicholai. Ask at the church if you would like a tour.

Return on Mission Avenue. Once you pass Overland, look to your left to see the Old Town Village, a number of recently built log buildings around a square. You can visit the gift shops, restaurant and ice-cream parlour and watch local artists give demonstrations. Past the village you come to the Bluffs, from which you overlook

Old Town Village in Kenai.

the canneries. Stay on Mission until you get to the Beluga Whale Lookout, where there are information panels about the whales. From here, if you like, you can use the walking-tour guide to lead you to further sites.

If you keep heading northward through Kenai, you find that the Kenai Spur Highway becomes the North Kenai Highway. This highway follows Cook Inlet northward to Nikiski and Captain Cook State Recreation Area. It is 7 kilometres (4.3 miles) from the Kenai city limits to Nikiski, an oil town whose population is employed largely on offshore rigs. Once you pass Nikiski Fire Station No. 2, it is about 14 kilometres (9 miles) to a campground and a picnic area just inside the recreation area. Continue to Stormy Lake for swimming, another picnic site and a boat launch. From the entrance to the recreation area, it is 5.1 kilometres (3.2 miles) to a T-junction; turn left for another larger campground or right to park while you beachcomb, hike or picnic.

On your way southward out of Kenai, turn onto the Soldotna–Homer Road, which puts you on the Kenai River Flats. In about 3 kilometres (2 miles) you reach a pull-out to your right where there is a boardwalk provided with information panels about the flats.

You cross a bridge over the Kenai River, 0.7 kilometres (0.4 miles) from the boardwalk, and just past that bridge there is a turn-off for the Kenai River Flats State Recreation Site on the right.

In 2 kilometres (1.2 miles) you reach Kalifornsky Beach Road. A left turn would take you back to Soldotna. Turn right instead to bypass the Sterling Highway between Soldotna and Kasilof. You drive past acreages and a few businesses, with Cook Inlet to your right. Though the inlet is mostly hidden by trees, look to the right at kilometre 6.5 (mile 4) for a view of it—and there is a pull-out at kilometre 11.2 (mile 7) from which you can also see it. If you are travelling this road early in the morning, watch for moose on and along the road.

Kilometre 26.6 (mile 16.5) brings you to the Sterling Highway and the community of Kasilof.

Kasilof to Homer

Kasilof and Clam Gulch

Turn right onto the Sterling Highway. Kasilof Mercantile is on the left side of the road and Kasilof Riverview Groceries is down the hill on the right. Kasilof began as a Russian settlement, which was called 'St. George,' in 1786. The Kenaitze Native peoples soon developed a fishing and agricultural village here, but the scattered residents of Kasilof are now mostly non-Natives.

You cross the Kasilof River 0.6 kilometres (0.4 miles) from the junction with Kalifornsky Beach Road and, at kilometre 13.3 (mile 8.3), you reach the turn-off to the right for the Clam Gulch State Recreation Site. Go down this road; just after the turn there is a place where you can rent buckets and shovels for digging razor clams. In less than 1 kilometre (0.6 miles) from the highway you reach a station where you pay your camping fees. (Although you do not need to pay to dig clams without camping, you do need a licence.) The campground is on a bluff above a beach on

---

'Clamming'

Although digging for clams, or 'clamming,' is allowed year-round, April through September are the most popular months. Because clamming is done at low tide, to avoid disappointment, consult a tidetable. You can pick one up at most visitor information centres and marine or fishing supply stores. The best time to dig for clams, because more beach is exposed, is during a so-called 'minus tide.' This tide occurs during the three to four days when the full moon exerts its strongest pull on the ocean waters.

All clammers tend to agree that for successful razor clamming you need a tidetable, a shovel and a bucket and gloves (because of the sharp shells). And they all concur that the way to find a clam is to watch for a small dimple or depression in the wet sand. However, the advice differs on what to do next.

Some people say that when you see such a dimple you should dig out a shovelful of sand about 15 centimetres (6 inches) to the side, preferably toward the ocean, because clams like to head toward water. Then, push your gloved hand into the hole and reach into the sand beneath the dimple and you should have yourself a clam.

Others claim you should face the shore and dig in front (shoreward) of the depression, while still others say you should dig out the sand directly beneath the dimple.

Experiment with different digging strategies to see what works best for you.

The clams are bigger, but not as plentiful, toward the southern end of Cook Inlet. Besides Clam Gulch, some other places that you might try are Ninilchik and Deep Creek.

To dig for clams, you must have a valid Alaska fishing licence. The maximum catch is 60 clams of any kind (or combination) per day, and you can have up to 180 in your possession. You must keep each clam that you dig up. No matter what its size or condition, it becomes part of your quota.

Although there have been problems with red-tide contamination in the Panhandle, there have been no such problems along this part of the state.

Cook Inlet. From the parking area, take the stairs to a narrow, steep four-wheel–drive road and follow it down to the beach.

After the turn-off for the recreation site, a sign along the highway announces that you are coming into the hamlet of Clam Gulch. Besides the usual visitor services, it offers clam cleaning and packaging.

At kilometre 15 (mile 9.3) from the recreation site there is a pull-out to your right. Look across the inlet from here to see some active volcanoes. They are, from left to right, Mount Augustine (which last erupted in 1986), Mount Iliamna (which might emit wisps of smoke), Mount Redoubt (which sent up a huge mushroom-shaped cloud during its 1989–90 eruption) and Mount Spurr (whose latest eruption was in 1992).

Ninilchik

At kilometre 12.2 (mile 7.6) from the volcano-viewing pull-out there is a road to your right. To reach Ninilchik's historic Russian Orthodox Church, turn onto this road and drive less than 1 kilometre (0.6 miles) up the hill to the parking area. Visitors are welcome to the church, but please respect the cemetery by staying out of it. You are not allowed to take pictures inside the church. A sign at the church states, 'Transfiguration of our Lord has been an active church since 1900.'

Besides the cemetery adjacent to the church, there is also an American Legion Cemetery, 'Dedicated to all veterans from all wars.'

Go back to the highway; the Ninilchik River Scenic Overlook State Recreation Site is to your left just after the road to the church. You can park here to enjoy a viewpoint overlooking the river, or you can walk down to the river itself on a short trail. There is also a campground.

Just after the highway crosses the Ninilchik River, turn to your right to visit the historic village of Ninilchik. When you reach a Y in the road, go right and cross the river again to arrive at the small village. According to some accounts, Ninilchik was settled as early as the 1820s by retired fur traders of the Russian America Company, though others say that settlement began in 1841–42. The early residents were of Russian and Native descent. They gardened, panned for gold, fished and hunted to survive. Many of their descendants still live in the village today. Some of the buildings still standing here today were built in the late 1800s.

Transfiguration of Our Lord Russian Orthodox Church in Ninilchik.

From the Y, take the left fork to get to the harbour. The Ninilchik River is to your right as it flows into the inlet. At the harbour there is a large camping area, along with a boat launch. You can dig for clams here, but watch the incoming tide, especially if you decide to try clamming on the offshore sandbars.

Shortly after you return to the highway, you drive through the new section of Ninilchik. You come to a viewpoint for Deep Creek to your left at kilometre 2.4 (mile 1.5) from the turn-off for historic Ninilchik. You then cross Deep Creek, which flows into Cook Inlet, and arrive at Deep Creek South Scenic Overlook, to your left after the bridge. From here, you can look down on Deep Creek.

Anchor Point

A sign welcomes you to Anchor Point 29.7 kilometres (18.5 miles) from Deep Creek. At kilometre 33.9 (mile 21.1) you can turn left onto North Fork Road if you want to bypass about 11 kilometres (7 miles) of the 24 kilometres (15 miles) of the highway between here and Homer. The North Fork Road follows the North Fork Anchor River and then heads southward to cross the South Fork Anchor River before rejoining the Sterling Highway.

Staying on the highway, as you drive through Anchor Point, the highway curves to the left. At this curve turn right off the highway onto School Road and then immediately turn left onto the Old Sterling Highway to reach the parking lot for the visitor reception centre. Across the road from the front of the visitor centre, a cairn with a plaque reads: 'Anchor Point, Alaska, most westerly highway point in North America. This point is Mile 157 Sterling Highway. Latitude 59°48.1' North. Longitude 151°50.21' West.'

(Note: Since the Nome–Teller Highway is much further west, this sign obviously refers to the most westerly point that is connected with the continent's network of other highways.)

In 1778, Captain James Cook and the crews of the *Resolution* and the *Discovery* sailed into Cook Inlet on their way up the West Coast in search of the reputed Northwest Passage. While trying to move one of their ships by hauling on a rope attached to a large kedge-anchor dropped from a rowboat a short distance away, the tidal currents proved too strong and they lost their kedge-anchor. They named the point of land where it happened 'Anchor Point.'

You can continue on the Old Sterling Highway until it rejoins the Sterling Highway 10.4 kilometres (6.5 miles) from Anchor Point. Along the way, you cross the Anchor River. For a side trip, just past the bridge over the Anchor River, turn right onto Anchor Point Beach Road (River Road), which takes you past four campgrounds along the Anchor River and the Halibut Campground on Cook Inlet. Follow this road past the Halibut Campground, to the parking area where the pavement ends. This spot is believed to be the most westerly point of North America that is reachable directly by road from the continent's highway network. Beach Access Road, which leads from the parking area to the beach, is not maintained and it can flood during extreme high tides.

Homer

At kilometre 20.5 (mile 12.7) along the Sterling Highway from Anchor Point, you begin going downhill. You can see Homer Spit extending into Kachemak Bay as you round a curve at kilometre 21 (mile 13). To begin your visit to Homer with a trip to the spit, stay on the Sterling Highway as it crosses Main Street and becomes Homer Bypass. Continue to follow it where it curves to the right and crosses the Slough Bridge and then curves left and becomes Ocean Drive. Another curve to the right and you are on Homer Spit Road.

Homer began as a coal-mining town. Although it was the Russians who began mining coal in the area in the early to mid-1800s, American companies continued the mining and, by 1889, they had established a town on the spit to house the workers. Alaska's first railroad was constructed to bring coal from the mines to the wharf at the end of the spit. When the gold rush began at Hope, prospectors arrived at the spit on their way to the gold-fields. A promoter named Homer Pennock formed the Alaska Gold Mining Company and arrived at the spit in 1896 with his crew. Although he stayed only one year, the town was named after him.

The coal business had died by 1902 and the town on the spit was abandoned. Fishing brought new settlers in the 1920s; they tore down some of the old town on the spit to build their own homes. In the early 1930s most of what was left of the old town burned down in a slow fire fed by an exposed coal seam and coal that had washed ashore. Fishing and a canning plant kept Homer alive until the 1950s, when the Sterling Highway was built.

Boardwalk on Homer Spit.

Homer became a city in 1964, just four days after the Good Friday earthquake sank the spit by as much as 2 metres (6 feet).

Now with a population of over four thousand people, Homer still makes much of its money from fishing, with help from forestry and seasonal tourism.

To your right, just as you get onto the spit road, is the Lighthouse Village, which contains a replica lighthouse, an art gallery and charter businesses. Signs on a patio here tell about the birds that migrate to the area. Keep a watch for eagles as you drive on the spit.

You pass three sawmills (each with a log sort) and the Spit Fishing Hole before coming to the commercial section of the spit, which has shops on stilts connected by boardwalks, provides parking for recreational vehicles and offers various tours and charters. What looks like a lighthouse on your left is actually the Salty Dawg Saloon. The tower was once a water tank and the bar was originally a grocery store and post office—one of the few buildings to survive the fire of the 1930s. You pass the Seafarers' Memorial and the Homer Spit Campground to your right and then you reach the Landsend Restaurant at the end of the spit.

If you want to try fishing for king and silver salmon without paying for a charter, return to the Spit Fishing Hole, though you still need to have a fishing licence.

For a view of Homer and the spit, return to Ocean Drive and,

Fishing lagoon on Homer Spit.

when it curves left to become Homer Bypass, continue straight ahead onto Lake Street. In three blocks you reach a stop sign. Turn right onto East End Road and then left onto East Hill Road in 0.3 kilometres (0.2 miles). You get great views already as you follow the winding road upward through a residential area. At kilometre 2.9 (mile 1.8), shortly after a sharp curve, turn left at the sign that reads 'Scenic Overlook.' You are now on gravel.

In 0.7 kilometres (0.4 miles) you come to the viewpoint, which is to your left. From here you can see Homer, the spit and way out over Kachemak Bay to the mountains on the other side. If you want more of these scenic views, return to East Hill Road and turn left onto it. It dead-ends after just 12.8 kilometres (8 miles), but the scenery is great.

To visit the Pratt Museum, go back to East End Road and stay on it as it continues past Lake Street and becomes Pioneer Avenue. When Pioneer curves left, go right onto Bartlett Street. The Pratt Museum, in a bluish-grey building, contains displays of the area's history, an art gallery, a number of aquaria and a tide-pool tank, as well as the skeletons of many whales, a sea otter and a sea lion. As you enter, look up at the 12.5-metre (41-foot) long skeleton of a beaked whale hanging over the reception desk. This whale washed ashore in the fall of 1977.

There are two regularly scheduled water trips that leave from Homer. One is to the village of Halibut Cove, located southeast of Homer on the south shore of Kachemak Bay, which you can reach by taking the twice-daily jaunt on the *Danny J*. At the cove you can visit the Saltry Restaurant and four galleries—many of the people who live here are artisans.

The second trip is via a vehicle ferry to Seldovia, a quiet, relaxing old fishing village to the southwest across Kachemak Bay. Stop in at Seldovia's visitor reception centre—located in Synergy Artworks, across Main Street from the small boat harbour—for a map of the village. A leisurely stroll takes you past the 12 signs that make up the outdoor museum. Although you can easily walk around the town, if you bring your recreational vehicle, the closest parking for it is at an RV Park about 2 kilometres (1.2 miles) to the north on Jakolof Bay Road.

From Homer you can continue on with Chapter 5 by driving back up through Anchorage and staying on Alaska Route 1 until you reach Palmer.

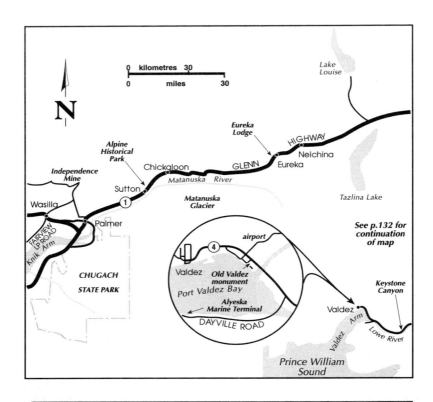

5
Palmer to Valdez to Tok

In this chapter you will drive on the oldest road in Alaska, on a road built over an old railroad bed and on the only two roads that lead into the world-famous Wrangell–St. Elias National Park and Preserve. You will have opportunities to visit a chapel on a hill, two ghost towns and two glaciers, and to hike part of the old Valdez-Eagle Trail.

Palmer to Glennallen

Palmer

As you come into Palmer from the southwest on the Glenn Highway (Alaska Route 1), turn east onto Evergreen Street. After you cross the railroad tracks, turn right onto South Valley Way. The visitor reception centre is in the log cabin on your left after you pass East Elmwood Avenue. If you are interested in the historic buildings of Palmer, pick up a walking-tour pamphlet at the visitor centre. The same building also houses the Colony Museum. Outside, there is a huge post with the names of various places and the distance that each is from Palmer.

Church of 1000 Logs in Palmer.

Palmer began as a place for miners to homestead after they returned from the 1913 gold rush in Nelchina. It was the building of a railroad station here on the Matanuska Branch of the Alaska Railroad in 1916, however, that really established the settlement. The next year the Department of Agriculture developed an experimental farm at Palmer and then coal was discovered in the area.

During the Great Depression of the 1930s, President Roosevelt sent over two hundred families from drought-stricken Michigan, Wisconsin and Minnesota to the Matanuska Valley to colonize the state and make it self-sufficient in food production. They became known as 'the Matanuska Colonists.' Each family was given a parcel of land—some sources say it was 16 hectares (40 acres) each and others say 65 hectares (160 acres). Though they began by living in cabins with log bottoms and canvas tops, they were given assistance in building permanent homes and barns. These barns are now known as 'the Colony Barns.' Although the settlers' lives were difficult, they succeeded in establishing Palmer as the centre of agriculture in the state.

From the visitor centre, turn onto East Elmwood and go two blocks to South Denali Street. The United Protestant Church, 'the Church of 1000 Logs,' is on the right corner. This church was built in 1936–37 by the Matanuska Colonists and is still used today.

In this land of long summer days, gardeners have grown 36-kilogram (80-pound) cabbages, 1-kilogram (2-pound) radishes, 4.5-kilogram (10-pound) onions and 57-kilogram (125 pound) pumpkins. If you want to see some of these hefty vegetables, visit the Alaska State Fair at the fairgrounds in Palmer at the end of August.

You can take a side trip from Palmer to climb to a viewpoint on a nearby feature known as 'the Butte' and to see a reindeer farm. To do so, leave Palmer on West Arctic Avenue, which becomes the Old Glenn Highway, and drive 11 kilometres

Muskox Farm near Palmer.

(6.8 miles) to the flashing light at Butte, where the Butte Trading Post and the Butte Cafe are on the left. Turn right here onto Bodenburg Loop Road and in about 1 kilometre (0.6 miles) the road curves left. Look straight ahead here for a sandy trail that goes up the hillside. Park beside the road. After a 45-minute climb, you arrive at the top. From here, you have a great view of the area and can see the Knik Glacier in the distance.

As you continue up the road, just after the curve you come to the turn-off to the right for the Reindeer Farm, which is located on one of the original colony farms. Here, you can walk up to the reindeer and pet and feed them. They are very tame and will nibble at your hands. Be sure to wear old running shoes or boots—or watch where you walk. You can let your children ride in a cart pulled by reindeer, while you stock up on reindeer souvenirs. Some of the reindeer are sold to farms in other states. The farm also sells meat, hides and discarded antlers.

If you continue on Bodenburg Loop Road, you pass by more of the colony farms and come out at the Old Glenn Highway again. Turn left and it is 9.3 kilometres (5.8 miles) back into Palmer.

As you leave Palmer on the Glenn Highway heading toward Glennallen, it is 2.5 kilometres (1.6 miles) from the junction of West Arctic Avenue to Palmer-Fishhook Road. If you did not visit the Independence Mine and Hatcher Pass and you still want to, turn left here (see Chapter 3). Otherwise, continue on.

Turn left off the highway onto Archie Road at kilometre 3.3 (mile 2.1) to go to the Muskox Farm, which you reach in about 0.5 kilometres (0.3 miles). At the Muskox Farm, tours that begin every half hour allow you to see the animals from walkways. You will learn about their history and how the Native peoples hunted them for food.

Every spring, muskoxen shed their inner wool or qiviut, a Native word that means 'down' or

The Muskox

Looking somewhat like a bison, the slow, shaggy muskox (*Ovibos moschatus*) is a member of the Bovidae Family to which sheep, goats, cattle and also bison belong. Well-adapted to life in northern regions, it is one of the oldest species on the continent, dating back to the last major ice age, approximately 12,000 years ago. The male stands 91 cm–1.5 metres (3–5 feet) high, has a length of 2.1–2.46 metres (7–8 feet) and weighs between 263-408 kilograms (579–900 pounds).

The first mention of the muskox by non-Natives was by Russian explorers in 1720. When threatened by wolves, a herd of muskoxen forms a protective circle around the young. This strategy made them easy prey for human hunters and, by the mid-1800s, all the muskoxen in Alaska had been wiped out. Now under strict protection, the muskoxen in Alaska today are descended from animals imported from Canada.

Foundations at the Alpine Historical Park at Sutton.

'underwool.' The herders use a hair pick to comb out the qiviut, which is eight times warmer than an equal amount (by weight) of sheep wool. It is sent to a cashmere spinning shop to be spun into yarn. The yarn is then sent to members of the Muskox Producers Cooperative, who live in small, isolated villages. The women of the cooperative knit it into clothing—each has her own special pattern. You can buy a hat or a scarf made from qiviut at the farm's gift shop. Though they are quite expensive, they are very soft and warm and they last for years.

The farm is open daily, 10 AM to 6 PM, May through September.

Wolf Country USA is on the right at kilometre 2.9 (mile 1.8) from the Muskox Farm. It is open all year, from 9 AM to 9 PM, with tours every 15 minutes. The wolves, called 'kissing wolves,' are quite tame. If you put something between your lips, one will stand on its hind feet and take it from your lips almost as if it was kissing you. Inside the gift shop you can buy souvenirs, crafts and hats or touques made from wolf hair.

The highway is very scenic as it winds along the Matanuska Valley. If you want fresh vegetables for a salad or sandwiches, Eska Farms is on your right, 11.8 kilometres (7.3 miles) from Wolf Country. You can purchase many kinds of seasonal vegetables here. They start the tomatoes and English cucumbers early, so you can buy ripe ones in June. If you would like to walk through their greenhouses and through their gardens with long rows of other vegetables, just ask. Lots of flowers in the yard make it very beautiful.

Sutton and Chickaloon

At kilometre 2.4 (mile 1.5) from Eska Farms, you cross Eska Creek and are in the community of Sutton, with the Sutton Store to your left. On the left, 1 kilometre (0.6 miles) from the store, you reach Alpine Historical Park. This park recounts the history of the area from early Native habitation through the mining of coal in the 1920s to the building of the Glenn Highway.

The Native peoples were the first to find coal in the Chickaloon area and they told others about it in the late 1800s. The Alaska Central Railroad built a line through here in 1904, hoping to use the coal to fuel their engines. The US Navy was also interested in the coal and asked the government to form the Wishbone Hill Coal Mining District. In 1922 the navy completed building the Sutton Coal Washery, in what is now Alpine Historical Park, to wash the coal that it mined.

The town of Chickaloon was established as a place for the miners to live but, by 1925, the US Navy decided that the coal was not good enough for use in its ships. The Chickaloon Mine was shut down and most of the miners moved away. The washery was taken down and moved to another site in the 1930s, leaving just the foundations.

Pathways at the park lead past pieces of old machinery with information panels in front of them. There are two boilers here—one was stationary when in use, while the other was portable—as well as steam engines and hoists. A number of historic buildings, such as the Chickaloon Bunkhouse, are open for viewing.

If you want to do some fishing, at kilometre 2.1 (mile 1.3) from the Alpine Historical Park, there is a map on the right that shows lakes in the area that have been stocked with trout.

You are driving with the Matanuska River to the right as you leave the sign. If you look to the right at kilometre 8 (mile 5) as you cross the King River, you can see its turquoise waters flow into the brownish Matanuska River.

Kilometre 24.3 (mile 15) brings you to Chickaloon, home of the Chickaloon Tribe of the Athabascan peoples. Then, as you cross the Chickaloon River, also turquoise, you can see it running below you and into the Matanuska River.

Matanuska Glacier and Eureka

You get your first glimpse of the Matanuska Glacier ahead just 23.3 kilometres (14.5 miles) from Chickaloon. A viewpoint is on the right at kilometre 40.4 (mile 25.1), from which you can see the glacier across the Matanuska Valley.

The Wickersham Trading Post, which sells gifts and has information, at 0.5 kilometres (0.3 miles) from the viewpoint, marks Glacier Park Road. If

Matanuska Glacier.

Historic Eureka Bunkhouse.

you want to visit the glacier (for a fee, courtesy of Glacier Park Resort), turn right down this steep, narrow, winding road, which offers great views. If you are pulling a trailer, leave it up at the highway. Turn right just after you cross a one-lane bridge over the Matanuska River, 1 kilometre (0.6 miles) from the highway. Pay your fee at the lodge and drive 3.2 kilometres (2 miles) to a parking lot. It is about a 15-minute hike to the toe of the glacier. The glacier is about 6 kilometres (4 miles) wide and 43 kilometres (27 miles) long, though it once stretched as far as Palmer.

There are viewpoints along the highway after you pass Glacier Park Road, the first being at kilometre 1 (mile 0.6). You can also see other mountain glaciers as you drive.

At kilometre 42.7 (mile 26.5) you reach the Eureka Lodge, to your left. On the same property sit the Eureka Roadhouse and the Eureka Bunkhouse, both built in 1936. The Eureka Roadhouse was the first roadhouse on the Glenn Highway. Eureka Summit is 2 kilometres (1.2 miles) past the lodge. With an elevation of 1013 metres (3322 feet), it is the highest point on the Glenn Highway.

 Alaska's Roadhouses

During the era when land transportation through Alaska was by dog sled or wagon, the first of Alaska's roadhouses were built, about one day's travel from each other. They provided shelter, a bed, meals and conversation for the traveller.

Hundreds of these roadhouses once dotted the scenery around the state. However, as the road system improved and people began using buses and private vehicles, many of the older road-houses shut down and the buildings were left to decay and fall apart. Although some of the road-houses remained in operation, many of the old buildings accidentally burned down or were replaced by new lodges, leaving only a few of the original buildings.

Nelchina and Tolsona

Nelchina Store is to the right at kilometre 11.2 (mile 7) from Eureka Lodge and the sign for the settlement of Nelchina is at kilometre 16.1 (mile 10). The community is mainly off the highway, but you do pass the elementary school on the left at kilometre 26.3 (mile 16.3).

At kilometre 39.1 (mile 24.3) you cross Mendeltna Creek and there is a Kamping Resorts of Alaska (K.R.O.A.) establishment to the right. Park here for a free visit to the Museum of Alaska's Drunken Forest. There is a path to the fenced-in 'forest,' which consists of trunks of trees with burls on them, or limbs that have grown askew and that have been put on display here.

The road to the Lake Louise Recreation Area is to your left at 11.1 kilometres (6.9 miles) from the Drunken Forest. The 31-kilometre (19-mile) road to the lake takes you past lodges, bed-and-breakfast operations and many trails, most of them less than 0.5 kilometres (0.3 miles) long and leading to lakes where you can fish for grayling and trout. At Lake Louise you can picnic, fish, camp or launch a boat.

After the turn-off for Lake Louise, you enter Tolsona, another community that is largely off the highway. On your left, 10 kilometres (6.2 miles) from the Lake Louise turn-off, there is a sign for 'Atlasta House.' The name of this log house reflects the owner's gladness at finally having a home.

The tall, snow-capped Wrangell Mountains now lie directly ahead. From left to right, the mountains that you can see are Mount Sandford, Mount Drum, Mount Wrangell and Mount Blackburn. Since the 1964 earthquake, Mount Wrangell, Alaska's largest active volcano, has been heating up. If you are here on a cold morning, watch for steam rising from its top.

Glennallen

At kilometre 33.1 (mile 20.6) from Atlasta House, you cross Moose Creek and pass the sign for Glennallen. Glennallen grew from a highway construction camp set up during the building of the Glenn Highway, which was built by the US Army during the Second World War to link Anchorage to the Alaska Highway via the Richardson Highway. It was named for two early 1900s army officers involved in leading explorations of the Copper River area, Major Edwin Glenn and Lieutenant Henry Allen.

After driving past Glennallen's business and industrial activities, which are spread along the highway, at kilometre 37.7 (mile 23.4) you reach a T-intersection where the Glenn Highway meets the Richardson Highway (Alaska Route 4). Glennallen's visitor reception centre is on the left in the sod-roofed Glennallen Log Cabin.

Though a left turn here will take you toward Fairbanks or Tok, this chapter continues with a right turn toward Valdez.

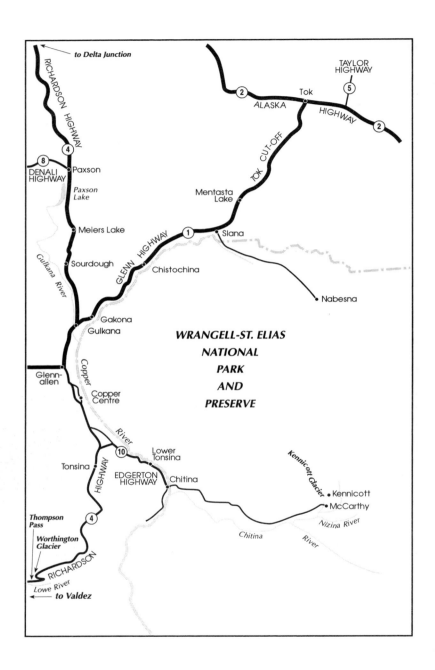

Tazlina to Valdez

Tazlina and Copper Center

As you travel from Glennallen to Valdez, with the Wrangell Mountains to your left and the Chugach Mountains to your right, you are following the oldest road in Alaska. First blazed in 1898, it was a part of what was known as 'the All-American Route' used by gold-rush stampeders heading for the Klondike (see sidebar on p. 134). Work on an actual road between Valdez and Fairbanks began in 1905, and it was completed in 1918. The work took this long because it was done mainly by human labour, since bulldozers and other road-building machines were at that time not yet available.

In 1.5 kilometres (0.9 miles) from the T-intersection, there is a sign for the community of Tazlina. You pass the Tazlina Store at kilometre 6 (mile 3.7) and then cross the Tazlina River.

To visit Copper Center, make a left turn at kilometre 13.5 (mile 8.4) onto a loop of the Old Richardson Highway that was bypassed during improvements to the highway. In 1.2 kilometres (0.7 miles) you reach the headquarters for Wrangell-St. Elias Park and Preserve (on the right), where you can pick up information on activities in the park. After you pass a grocery store, an art gallery and a post office, make a second left turn at kilometre 4 (mile 2.5) to continue to Copper Center. If instead you stayed on the Old Richardson Highway past this turn-off, you would come to the Chapel on the Hill. Completed in 1943, it is the oldest log chapel in the Copper

Copper Center Roadhouse.

River area. You can leave your vehicle beside the road and climb the path up the hill to the chapel, where you can watch a free slide show about its history and that of the area.

The second left turn has put you onto another loop, this one off the Old Richardson Highway. At 3.2 kilometres (2 miles) from the second left, you reach the Copper Center Lodge, which offers dining seven days a week. Go next door to the lodge's Bunkhouse Annex, which contains the George I. Ashby Memorial Museum, to see artifacts from gold-rush times. It is open 1 PM to 5 PM, Monday to Saturday, from June 1 to September 1.

Copper Center began with a roadhouse in 1896. During the Klondike Gold Rush, prospectors arrived here after trudging over the glaciers from Valdez and

An All-American Route to the Klondike

When the rush to the Klondike was on, the Canadian government imposed some strict regulations on the gold-rush stampeders. To avoid these regulations, over four thousand people headed for Valdez. They had heard about an old Native-Russian trail from Valdez to Yukon that was supposed to be an 'All-American Route' that would bypass the Canadian authorities and was also said to be shorter.

The men arrived at Valdez and began crossing the Valdez Glacier, an obstacle that most had not counted on, so they were not prepared for the arduous trek. Some did not bring water or wood for cooking and warmth. Others did not even know how to carry their packs properly. Fierce storms, snowblindness and treacherous crevasses took their toll on the gold-seekers.

Hundreds turned back with scurvy or frostbite. Only a few managed to reach the other side and get off the ice. Of the ones who made it this far, some lost their footing while crossing the run-off waters and drowned, unable to release their heavy packs in time to escape. Those still surviving built makeshift boats and sailed down the Klutina River to Copper Center.

From the Klutina River, the route continued to the Copper River, northeast to Mentasta Pass, to the Fortymile River, to the Yukon River at Eagle and from there to Dawson City. Only about three hundred of those who started from Valdez actually made it all the way to the Klondike.

many spent the winter. Those who were able to do so continued via the Eagle Trail to Dawson. However, it is said that hundreds died of scurvy and many others turned back totally discouraged.

First, follow one loop road and then the other to return to the Richardson Highway, which you reach in 1 kilometre (0.6 miles).

Chitina, MaCarthy and Kennicott

Once you are back on the Richardson Highway, it is 12.7 kilometres (7.9 miles) to a gravel road on your left, the Old Edgerton Highway. You can turn onto it if you want to drive through some lovely homestead country before hooking up with the Edgerton Highway at Kenny Lake. Otherwise, stay on the Richardson Highway for another 17.2 kilometres (10.7 miles) from the gravel road, when you reach the new, paved Edgerton Highway, which goes to Chitina.

Turn left onto the Edgerton Highway and in 1.5 kilometres (0.9 miles) from the Richardson Highway you crest a hill from which you can see far ahead. On a clear day, the beautiful, stark-white Wrangell Mountains across the valley are outlined against the blue sky. You enter the settlement of Kenny Lake at kilometre 8 (mile 5) and at kilometre 11.8 (mile 7.3) you pass the southeastern end of the gravel-surfaced Old Edgerton Highway.

Kilometre 38.3 (mile 23.8) brings you to Liberty Falls State Recreation Site, which is to your right. From the parking lot, walk out onto the wooden bridge to see Liberty Falls; you can continue across the bridge and walk along the creek for a closer look.

Just after you get back onto the highway, you cross Liberty Creek. You begin going downhill and in 9 kilometres (5.6 miles) you enter a rock-walled canyon, with Threemile Lake to your left. Twomile Lake is to your right at kilometre 10.8 (mile 6.7) and Onemile Lake, also on the right, is at kilometre 13 (mile 8.1).

At kilometre 15.3 (mile 9.5) you reach Chitina and its historic buildings. The Chitina Emporium sells woven baskets, quilts and stained glass articles, while the Chitina Artworks offers other craft items, including paintings and beadwork. Browse through both of them.

Chitina (the second 'i' is silent) is at the confluence of the Copper and Chitina rivers. 'Chitina' was formed from two Athabascan words, chiti, meaning 'copper,' and na, meaning 'river.' Local Native peoples used the copper in the area to make tools for shaping other pieces of copper into plates for trade with other bands.

The Copper River & Northwestern Railroad, constructed to take copper ore from the Kennecott Mines to the seaport that became Cordova, saw Chitina established along it in 1910. The town prospered as a stopover for travellers who came by ship to Cordova, caught the train to Chitina and then headed to Fairbanks by stage. The age of prosperity lasted until 1938, when the Kennecott Copper Corporation closed its mining operations and the railway quit running. (Incidentally, the Kennicott Glacier and the nearby town were named in honour of an Alaskan explorer, Robert Kennicott. The mine was supposedly named after the glacier, but somebody misspelled the name with an 'e' where there should have been an 'i' and the mistake was never corrected.)

Continue on the road through Chitina and you soon reach the end of the pavement and begin driving the McCarthy Road. This road, which takes you into the Wrangell–St. Elias National Park and Preserve, is in poor shape and it could take you four or more hours to make the 97-kilometre (60-mile) trip to the end of the road. There are residences, campgrounds, trail rides and rental cabins along the road, but no service stations. Because the road is built on an old railroad bed, watch for the spikes that sometimes work their way to the surface. There are only two places where you can get a tire repaired, so make sure that you have a good spare and a working jack. If you wish to save your vehicle the hardship of the drive, there is a tour that leaves from Chitina.

The beginning of the road is constricted by two rock walls about three vehicle lengths long that are spaced just far enough apart for one vehicle to pass. The Copper River flows by on your right until you cross it at kilometre 1.7 (mile 1.1). At kilometre 2.4 (mile 1.5) there

Chitina Emporium.

The Copper River Highway

The accidental discovery of copper next to the Kennicott Glacier in 1900 had by 1908 led to the beginning of construction on the Copper River & Northwestern Railroad's line (from Cordova at tidewater through Chitina to the Kennecott Copper Mines at Kennicott). The track was finished in 1911 and was in use until 1938, when the mine closed.

The Kennecott Copper Corporation donated the 315-kilometre (196-mile) railroad right-of-way to the federal government in 1941, with the stipulation that it be made into a public road from Cordova to Chitina. Construction of the Copper River Highway began in 1945. Even though workers had the railbed as a starting point, the going was slow. It was not until 1958 that the road was completed from Cordova even as far as the bridge over the Copper River 77 kilometres (48 miles) away. This bridge is called 'the Million Dollar Bridge' because it cost over one million dollars to build in 1910. The old decking on the bridge was replaced with concrete and work continued on the other side.

However, the earthquake of 1964 collapsed one of the four spans of the bridge and warped the other three. Nothing has been done since then to complete the Copper River Highway (Alaska Route 10).

The portion of the right-of-way between Chitina and Kennicott has become the McCarthy Road.

is a Y. Take the right fork of the Y to go to McCarthy. The left fork goes to a wide-open flat beside the river. During the salmon run in June, Alaskans come here to dipnet for fish. Huge nets set at the ends of 3-metre (10-foot) long poles are dipped into the water to catch the red and king salmon that return to this river.

You are now following alongside the Chitina River. At kilometre 8 (mile 5) there is a viewpoint from which you can look down on it. Silver Lake—with fishing for rainbow trout, boat rentals and camping—is to your right at kilometre 17.5 (mile 10.9). If you need a tire repaired or want to buy tires, you can also do that here.

At kilometre 27.4 (mile 17) there is a pull-out on your right from which you can take pictures of the bridge over the Kuskulana River, just ahead, and the canyon below.

One more pull-out is before the bridge, but the view includes only the bridge and not the canyon.

Slow to 25 kilometres per hour (15 miles per hour) and be prepared to yield to oncoming traffic as you approach this one-lane bridge. Built in 1910 for the Copper River & Northwestern Railroad, it is 160 metres (525 feet) long and 72.5 metres (238 feet) above the Kuskulana River. The guardrails were added in 1988.

For most of its length, the McCarthy Road is wide enough for two vehicles to pass and there are many pull-outs that you can use if vehicles are too big or wide to pass comfortably. At kilometre 30 (mile 18.6), however, you reach a stretch that is just one lane wide for about 150 metres (500 feet). It is on a curve with a rock wall to the left and a drop-off to the right, so drive slowly and carefully.

At kilometre 46.9 (mile 29.1) you round a curve and can see an old railroad trestle spanning the Gilahina River ahead. You work your way down to the Gilahina River and cross it at kilometre 47.3 (mile 29.4). Just before the bridge there is a parking area that you can use if you want to take pictures of the trestle or do some fishing.

From time to time you drive through forest where the trees are close to the edge of the road and where their overhanging branches meet overhead. To the left, 74 kilometres (46 miles) from the beginning of the road, you pass Long Lake and the Long

Rock wall at beginning of McCarthy Road.

McCarthy Museum.

Lake Wildlife Refuge. To protect spawning salmon, boat motors used in the lake must be less than 10 horsepower.

At kilometre 91.8 (mile 57) you cross the first of a number of small streams that supply drinking water to local residents. Please help the residents protect the quality of the water by not bathing or washing in any of the signposted streams and by keeping your dog leashed.

At kilometre 97 (mile 60.3) the road ends at a parking lot on the bank of the Kennicott River. A sign here reminds visitors that most of the McCarthy–Kennicott area is privately owned. Walk over to the Tram Station to pay your parking fees and perhaps to book a seat on the shuttle-bus from the other side of the river to McCarthy and Kennicott. You can also rent a bicycle to tour the area or sign up for a flight over the glaciers and mountains of the Wrangell–St. Elias National Park and Preserve. The wood for the Tram Station came from the timbers of the bridge over the Nizina River, which was built in 1933 and collapsed on July 3, 1993.

From the Tram Station, look up at the mountains to see the Kennicott Glacier. At one time the glacier covered the spot where you are standing—you can see the black piles of ground rock that it left behind near the parking lot.

Leave the Tram Station and walk across the Kennicott River on the steel-decked footbridge, through which you can see the water rushing below. This bridge was opened in May of 1997 to replace the hand-operated, open-platform tram that you can see to the right of the bridge. Before 1997, visitors crossing the river had to sit on the platform and pull themselves across using a cable.

At the end of the bridge, there is another gravel road. The shuttle-bus will pick you up here if you bought a ticket, or you can enjoy the scenic walk (or bicycle ride) into McCarthy. You pass the McCarthy–Kennicott Community Church—open at 10 AM each Sunday for all faiths—on the right and then reach a second footbridge over another channel of the river. Look to your left while on this bridge to see the hamlet of Kennicott way in the distance at the foot of the mountain.

After about a 15-minute walk, you arrive at a red building that houses the McCarthy Museum, which has artifacts and displays related to the mining history of the area. (If the museum is closed, check its schedule at the McCarthy Lodge.) From the museum you can turn left and walk 7.2 kilometres (4.5 miles) to Kennicott or turn right to go into McCarthy.

Kennecott Mill at Kennicott.

McCarthy was established to provide services that were not available in the rather strict company town of Kennicott. It offered saloons, pool halls, shops, restaurants and hotels and even a red-light district. When the mines shut down in 1938, both towns lost most of their residents. Today, there are only about 25 people in McCarthy and 10 in Kennicott.

The McCarthy Lodge, which has a restaurant/saloon, is in a building that was constructed in 1917 and was used for a time as a photographer's studio. Inside there are pictures from the days of the mine's operation. In other buildings in the hamlet you will find an air charter service, another restaurant, a pizza parlour, an ice cream vendor and the Ma Johnson Hotel, which rents rooms and has a gift shop. If you continue down the main street, you will reach the section of town that held the red-light district. Now there are just a couple of dilapidated log buildings overgrown by trees.

Although you can walk to Kennicott, a shuttle-bus runs every two hours, beginning at 10 AM. The most impressive building in Kennicott is the Kennecott Mill, which climbs 14 storeys up the mountainside. It processed the ore from the copper mines in the area and, when it closed, the miners and the company left the buildings, equipment and tools where they lay.

Besides seeing the buildings, you can try rafting, take a glacier-viewing flight or go on a guided hike. There are bed-and-breakfast operations in some of the town's original houses and the Kennicott Lodge offers a restaurant for refreshments.

When you are done with Kennicott and McCarthy, return to the Richardson Highway.

Worthington Glacier and Valdez

Continuing southward on the Richardson Highway, 5.1 kilometres (3.2 miles) from the Edgerton Highway junction you cross Squirrel Creek. There is a service station to your right here—watch for the giant squirrel.

At kilometre 29.1 (mile 18.1), the Alaska Pipeline's Pump Station 12 is to your left and there is a road to your right that goes uphill to a viewpoint overlooking the Alaska Pipeline. Continue southward and at about kilometre 22 (mile 14) from the pump station you begin to notice a mountain ahead that has a huge glacier at its middle. It is Mount Billy Mitchell, named for then-Lieutenant William Mitchell, who was in charge of the US Army Signal Corps contingent that built the telegraph line that connected all the military posts in the state by 1903. Known as the Washington–Alaska Military Cable and Telegraph System (WAMCATS), it also allowed Alaska to communicate with the rest of the US.

Kilometre 48.4 (mile 30.1) gives you a great view of the Worthington Glacier. You can turn off for the Worthington Glacier State Recreation Site at kilometre 57.8 (mile 35.9). The parking lot is adjacent to a viewing area that overlooks the glacier and has a number of interpretive panels about it.

From the viewing area you can walk down to the toe of the glacier, where a lake has formed, or you can follow a path to the side of it. From the parking lot, a viewpoint trail climbs above the glacier. In the late 1800s, the glacier was about 30 metres (100 feet) higher and 300 metres (1000 feet) longer than it is today.

At 4.3 kilometres (2.7 miles) from the Worthington Glacier, you reach Thompson Pass, elevation 816 metres (2678 feet). This pass holds two of Alaska's records for snowfall: in December of 1955, 1.6 metres (5.2 feet) of snow fell in one 24-hour period and, during the winter of 1952–53, a total of 24.7 metres (81 feet) of snow dropped onto the pass. This large amount of snowfall is the result of warm, moisture-laden air that comes from the coast and drops its moisture as snow as it rises over the pass.

Worthington Glacier.

After the pass, you begin a long, slow, winding descent to Valdez. The hills are bare of trees, allowing you to see the beautiful mountain scenery. At kilometre 16.1 (mile 10) you cross Sheep Creek. Look to your right to see the canyon that the creek has made. Although you are still far from downtown Valdez, you pass the city limits sign at kilometre 19.2 (mile 11.9).

You enter Keystone Canyon at kilometre 21.7 (mile 13.5). You cross the Lowe River, which hits a rock wall and doubles back on itself, for the first time at kilometre 22.5 (mile 14). On a curve as you come around a rock wall at kilometre 23.2 (mile 14.4), look for a pull-out to your left.

Beside the pull-out there is an old, partially completed railway tunnel. This tunnel was made by hand during the race to build a track from the coast to the Kennecott Mines. A feud broke out between two of the nine competing companies and one man was shot. In the fervour over the shooting, the tunnel was never finished. The railroad to the mines, instead of beginning at Valdez, as it might otherwise have, starts at Cordova instead.

Inside the short tunnel, water runs down the walls and accumulates in a large pool on the ground. By stepping on stones, you can get part-way to the small opening at the other end.

You cross the Lowe River again after the tunnel. Then, between kilometre 25 (mile 15.5) and kilometre 25.5 (mile 15.8), you pass Bridal Veil Falls and Horsetail Falls. Both are on the left, with pull-outs for them on the right.

Bridal Veil Falls.

These falls are a 'must-stop' and both are of such a great height that you may not get the entire waterfall in one photo.

You reach Dayville Road, on the left, 18 kilometres (11.2 miles) from Bridal Veil Falls. Take a side trip down this road if you are interested in touring the Solomon Gulch Fish Hatchery (look for the blue buildings) or, if it is July, fishing for returning pink salmon in the adjacent waters. The road goes along the south shore of Port Valdez Bay until it ends at the Alyeska Marine Terminal, where oil that has come all the way from Prudhoe Bay is finally pumped into huge tanker ships. You can also tour the terminal—consult the visitor reception centre in Valdez for times and reservations or contact the Alyeska Pipeline Service Company's visitor centre at the Valdez Airport.

As you continue on the highway toward Valdez, you can see the harbour to your left, the pipeline terminal and maybe a tanker waiting to be loaded with the oil. In 4.4 kilometres (2.7 miles) from Dayville Road, turn left onto Alaska Avenue to visit the site of Old Valdez. One-half kilometre (0.3 miles) down the road there is a memorial, a large concrete area with flower boxes set on it.

Of Alaska's coastal towns, Valdez was the hardest hit by the 1964 earthquake, losing 28 citizens, with three more people dying on the steamship *Chena* in the harbour. The city was only 72 kilometres (45 miles) from the epicentre of the quake, which registered 9.2 on the Richter scale and lasted four minutes. This site of Valdez was almost levelled by the earthquake and the resulting tidal waves.

Although there was already a trading post at Valdez even before the Klondike Gold Rush of 1898, it was not until 1900 that the army set up Fort Liscum (where the oil terminal is now) to deal with the influx of gold miners. The army stayed until

1922 and during those years the trading post grew into a town. It took its name from Port Valdez, which had been named in 1790 by Spanish explorer Don Salvador Fidalgo for Antonio Valdes y Basan, marine minister for Spain at the time.

Once you return to the highway, it is about 5 kilometres (3 miles) into Valdez. As you come into the city, turn left onto Pioneer Drive and turn left once again onto Chenega Avenue when you reach it. The visitor reception centre is on the corner at Fairbanks Drive. Continue one block down Pioneer to Tatitlek Avenue and turn left. In two blocks you reach the Valdez Museum, which is on your left.

The museum's self-guiding tour takes you past displays of the area's history— the gold rush, the earthquake, the construction of the pipeline and the 1989 Exxon Valdez Oil Spill. In the yard of the museum, you can see Lifeboat #4 from the cruise ship *Prinsendam*, which sank on October 11, 1980. A week earlier, on October 4, her crew had sent out a distress call from the Gulf of Alaska, reporting a fire in her engine-room. In what Alaska search-and-rescue crews consider to be among the 'Top 10 Rescues of the Past 50 Years,' the passengers and crew were rescued from their lifeboats by helicopter and deposited on the deck of the supertanker *Williamsburg*. The *Williamsburg* docked in Valdez, and the passengers were taken into the homes of the townspeople, earning Valdez recognition as an 'All-America City.'

One of the highlights of visiting Valdez is the opportunity to tour Prince William Sound and see the Columbia Glacier, the largest tidewater glacier in the sound and the second largest in North America. If you have the time, it is well worth the money to take one of the charters available from Valdez. As you travel through the iceberg-filled waters, watch for porpoises swimming beside the boat, sea lions resting on buoys and otters on their backs, either breaking open shellfish on rocks on their stomachs or just lying with their front paws folded on their chests. And, of course, the best part is seeing the glacier calve into the water.

Glennallen to Tok

Gulkana and Paxson

This chapter now continues from back at the T-intersection in Glennallen, where the Glenn Highway meets the Richardson Highway. As you head northward, you cross the Gulkana River 19.9 kilometres (12.4 miles) from the intersection and the village of Gulkana is to your right after the bridge. At kilometre 22.7 (mile 14.1) you reach Gakona Junction. The Tok Cut-off (Alaska Route 1) goes to the right here, but you can begin with a side trip up this part of the Richardson Highway (Alaska Route 4), which continues straight ahead to Paxson (mentioned in Chapter 3 as being at the eastern end of the Denali Highway), Delta Junction and Fairbanks.

There is lovely scenery on the way to Paxson—and many viewpoints. You cross Sourdough Creek at kilometre 31 (mile 19.3). The Sourdough Roadhouse is on the left. The original Sourdough Roadhouse, built in 1903 and the last one that remained from the over 40 that once stood along the gold-miners' trail from Valdez to Fairbanks, burned down in 1992. The building the roadhouse is in now and two old log cabins in the yard are from the same era. The one closest to the roadhouse was a schoolhouse and the one next to it was a carriage house. If you want to sleep in a bit of history, rent one of those two cabins for the night.

Old school building at Sourdough Roadhouse.

Meiers Lake and the Meiers Lake Roadhouse are to your left at kilometre 67.2 (mile 41.8). Watch for swans as you drive beside the lake. Then you pass Paxson Lake and you reach the junction with the Denali Road at kilometre 97.7 (mile 60.7) from Gakona Junction. On the far left corner stands the Paxson Lodge, with a post office, rooms to rent and a restaurant, all in one large building. If you continue on to Delta Junction, you will cross Isabel Pass, said to be the most scenic pass in Alaska, if the weather co-operates.

Gakona and Chistochina

Canoeing the Gulkana River

The Gulkana River, designated a National Wild River, is one of the easier rivers when it comes to putting in or taking out a canoe (or raft). However, you should be experienced with whitewater before attempting it and there should be at least two canoes in your party.

A favourite put-in spot is at the Paxson Lake campground. From there you paddle southwest on the lake for about 5 kilometres (3 miles) before reaching the outlet of the Gulkana River. Once on the river, you have Class II and III rapids as the river drops at a rate of 7.2 metres per kilometre (38 feet per mile).

After the Middle Fork confluence, the river slows until you reach the Canyon Rapids, which, if you have an open canoe (or small raft), you should portage around on the left side. If you are an experienced canoeist and do decide to run these Class IV rapids, portage your gear around them first.

You encounter Class II and III waters again below the rapids and then you have about 27 kilometres (17 miles) of Class I to the take-out at the Sourdough Creek Campground.

Expect to have to go around overhanging branches and watch for boulders and fallen trees. If you meet a motorized boat, keep to the shallow side so that the other boat has the deeper water. Hopefully, the boat will slow down so as not to swamp your canoe with its wake.

Back at Gakona Junction, turn toward Tok. In 0.4 kilometres (0.2 miles), a sign says that you are entering Gakona. Stop in at the Gakona Roadhouse, built in 1929, to your left at kilometre 3.1 (mile 1.9). The old original roadhouse, completed in 1905, and the barn, circa 1910, are to the left of the 'new' roadhouse as you face it.

Paxson Lodge.

The current owners plan to restore these two old buildings. The Carriage House restaurant is to the right of the roadhouse, in the actual carriage house from the early 1900s. The Trapper's Den, a bar, is in a 1940s bunkhouse.

Chistochina, marked by the Chistochina Trading Post, is 49.5 kilometres (30.7 miles) along the highway past Gakona. It is mainly an Athabascan Ahtna community. You cross the Chistochina River at kilometre 56.8 (mile 35.3) and again at kilometre 57.1 (mile 35.5).

At kilometre 96.2 (mile 59.8), turn right onto the Nabesna Road (which has no service stations along it). It goes to Slana and Nabesna and is the only road besides the McCarthy Road that leads into the Wrangell–St. Elias National Park and Preserve. Less than 1 kilometre (about 0.5 miles) after the turn-off, stop in at the Slana Ranger Station, which is open from 8 AM to 5 PM, to inquire about the road conditions ahead (the road is sometimes impassable) and to find out more about the park.

In 1.2 kilometres (0.8 miles) from the highway, you reach the Hart D Ranch, on whose property you can browse through an art gallery, mail a letter at the Slana Post Office or camp for the night. At kilometre 4.1 (mile 2.5) from the ranch, you enter the Wrangell–St. Elias National Park and Preserve. There are no formal campgrounds along this road—you can stay wherever you find a nice spot as long as you carry out your garbage. Do respect private property within the preserve, however.

You reach the first of two lodges, the Silvertip Lodge, at kilometre 40.5 (mile 25.2). The second, the Sportsmen's Paradise Lodge, is at kilometre 44.8 (mile 27.8). Both lodges offer fishing, rooms or cabins to rent and charter flights over the area or to other fishing lakes. After the second lodge, the road becomes almost impassable and is suitable only for four-wheel–drive vehicles, but the scenery of Wrangell–St. Elias National Park is great. Of the many creek crossings, the hardest is at Lost

Gakona Roadhouse.

The Wrangell–St. Elias National Park and Preserve

The Wrangell–St. Elias National Park and Preserve receives about 25,000 visits per year and is the largest park in the US. It covers nearly 5.34 million hectares (13.2 million acres), of which just over 63 percent is park and the rest is preserve, where 'sport' hunting and trapping are allowed. Within both the preserve and the park, local residents are permitted to practise subsistence hunting and trapping.

The park borders Canada's Kluane National Park on the east and the Tetlin National Wildlife Refuge on the north. The Copper River marks most of the western boundary and the southern boundary is jagged. The park and preserve has nine of the 16 highest mountains in the US within its limits.

The area was originally made a national monument in 1978 and then proclaimed a national park and preserve on December 2, 1980.

Given Wrangell–St. Elias's approximately 3.6 million hectares (9 million acres) of true wilderness and its absence of marked hiking trails, limited facilities, difficult terrain and quick weather changes, anyone venturing away from the road should be both self-sufficient and experienced.

Creek, which is wide and has a loose gravel bottom. Nabesna, about 36 kilometres (22 miles) from the second lodge, is a small mining community of about 25 people.

Continuing along the highway toward Tok, at kilometre 25.5 (mile 15.8) from the Nabesna Road, you come to the bridge over the Slana River and then cross Slana Slough and follow it to your left for a ways. On the left at kilometre 34.6 (mile 21.5), you pass the 11.2-kilometre (7-mile) road to the Native village of Mentasta Lake.

Kilometre 78.9 (mile 49) brings you to the Eagle Trail State Recreation Site on your left. If you want to do a short hike, turn in and drive past the road to the campground. At 0.4 kilometres (0.2 miles) you reach a picnic shelter on your left. A posted map shows the two self-guided trails that begin here. The Eagle Trail is an easy 30-minute hike in a loop back to the picnic area. This 1.6-kilometre (1-mile) path has 18 numbered stations. After you reach the eleventh one, you are following part of the old Valdez–Eagle Trail, built for the gold miners in 1899. The other trail is the Tok River Valley overlook trail.

After the recreation site, it is just 25 kilometres (15.5 miles) to the junction with the Alaska Highway in the centre of Tok and the Tok visitor reception centre just ahead.

To continue on with Chapter 6, turn right onto the Alaska Highway and drive to Tetlin Junction, a distance of 20 kilometres (12.4 miles) along the highway.

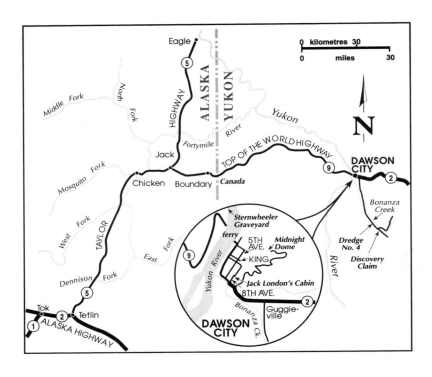

6
Tetlin Junction to Dawson City

This chapter covers the Taylor Highway (Alaska Route 5), which gives you great panoramic views of valleys and mountains. Once you get past the settlement of Chicken, you will be driving over dome-shaped hills from which you can look down on some of the most magnificent scenery you have ever seen.

You will be travelling through some of the earliest and richest gold-mining areas in the North: Chicken, Jack Wade, Eagle and Dawson City all saw their gold rushes, Dawson City's being the biggest and best. There is still active mining along the way, so watch for mining equipment alongside the road as you travel.

Tetlin Junction to Eagle

Tetlin Junction

Tetlin Junction is 20 kilometres (12.4 miles) east of Tok on the Alaska Highway. Turn north onto the Taylor Highway, which goes to Eagle and the area known as 'the Gateway to the Fortymile Mining District.' The road surface is chip seal as you follow the winding highway up out of the Tanana River valley. At about kilometre 19 (mile 12), you enter part of the area devastated by the 1990 Tok Burn (see p. 57).

Fortymile River and Chicken

At kilometre 37.3 (mile 23.2) the chip seal ends and you are on well-packed gravel.

West Fork Campground is to your left at kilometre 78 (mile 48.5), and you cross the West Fork of the Dennison Fork of the Fortymile River just past the entrance. At kilometre 102.9 (mile 63.9) you cross the Mosquito Fork of the Fortymile River.

These tributaries of the Fortymile River, as well as the South Fork on the other side of Chicken, are popular with canoeists. You can put in on any of them and paddle for just a few hours or carry on to where the Fortymile enters the Yukon River, downstream from Dawson City (check in with US and Canadian customs), but note that there are a number of hazards, including rapids up to Class III after heavy rains. If you are really enthusiastic, you can follow the Yukon all the way to the Bering Sea. Be sure to acquire the appropriate maps and guidebooks and provision yourself accordingly for the length of your trip.

Chicken Emporium.

The road narrows and gets rougher after the bridge across Mosquito Fork. At kilometre 105.5 (mile 65.6), a sign reads 'Chicken Community.' You pass a post office to your left and reach the sign for downtown Chicken. Turn right to visit the Chicken Mercantile Emporium, the Chicken Liquor Store, the Chicken Creek Saloon and the Chicken Cafe, which are all in a row and connected by a boardwalk. At the emporium you can purchase souvenir T-shirts and other items. You can become part of a tradition at the saloon by putting your business card or anything else that you have (shorts, panties, shirt, bra, licence plate, cap, etc.) on the ceiling or wall. Finally, the apple pie at the cafe is very popular—get there before lunch-time or they might be sold out.

After leaving Chicken, turn right onto the Taylor Highway. On your right is The

The most often-told story of how Chicken got its name goes like this: During the mining activity that took place here in the early 1890s before the Klondike Gold Rush, the miners wanted to name their town after the ptarmigan, a plentiful gamebird in the area. However, as no one knew how to spell 'Ptarmigan,' they settled for 'Chicken,' a common nickname for ptarmigan in the North.

Another story, not so well known, has it that the early miners found nuggets the size of the dried corn that they usually fed to the chickens, hence the name.

A third tale is that, seen from above, the sand bars in the river looked like the claws of a chicken's foot. There is some dispute about the plausibility of this last explanation—in a pre-aviation age, it is unlikely that miners saw the sandbars from above.

Goldpanner, where you can day-camp (for free), pan for gold and buy souvenirs and gasoline. Then you cross Chicken Creek and begin to climb steeply on a narrow, winding road. Look downward to see the original Chicken townsite, now on private land. When you come to Lost Chicken Creek at kilometre 4 (mile 2.5) from Chicken, look to your left for a sign that says 'Lost Chicken Hill Mine, 1895.' It has arrows that point one way to Dawson and the other way to Fairbanks and Chicken. On a hill behind the sign there are some old mine buildings. However, because this mining area is currently active, do not trespass.

You cross the South Fork of the Fortymile River at kilometre 14.3 (mile 8.9) and in 24.9 kilometres (15.5 miles) you reach the bridge over the Walker Fork of the Fortymile River.

The Jack Wade Dredge and Eagle

Gold was discovered in the Fortymile Mining District in 1886, over a decade before the Klondike Gold Rush. The first claims on Jack Wade Creek were discovered in 1892 by Jack Anderson and Wade Nelson, hence the name. There has been ongoing gold mining on the creek since that first discovery.

At kilometre 31.5 (mile 19.6) from Chicken, there is a pull-out to the right for Dredge No. 1, also called 'the Jack Wade Dredge.' It is a lot smaller than both Dredge No. 8 near Fairbanks and Dredge No. 4 near Dawson City.

The dredge has sat here since it quit working in 1942, and it is still as solid as the day it was abandoned. However, you can see where flooding by the adjacent creek has left silt on the floor of the dredge and where vandals have stolen some of its machinery, wrecking one wall to do so. If you walk on the dredge, you do so at your own risk.

At kilometre 47.2 (mile 29.3) from Chicken, you reach Jack Wade Junction. The Top of the World Highway, straight ahead, goes to Dawson City. Turn left here to stay on the Taylor Highway and head for Eagle. The road climbs and you drive over dome-shaped hills where the trees are sparse and the vegetation is mainly small bushes and grass. You can see some breathtaking scenery as you look down on everything from up here. In places you can see the road snaking ahead.

By kilometre 15.8 (mile 9.8) from the junction, you begin an 11-kilometre (7-mile) winding descent into a canyon to cross the Fortymile River at kilometre 27.9 (mile 17.3).

At kilometre 48.5 (mile 30.1) you reach O'Brien Creek Lodge, which has a service station and a store and offers camping. You cross King Solomon Creek at kilometre 58.8 (mile 36.5) and North Fork King Solomon Creek at kilometre 65.5 (mile 40.7).

Woody's Place (American Summit Liquor) is a little store to the right at kilometre 76.6 (mile 47.6) just before American Summit, where there is a pull-out from which you can enjoy the view of the surrounding hills and valleys. When you reach Telegraph Hill Services, a gas station on your left at kilometre 103.3 (mile 64.2), stop in to get a map of Eagle, the community that you are just entering. It was named for the large number of eagles that nest on nearby Eagle Bluff.

Eagle was established in 1881 after a French Canadian named Francis Mercier set up an independent trading post in competition with the Hudson's Bay Company posts of Fort Yukon and Fort Reliance. During the Klondike Gold Rush, when the

Mule Barn at Fort Egbert in Eagle.

Canadian government imposed taxes and regulations on the miners, the miners set up a supply town here. It grew because it was a major port on the Yukon River, supplying goods and services to Interior Alaska.

Fort Egbert—one of a number of military posts set up in Alaska to provide law and order and protect businesses from aggressive miners and Natives—was built near the townsite in 1899. In 1902 the first federal court in interior Alaska was set up at Eagle under Judge James Wickersham. Also in that year, the region's first telegraph line (the Washington-Alaska Military Cable and Telegraph System, WAMCATS) was being constructed from Valdez to Eagle. However, gold strikes in Nome and Fairbanks lured away the miners and in 1911 Fort Egbert all but closed, leaving only the five men who operated the telegraph. The court moved and so, by 1959, only 13 people lived here.

In recent years, an increase in gold mining in the area and the growth in tourism have revitalized Eagle. The highway becomes Amundsen Drive as you enter the village. To get to Fort Egbert, turn left onto 4th Street. Fort Egbert, with its five restored buildings (of the 45 that originally stood here) is on your left in just three blocks.

The green building, the quartermaster's storehouse, was a very important part of the fort. Because the fort received all of its supplies by steamboat, and because the Yukon River is navigable only in summer, the fort had to stock up with rations to last the whole winter, as well as emergency supplies that would sustain the fort for at least six months.

The large, white building, 'the mule barn,' once housed 60 mules and 21 horses and there were 30 dogs in the sheds built on one side. The top floor was a hay loft,

Jack Wade Dredge.

Waterhouse in Eagle.

fitted with chutes for dropping hay down to the stalls. The sled dogs were used by the crews constructing the WAMCATS line under the direction of William 'Billy' Mitchell, at that time a young lieutenant in the Army Signal Corps.

Return to Amundsen Drive and continue on to 1st Street. A cairn and a park on the right corner at this intersection are dedicated to Roald Amundsen, the Norwegian Arctic explorer. When his sloop, the *Gjoa*, was frozen into the ice off the north coast of Alaska late in 1905, he arranged to join a dog-sled party bound for Fort Yukon to seek medical advice for an ailing crew member. When told that a telegraph was available at Eagle City, he continued up the Yukon River to send word back to Norway that he and his crew were the first to successfully navigate the elusive Northwest Passage, and to ask his brother to wire money. He had crossed 800 kilometres (500 miles) of wilderness to reach Eagle, where he sojourned for two months while he waited for the money to arrive, before returning to his ship.

Turn left on 1st Street and you come to the town's water well, which is said to date from 1903 (though some sources say 1901 or 1909). It still supplies water for many of the residents and you can stock up on water yourself here. You can visit the adjacent old Wickersham Courthouse, which is now a museum. Be at the courthouse by 10 AM and, for a nominal fee, you can join the Eagle Historical Society's daily walking tour, which takes you past many other historic buildings from the early 1900s—or see them on your own.

Before you leave Eagle, take a few moments to sit on one of the benches that overlooks the Yukon River. Canyon walls rise to your left and Belle Island is in front of you. If you decide to stay the night, there is a Bureau of Land Management (BLM) campground 1 kilometre (0.6 miles) past Fort Egbert.

Boundary to Dawson City

Boundary

Return to Jack Wade Junction and take the Top of the World Highway toward Dawson City (note that this highway is closed in winter). You are again driving over dome-shaped hills and can see far into the distance all around you.

In 15.5 kilometres (9.6 miles), you reach the community of Boundary. For years the Boundary Lodge was operated by a man known as 'Action Jackson.' It was a rowdy place and Jackson would occasionally tame the patrons down by taking his six-shooter out of the holster on his hip and shooting into the ceiling. The lodge was so popular that people would come from Dawson City to party. A new building now houses a restaurant, Boundary Inc., at this location and Action Jackson's Bar has been moved into the back of the yard, where it is being used for storage. In keeping with history, however, a gift shop has been set up in an old log building from Jackson's time.

Poker Creek Customs and Little Gold Creek Customs

Because of the elevation, which is generally around 900 metres (3000 feet), the weather along the Top of the World Highway is usually overcast, drizzly or misty. At kilometre 5.5 (mile 3.4) from Boundary, a viewpoint with a platform overlooks a magnificent valley. At kilometre 6.5 (mile 4), you reach Poker Creek Customs, the most northerly border port in the US. Just past the US customs post, you arrive at the Little Gold Creek Canada Customs post. Both customs posts are open from 8 AM to 8 PM Alaska time, which is 9 AM to 9 PM Yukon time.

Top of the World Highway to Dawson City.

Shortly after Little Gold Creek, a road to the right goes to a rest area. If you want to get to the top of 'the top of the world,' stop in at this rest area, walk across the highway and follow a path up the hill. At the top you are at the highest point along the highway. On a sunny day you have a magnificent view of the short grass and small flowers of the alpine tundra stretching into the distance around you.

Since you entered Yukon, you have been on Yukon Highway 9, which follows an old pack trail that ran from Dawson City to Sixtymile (an old mining area where there is still active mining) and some gold-bearing creeks in the area. When it was improved, it was named 'Ridge Road,' because of the ridge it runs on. Dredgemaster Gold Mines Sixtymile Road, to your right at kilometre 19 (mile 11.8), leads to private land.

Border cairn at Poker Creek Customs.

Look to your left at kilometre 19.4 (mile 12.1) to see a log cabin that was once a stop for the McCormick Transportation Company. There is a spruce tree growing on its sod roof. At kilometre 46.8 (mile 29.1), the unmaintained road to your left goes to the site of Clinton, a settlement for the workers at an asbestos mine that closed down in 1979.

A rest stop with an information panel about the ferry that crosses the Yukon River to Dawson City is to your right at kilometre 92.5 (mile 57.5). Beyond this sign a platform overlooks the Yukon River.

Another write-up at the rest stop tells about the Fortymile Herd, which at one time numbered over

Ferry at Dawson City.

one-half million caribou. They were named after the Fortymile River, which flows into the Yukon River downstream from Dawson City. During this herd's migration times, boats on the Fortymile River had to wait for hours—even days—while the herd crossed the water. Because easy access by road allowed over-hunting, by the 1970s the herd had been reduced to a small fraction of its original size. However, the size of the herd has now increased to over 20,000.

Just past the rest stop, a sign welcomes you to Dawson City and you begin heading downhill to the Yukon River. At kilometre 102 (mile 63.4), look to your right for a view of the river and Dawson City.

There is a Yukon government campground to your left at kilometre 107 (mile 66.5). A path from the far end of the site leads to 'the Sternwheeler Graveyard.'

 ## The Beginning of the Klondike Gold Rush

There are a number of variations on the story of how gold was discovered in the Klondike, all involving the same central characters. Here is one version: In the spring of 1894, Bob Henderson, a would-be prospector from Nova Scotia, arrived in the Yukon. He panned for gold for two years and in the spring of 1896 he heard stories of gold on two rivers: the Klondike (distorted from Thron-diuck, a Native name that reflected the traditional salmon-trap poles that were pounded into the river's bed) and the Indian. These rivers are separated by Midnight Dome, a small, round-topped mountain that overlooks the confluence of the Klondike and Yukon rivers. Henderson climbed this mountain and saw many creeks running down from Midnight Dome.

He walked down the mountain and panned some gravel in one of the creeks, where he found enough gold to call it 'Gold Bottom Creek.' As was the custom of the day (to give other prospectors a chance to strike it rich too, and thereby to help prevent stealing and murder over good claims), Henderson proceeded to tell everyone he met about his find. He met George Washington Carmack and his two Native brothers-in-law, Tagish Charlie and Skookum Jim Mason, who were on their way to Rabbit Creek. Henderson, who did not like Natives, told Carmack in private about Gold Bottom, suggesting that he stake his claim alone. Carmack said that they would find their own creek but promised to let Henderson know if they found anything. Before the parties separated, Carmack's companions asked Henderson for tobacco, but he refused to sell any to them.

On August 17, 1896, where Rabbit Creek empties into the Klondike River, Carmack found gold worth a whopping $4 in his pan. Carmack and his two brothers-in-law staked claims on Rabbit Creek. On their way to record the claims in Fortymile, they told everyone they met about the creek, which they renamed 'Bonanza Creek.'

Henderson, however, did not hear of the strike until all the rich claims had already been staked.

At freeze-up every year, any boats that happened to be in Dawson City were docked here until spring, but some, because of ice damage or because they were replaced by newer boats, were never used again. Not many of them are left to be seen.

Old Canadian Imperial Bank of Commerce building in Dawson City.

If you are going to stay in Dawson City for few days, you may consider finding a camping spot here and parking your vehicle, because Dawson City is small enough that you can walk wherever you wish to go. There is also a private campground, the Gold Rush Campground, on the other side of the river, at the corner of York and 5th Avenue.

Past the campground you arrive at the Yukon River. West Dawson was established here in 1899 by residents who wanted to avoid the typhoid outbreaks caused by over-crowding in downtown Dawson City. A ferry has been operating from this site since 1902. There is usually a wait for the ferry but it only takes about five minutes to make the crossing, so the wait should not be too long. Like the Top of the World Highway, the ferry closes down for winter.

As you leave the ferry, you are on Front Street. Dawson City has kept its old-time flavour with dirt streets and wooden boardwalks. The visitor reception centre is in the two-storey log building on the corner at King Street. If you plan to 'do the Dempster Highway' (Chapter 7), cross Front Street and drop in at the Western Arctic Visitor Centre to ask about road conditions.

During the Klondike Gold Rush, Dawson grew quickly to become the largest city north of San Francisco, and it became known as 'the Paris of the North.' It had hotels, dance halls, daily newspapers and saloons for its 30,000 inhabitants. Fresh eggs were brought by raft on the Yukon River and whisky came in by the boatload before freeze-up. Gambling made rich men out of some and paupers out of others, dancehall girls charged $5 in gold for each minute they danced with a miner and even the janitors made up to $50 per night when they panned out the sawdust off the bar-room floors.

In 1898 the Yukon Territory was separated off from the rest of the NWT and Dawson became the capital. The old Territorial Administration Building on 5th Avenue, between Church and Turner, now houses the Dawson City Museum. The building was constructed in 1901 for the territorial seat of government, and was the centre of government administration until 1953, when the capital was moved to Whitehorse.

There are so many places to visit in Dawson City that it is hard to know where to begin. Why not start with the Robert Service and Jack London cabins and the Pierre Berton House, all on 8th Avenue between Mission and Grant Streets?

Diamond Tooth Gertie's in Dawson City.

Robert Service was born in England and raised in Scotland, where he trained to be a bank teller. He moved to Canada in the mid-1890s and then went down to the US, where he lived for six years. In 1903 he began working for the Bank of Commerce in Victoria, BC. Late in 1904 he was sent to their branch in Whitehorse. Four years later, just after his first book of Yukon-inspired poems had been published, he was transferred to Dawson. His second book was published in 1909. Intending to live on the revenue from his writing, he quit his job at the bank. He left Dawson City in 1912 to become a war correspondent and eventually settled in France, never to return to the North. No one has lived in his cabin since.

In 1897 Jack London came to the Yukon from West Oakland, California, to look for gold. He and his partners built a cabin and stayed through winter, during which London got scurvy. He went to Dawson City for treatment in the spring of 1898 and left from there to return home to California. Although short, his sojourn in the Yukon inspired the start of a spectacular writing career that resulted in over 50 books. In 1932 Jack London's cabin was found to be still standing along Henderson Creek, where it was left until 1969, when two replicas were made of the cabin, each one with one-half of the logs from the original one, plus other logs. One cabin was moved to Jack London Square in Oakland, California, and the other now sits in Dawson City.

Readings are given every day at the Service and London cabins.

The Pierre Berton House is the childhood home of Pierre Berton, noted author of over 40 books. His parents bought the house for $500 in 1920. Mr. Berton repurchased it from a subsequent owner in 1989 for $50,000 (his parents had sold it for just $400 in 1932) and donated it to the Yukon Arts Council for use in a writer-in-residence program.

Two of the more popular places in Dawson City are the Palace Grand and Diamond Tooth Gertie's. The Palace Grand, made from the hulls of two beached sternwheelers, was built in 1899 by 'Arizona Charlie' Meadows. It had shows that ranged from wild west to opera. It was restored in 1962 and now you can see a musical comedy on stage every night.

Diamond Tooth Gertie's gambling hall, run by the Klondike Visitors' Association (KVA), is in the building constructed in 1901 to be the city's Arctic Brotherhood Fraternity Hall. Once a popular and colourful secret society and social club, the brotherhood slowly faded away as its members left the North or died and its buildings across the North were put to other uses.

When the KVA took over the building, it named its casino after Gertie Lovejoy, one of the most famous dancehall girls of the gold-rush era, who gained her nickname when she had a diamond inserted between her two front teeth. Today at Gertie's you can watch a can-can show or play the slot machines, roulette or blackjack and know that any money that you spend is helping to support Dawson's historic sites and tourist attractions.

Some other historic buildings to see are the Yukon Hotel, built in 1898; Ruby's Place, which began as a laundry in 1903 and was then a brothel from 1935 until 1961, under the management of Mathilda 'Ruby' Scott; and the beautiful restored post office, which was built in 1900. Most of the city's historic buildings have signs that identify them. One place on Princess Street at 7th Avenue has a sign that describes how it was 'built in 1900 using beached riverboat lumber,' and how the parks service is restoring additional historic buildings.

If you want to see a cemetery where members of the North-West Mounted Police (NWMP) and Royal North-West Mounted Police (RNWMP) were buried, take King Street out of the city. In 0.5 kilometres (0.3 miles), the cemetery, with its bright white markers, is to your right.

To get to Midnight Dome, follow the Klondike Highway (Highway 2) eastward out of town. In 2.1 kilometres (1.3 miles) from the visitor reception centre at King Street, you reach Dome Road. Turn left

Dawson City and the Klondike and Yukon rivers from the Dome.

and it is 7 kilometres (4.3 miles) from the highway to the top. From here you can look over Dawson City, the Klondike and Yukon rivers and the hills around you. You can also see the piles of gravel (tailings) left along the Klondike River by the gold dredges.

Klondike City (also known as 'Lousetown') once stood across the Klondike River from Dawson City. Men from Dawson wishing to visit the 'ladies of the

Klondike Kate

Many of the women who went to the Klondike were named 'Kathleen' or 'Katherine' and there are least 17 different women who have been called 'Klondike Kate.' One of them is Kathleen Eloisa Rockwell.

Kathleen was born in Junction City, Kansas, and was in her mid-teens when she became a chorus girl in New York. She took a job with a vaudeville company and moved to Spokane, Washington. However, along with singing and dancing, the work also included encouraging men to drink more whisky, which she did not enjoy, at first.

When gold was discovered in the Klondike, she quit her job and headed north. She worked in Skagway and Whitehorse before reaching Dawson City in 1900. She got a job at the Palace Grand as a singer and dancer and her red hair made her a favourite among the spectators.

Soon she became involved with Alexander Pantages, the owner of the Dawson Orpheum Theatre, who persuaded her to invest in expanding his theatre empire. However, Kate felt used and betrayed and the relationship ended in a breach-of-contract suit. She left the city in 1905.

Kate married and divorced a number of times after that. She began to publicly call herself 'the Belle of Dawson' and 'the Klondike Queen' and was able to make a living by telling stories of the gold rush and her part in it as 'the Queen of the Yukon.' She died in 1957, at the age of 81.

evening' who had their establishments there had to cross a narrow wooden bridge that spanned the river. Some would-be visitors were too inebriated to make the crossing and were swept out into the Yukon River to drown or, if they were lucky, to wash ashore still alive somewhere downstream.

After the gold rush ended, gold companies continued to mine the creeks, using dredges to dig up the creek bottoms and leaving behind piles of gravel. The dredging lasted until the 1960s, when declining gold prices made these operations uneconomical. Mining is now done with big trucks, huge sluices and backhoes.

If you want to see the largest wooden-hulled bucket-line gold dredge in North America, return to the Klondike Highway and follow it east for 1.7 kilometres (1.1 miles) from Dome Road and take the right turn onto Bonanza Creek Road. On your left is Guggieville, once a mining camp for the Yukon Gold Company, which was financed by the Guggenheim family of New York. It is now the site of an RV park.

As the gravel road winds through tall piles of tailings and active mining areas, do not go off the road onto private claims.

At kilometre 10 (mile 6.2), you reach Claim No. 33, where small, colourful shops sell cold pop, snacks and souvenirs and where you can try gold-panning. You reach Dredge No. 4, still standing where it ceased work in 1960, at kilometre 12.4 (mile 7.7). This huge blue structure sits on 'Claim No. 17 Below Discovery.' The name reflects the custom of numbering claims sequentially above and below the first or 'discovery' claim on each creek or river. For example, the first claim upstream from the Discovery Claim was 'Claim No. 1 Above Discovery' and the first one on the downstream side was 'Claim No. 1 Below Discovery.'

Dredge No. 4, built in 1912, was the largest wooden-hulled dredge in North America. It operated from the Klondike Valley to Hunker Creek, east of Dawson

City, between 1913 and 1940. It was rebuilt on Bonanza Creek in 1941 and worked there until 1960. It could dig 14.6 metres (48 feet) below the water level of the stream it was on and 5 metres (17 feet) above.

At the dredge there is a Parks Canada visitor reception centre where you can pay to take a tour of the site. You can also book a tour here for the Discovery Claim, on which you learn how the original miners worked when they first arrived. On the tour you have the opportunity to work some of the ground of the Discovery Claim for yourself, dig dirt from a shaft and operate a rocker sluice. To get to the Discovery Claim—the one that started the Klondike Gold Rush—continue along the road and in 2 kilometres (1.2 miles) you come to a Y. Take the right fork and, in less than 0.5 kilometres (0.3 miles), look to your left for the cairn that marks the Discovery Claim. If you wish, you can have lunch at this historic site, which has picnic tables.

To continue on with Chapter 7, go back to the Klondike Highway (Highway 2) and head eastward on it for

Dredge No. 4.

37 kilometres (23 miles) until you reach the intersection with the Dempster Highway. If you would rather not explore the Dempster Highway, skip ahead to Chapter 8.

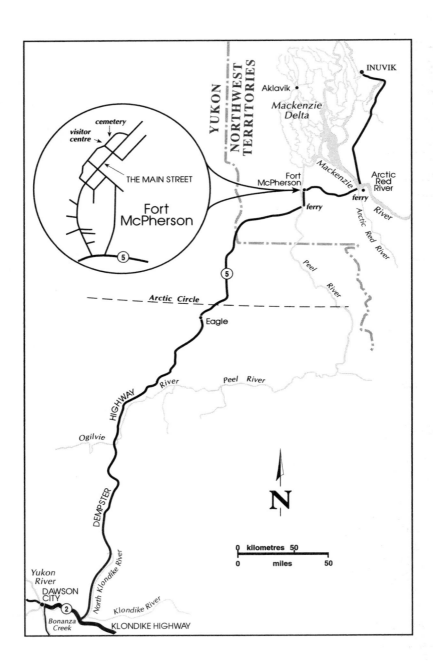

INUVIK

Aklavik •

Mackenzie Delta

YUKON

NORTHWEST TERRITORIES

Mackenzie River

Arctic Red River

Fort McPherson

ferry

ferry

Arctic Red River

⑤

Peel River

Arctic Circle

Eagle

Peel River

River

HIGHWAY

Ogilvie

DEMPSTER

N

kilometres 50

miles 50

North Klondike River

Yukon River

DAWSON CITY

②

Bonanza Creek

Klondike River

KLONDIKE HIGHWAY

cemetery

visitor centre

THE MAIN STREET

Fort McPherson

⑤

7
'Doing the Dempster'

You do not 'drive the Dempster Highway,' you 'do the Dempster,' but no one is sure where that expression came from. The Dempster Highway, opened on August 18, 1979, is the first Canadian highway into the Arctic. This drive will take you from the Klondike River, through the Ogilvie, Tombstone and Richardson mountains and across the Arctic Circle to end in Inuvik, NWT. Along this highway is a good place to see Canada's largest owl, the great grey owl. The speed limit is generally 90 kilometres per hour (55 miles per hour), but you will sometimes have to slow down for rough sections. Also, watch for the many bicyclists who cycle this road each summer. It will probably take you about three days to make this round trip, taking into account road conditions, stops and scenery. You can check how far you have come using the distance markers that are spaced sporadically along the highway. Have a spare tire, some extra food and plenty of gas with you—services are few. Also make sure that you bring plenty of insect repellent because, as soon as you stop, your vehicle will be surrounded by mosquitoes.

Dempster Corner to North Fork Pass

The Dempster Highway joins the Klondike Highway 40.8 kilometres (25.4 miles) east of the visitor reception centre in Dawson City or 37 kilometres (23 miles) from Bonanza Creek Road. You will want to gas up at a service station at this junction, called Dempster Corner, before heading north.

Dempster Highway sign at beginning of the Dempster Highway.

At the beginning of the Dempster Highway, a large sign and information panel are to your right. There are write-ups about the birds and animals of the north country, permafrost and the Native peoples. Beside the sign there is a metal replica of a dog sled, which was the main mode of winter transportation in the North for hundreds of years, both for Natives and non-Natives alike.

Immediately after the sign and information panels, you cross the Klondike River. This wide, curving gravel road through the hills leads past mountain scenery. Black spruce and poplar alternate with areas of short bushes, low grass, mosses, sedges and lichens.

North Fork Road is to your right at kilometre 7.6 (mile 4.7). The North Fork Ditch, about 1.5 kilometres (0.9 miles) to the south, was dug to divert water from the North Klondike River to a hydroelectric plant 25 kilometres (16 miles) to the east. From the early 1900s until 1960, it also provided water and power for gold-dredging operations further down the valley. If you want to see a demonstration of 'heap leaching,' a process by which chemical solutions are used to extract gold from ore, turn right onto North Fork Road and drive 20 kilometres (12 miles) to the Brewery Creek Mine. Note that this rough road is not suitable for motorhomes or trailers. Tours are 1.5 hours long and begin at 10:30 AM on Tuesdays and Fridays.

There are many creek crossings, and then kilometre 72 (mile 44.7) brings you to the Dempster Interpretive Centre and the Tombstone Mountain Campground on your left. Stop in here for information about the highway and the conditions along it.

The Dempster Highway

In 1954 the first exploration oil well was dug in the Eagle Plains area. Prime Minister John Diefenbaker ordered that a road be built to the oilfields. The road was surveyed in 1958 and, by 1961, 116 kilometres (72 miles) of it had been constructed. However, the oil discovery at Eagle Plains proved to be poor, and the road-building was halted.

Construction resumed in 1971, when oil was discovered in the Beaufort Sea and a road was needed to haul supplies. The Dempster Highway was opened to public travel in 1979.

The highway is named for Corporal W.J. Dempster of the Royal North-West Mounted Police, who patrolled in this part of the North, by dog sled in winter, in the early 1900s. (Also see sidebar, 'The Lost Patrol,' on p. 167.)

Ten kilometres (6.2 miles) from the interpretive centre, where a side road joins the highway, look to your right for a white metal post with a blue top and a picture of a set of binoculars on it. This marker is the first of seven along the Dempster that indicate places of interest. In this case you are at North Fork Pass, the highest place on the Dempster Highway. The pass is on the dividing line between rivers that flow northward to the Mackenzie River and onward to the Beaufort Sea and rivers that flow southward, heading via the Yukon River to the Bering Sea. Stand with your back to the picture of the binoculars to survey the part of the highway that you have just travelled. Drive along the side road, which leads to a gravel pit just off the highway, for a better view of the area.

Two Moose Lake, Chapman Lake and Jeckell Bridge

To your left, at kilometre 103.8 (mile 64.5), notice Two Moose Lake, a 'thaw lake.' A thaw lake forms when a patch of vegetation growing on top of the permafrost, which is up to about 90 metres (300 feet) deep in this valley, is disturbed and the soil thaws. Over time, a hole forms, gradually fills with water and grows to become a lake. Watch for the Alaska/Yukon moose (sometimes known as 'the tundra moose'), the largest moose subspecies in North America, to come here and feed.

You reach Chapman Lake at kilometre 117.1 (mile 72.8). Chapman Lake, which has a small tundra island in the middle of it, may have swans swimming gracefully on its waters. A sign here tells about the Centennial Patrol, which in 1995 made a special commemorative trip that followed the exact route of the early North-West Mounted Police dog-sled patrols.

The white post that marks Windy Pass is 37 kilometres (23 miles) from Chapman Lake. It is to your right and a bit off the road. When you turn your back to the marker to look at the pass, you will usually feel the wind at your back.

The grey scree slopes (consisting of small, loose stones) that you are driving past were formed by water freezing and cracking the rock outcroppings above, causing pieces to break off and slide down the slope.

Windy Pass Moths and Butterflies

Windy Pass was part of ice-free east Beringia during the late Wisconsinan ice age (see the sidebar 'Beringia,' p. 42). It was the habitat of many species of butterflies and moths, and many of these species still live at Windy Pass. Some of the butterfly species are the polaris fritillary, the swallowtail and the noctuid. Two of the moth species are the arctiid and the black arctiid.

The female moths of Windy Pass are wingless and spend most of their time hiding under rocks, coming out only to eat and to breed (from mid-June to mid-July). The eggs are laid under rocks and, in 8 to 10 days, the caterpillars hatch. They hide during the day to avoid predators. The caterpillars pupate into adult moths and start the cycle again.

To see either the moths or the butterflies for yourself, walk down Windy Pass as far as your enthusiasm takes you. You might see male moths flying, or you might find a small dome made of males huddled together.

Arctic Circle sign on Dempster Highway.

When you see the 158-kilometre marker to your right at kilometre 43 (mile 26.7) from Chapman Lake, look nearby for the third of the seven white metal posts, which marks the gyrfalcon aerie. Stand with your back to the marker and look up the rock wall to see the gyrfalcon nest. The birds and the nest are both brown and blend in with the rock but, if you watch patiently, you will see one or both of the birds flying around the nest. Please do not get closer, because you may disturb them.

At kilometre 53.5 (mile 33.2), you cross Red Creek. It runs into Engineer Creek, which is next to the highway. Look at the red rock, its colour caused by iron oxide, in both creeks. Watch for the white post at kilometre 55.1 (mile 34.2). The water trickling down the bank across the road from it is a sulphur spring. You can see the red coloration of the rocks gradually lighten as you drive further along Engineer Creek.

At kilometre 62.4 (mile 38.8), you reach the fifth marker post, which says 'Sheep Lick and Trails.' On the side of the hill, look for the trails that Dall sheep use to come down to the creek to eat mineral-rich mud. The sixth marker, at kilometre 70 (mile 43.5), indicates a second sheep lick. Each lick extends for about 2 kilometres (1.2 miles) along Engineer Creek.

Engineer Creek Campground—where you can camp, picnic or fish for arctic grayling—is to your right at kilometre 78.8 (mile 49), and at kilometre 80.1 (mile 49.8) you cross Engineer Creek.

Just before you cross the bridge over the Ogilvie River at kilometre 81.6 (mile 50.7), look to your right for a big, grey rock located at a small pull-out. A plaque on it commemorates the construction of the Jeckell Bridge by the 3rd Field Squadron in 1971.

At kilometre 87.6 (mile 54.4) you reach the seventh and final white post along the Dempster Highway. It marks Rampart Hill, where a peregrine falcon family lives. You will have to use your binoculars to find the nest on a ledge on the cliff.

Next follow the Ogilvie River through a narrow valley, and try fishing for arctic grayling at pull-outs along the river. Then you leave the valley and begin to drive atop a ridge on the Eagle Plains plateau, which is really rolling hills and not as flat as you might expect.

Arctic tundra along Dempster Highway.

Eagle Plains and the Arctic Circle

Around kilometre 185 (mile 115), you begin to see sections of an old burn area. At kilometre 256 (mile 159.1), you reach Eagle Plains Lodge, which has a hotel, gas pumps, an RV park and a restaurant, and sells groceries, too. The next services are about 189 kilometres (117 miles) from here, at Fort McPherson.

Enjoy the gorgeous views as you go downhill from Eagle Plains to the Eagle River, which you cross 11.7 kilometres (7.3 miles) from the lodge. At kilometre 23.4 (mile 14.5) the road widens a bit and becomes an emergency airstrip, so do not stop for the next kilometre (0.6 miles), just in case a plane needs to land.

At kilometre 40 (mile 24.8) you reach the Arctic Circle, where there is a picnic area with a large sign. This site is one place where you will definitely need your insect repellent.

You reach the Rock River campground, to your left at kilometre 40.6 (mile 25.2) from the Arctic Circle, and then cross the Rock River at kilometre 41.4 (mile 25.7). For the last while, the scenery has been alternating between trees and tundra, but at kilometre 50 (mile 31) you come out of the forest and are in tundra for about the next 40 kilometres (25 miles). A pull-out to your left at kilometre 59.5 (mile 37) has a stone cairn and a write-up about Wright Pass, which was named after Allen A. Wright, who mapped the route taken by the Dempster Highway.

'The Mad Trapper' of Rat River

Albert Johnson, if that was his real name, arrived in the North in 1931. In a land where friendliness, helpfulness and accessibility were the way of life, he was unfriendly to the point of being hostile, choosing to spend his time alone in his cabin on Rat River.

The area was in the territory of the Gwich'in (Loucheux) people and two of them lodged a complaint with the Royal Canadian Mounted Police (RCMP) about Johnson trapping on their traplines. A police officer was sent out to question him but Johnson refused to talk with the man. When the Mountie returned with a search warrant, Johnson shot and seriously wounded him.

The Mounties came to arrest Johnson and beseiged his cabin for three days, even blowing off the roof with dynamite. He kept them away with gunfire and they finally had to return to their camp for more supplies and ammunition.

When they got back, Johnson was gone—and thus began a 240-kilometre (150-mile), 40-day manhunt in the dark, cold days of winter through the deep snow of the Richardson Mountains and the valleys of the Peel and Eagle rivers. Johnson travelled lightly on snowshoes and lived off the land while the search party travelled with dog sleds. They caught up with him once—during the shoot-out, one Mountie, Constable Edgar Millen, was killed. They finally surrounded him but he wounded another officer before he himself was shot, 80 kilometres (50 miles) downstream from the bridge across the Eagle River. His body was buried in the cemetery at Aklavik, a little over halfway between Fort McPherson and the Arctic Ocean.

No one knows who Albert Johnson really was or where he had come from.

The Border and Fort McPherson

At kilometre 60.1 (mile 37.3) from the Arctic Circle you leave the Yukon and enter the Northwest Territories (NWT). The border at this point is on the

Continental Divide—the waters to the west flow through the Yukon to the Bering Sea while the waters to the east go through the NWT to the Beaufort Sea. Set your watch one hour ahead here.

The road widens to double as an emergency airstrip once again at kilometre 60.1 (mile 37.3) from the Yukon border. To your right at kilometre 66.2 (mile 41.1) is the Tetlit Gwinjik Wayside Park. Signs here explain about the Mackenzie River and the huge delta of approximately 12,000 square kilometres (4630 square miles) that it forms.

Ferry over the Peel River.

Climb the hill to a platform, where additional signs here tell about various plants and birds, beluga whales, caribou and wolves.

You reach the ferry across the Peel River at kilometre 135 (mile 83.9); it operates from 9:30 AM until 12:30 AM. At kilometre 8.9 (mile 5.5) from the ferry, a sign welcomes you to Fort McPherson. Turn left to go into the village at kilometre 11.2 (mile 7). Probably the first thing you will notice is that houses in the village are on stilts or blocks that raise them above the ground, because of the permafrost.

 Midnight Sun, Midday Darkness

The Arctic Circle defines the southern edge of the Arctic through Canada, Alaska, Scandinavia and Russia. An imaginary line at 66°30' north latitude, it marks the most southerly extent of 24-hour daylight on the longest day of the year, June 21.

The further north of the circle you go, the more days of total daylight you will get in summer. In northern Norway, for example, there is continuous daylight from May until July. This phenomenon occurs because the earth's axis of spin is not at right angles to its axis of rotation around the sun. It is tilted to such a degree (23°30') that the geographic North Pole itself gets continuous daylight from March 20 until September 22.

The bad news, if you like lots of daylight, is that during the other half of the year the opposite happens. On December 21, no daylight at all reaches any point north of the Arctic Circle, even at midday. The North Pole itself does not get any daylight for six whole months! However, while the Northern Hemisphere is experiencing darkest winter, the area south of the Antarctic Circle, at 66°30' south, is receiving its share of 24-hour-per-day daylight.

To get to the visitor reception centre, follow the signs—the streets and avenues in Fort McPherson have no names posted. To see the cemetery where members of 'the Lost Patrol' are buried, begin by facing the visitor centre and go about 15 metres (50 feet) to your right to one end of the cemetery. Or drive past the visitor centre for one block to the right and you will see a big white church and the cemetery's other entrance on your left.

In the early part of the twentieth century, the detachment of the North-West Mounted Police (which was awarded the prefix 'Royal' in 1904) stationed at Dawson City would make an annual winter patrol by dog sled from Dawson to Fort McPherson. In the winter of 1910–11, however, it was decided to run the 765-kilometre (475-mile) patrol in reverse.

In December of 1910, Inspector F.J. Fitzgerald, along with Constables Kinney and Taylor, Special Constable Carter and a Native guide, left Fort McPherson for Dawson City. Some accounts state that Fitzgerald wanted to set a time record for this run and therefore kept supplies at a minimum to lighten the load. As for the guide, one story is that he missed an important turn on the trail and led the patrol astray. Another story has it that Fitzgerald, believing that he didn't need any help finding the route, sent the guide back after a few days of travel, but that he was unable to follow the trail without the guide's help.

Whatever the true account of how the patrol got off course, it was the blizzards and the freezing temperatures that really hampered the men's progress. Eventually, their food ran out and the men ate their dogs, one by one as they died. They even boiled their leather shoelaces and the leather thongs from their sleds in the hope of extracting nourishment.

Lost Patrol gravesite in Fort McPherson.

The patrol finally decided to head back to Fort McPherson. Weak and exhausted by days of gruelling travel, Taylor and Kinney were unable to go further and were left in a tent. Fitzgerald left his diary with them and tied a handkerchief to a tree to mark the camp. However, as Fitzgerald and Carter continued onward to get help, Kinney died and Taylor then shot himself.

The Native guide, who had separated from the party, arrived in Dawson City by a different route in March and was surprised to hear that the patrol had not arrived. A search party was sent out and it found Taylor and Kinney first, 56 kilometres (35 miles) from Fort McPherson. Fitzgerald and Carter had made another 16 kilometres (10 miles) toward the fort before they had died.

The man who led the search party was Corporal W.J. Dempster.

The Arctic Red River and Inuvik

The trees after Fort McPherson are all scrubby black spruce, poplar or birch, and there are no mountains or hills. The Mackenzie River Wayside Park, which has picnic tables, is on your right at 56.4 kilometres (35 miles) from the turn-off for Fort McPherson. Park and follow the path that leads to a large viewing building built with logs. From the ground floor, you can already see the Mackenzie River and, if you go up to the top floor, you can see the Arctic Red River flowing into the Mackenzie. On a bluff above the rivers is the hamlet of Arctic Red River, called Tsiitehnjik or Tsiigehtchic by the Gwich'in people. The church with the red roof that sits on the edge of the bluff was built in 1920 by the Oblate Missionaries.

Arctic Red River merging with the Mackenzie River at Arctic Red River.

One-half kilometre (0.3 miles) from the park, you arrive at a ferry dock. Depending on the destinations of the passengers, the ferry crosses either the Arctic Red River, to the hamlet of the same name, or the Mackenzie River, which puts you on the highway to Inuvik. Because most of the traffic is bound for Inuvik, if you want to visit Arctic Red River, be sure to tell the deckhand when you board.

As in Fort McPherson, at Arctic Red River the houses and buildings are also on stilts and blocks. Look for the bell, held on a rope between two upright, burled logs, that was given to the residents of Arctic Red River by the mayor, city council and residents of Winnipeg (which is situated along another Red River) in 1967 to commemorate Canada's Centennial.

Next to the red-roofed church that you saw from the viewing building, a picnic table overlooks the confluence of the Arctic Red and Mackenzie rivers. During spring break-up, the water in the rivers rises about 10 metres (over 30 feet) and the ice jam can extend up the Arctic Red River for as much as 50 kilometres (30 miles) from the Mackenzie.

Because of its beauty, the Arctic Red River was named a Canadian Heritage River in 1993. The river got its name from the reddish water that occasionally comes down from the iron deposits in the Mackenzie Mountains, where the river begins.

RCMP constable Edgar Millen was stationed at Arctic Red River when he was shot by 'the Mad Trapper' on January 30, 1932, as was described in the sidebar on p. 165.

After you get off the ferry to continue along the Dempster Highway toward Inuvik, you intermittently follow the Mackenzie River. The flat landscape is forested in black spruce. A number of day-use areas and parks are along this part of the highway; each name is indicated in both English and the Gwich'in language.

At kilometre 113.6 (mile 70.6) from the ferry, you reach pavement and a Y intersection. To the left is the airport. To continue to Inuvik, take the right branch and then take the turn-off in 10 kilometres (6.2 miles).

You are on Mackenzie Road as you come into Inuvik. It is just a short

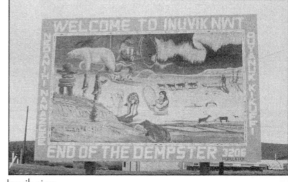
Inuvik sign.

Igloo Church in Inuvik.

distance to the visitor reception centre. Then continue down Mackenzie and, just before the traffic lights, look to your left for the Inuvik Research Centre. This centre was built to encourage, support and document sociological and environmental research in the western Arctic and northern Yukon. For example, studies done through this institution have investigated the change of lifestyle in the North since the oil discovery in the Beaufort Sea and the impact that it has had on the people and animals of the area.

Look over at the left corner at the traffic lights to see the giant inukshuk there. The inukshuk are made of rock and shaped to resemble humans beings. They were built in strategic configurations by the Inuit so that the caribou that they were chasing could be funnelled into a lake and killed more easily.

Our Lady of Victory Church, also called 'the Igloo Church' because of its shape, is to your right just after the lights.

Inuvik is a relatively new town. In the early 1950s, because of flooding at Aklavik, the site of the regional administrative centre at that time, the government chose a new location for its offices on the other side of the Mackenzie River. Construction began in 1955. By 1961 the town of Inuvik was finished. It now has a mixed population (Natives and non-Natives) of around 3300.

This far north you can enjoy seeing the sun constantly for eight weeks, four on each side of June 21. If you wish to shop for souvenirs, there are galleries and craft shops all along Mackenzie Road. If you are interested in visiting other northern communities in the region or taking a nature tour, you can also find a number of tour companies here.

Return back down the Dempster Highway to continue with Chapter 8.

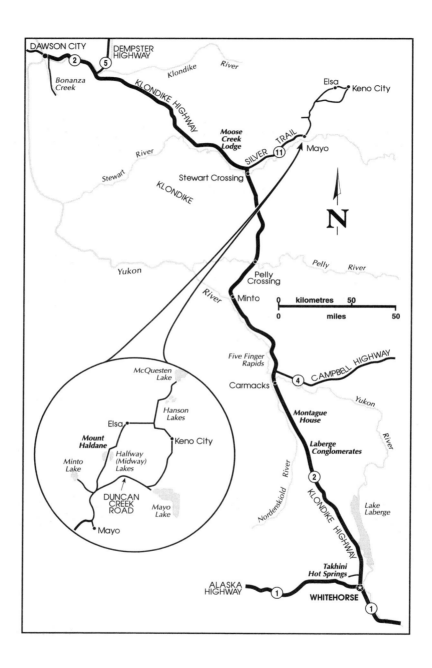

8
Dempster Corner to Whitehorse

During the Klondike Gold Rush, prospectors headed northward down the Yukon River from Whitehorse to Dawson City. As you head southward on the Klondike Highway, you will be taking a parallel route in the reverse direction, though you will not see the Yukon River again until you reach Minto, around the midpoint of the highway. Previous chapters have helped you visit towns and mines that grew from the discovery of gold and copper. In this chapter you will see towns and mines founded on silver.

Dempster Corner to Elsa

Partridge Creek Farm and Moose Creek

This chapter begins at Dempster Corner—40.8 kilometres (25.4 miles) east of the visitor reception centre in Dawson City or 37 kilometres (23 miles) from Bonanza Creek Road—where the Dempster Highway meets the Klondike Highway (Highway 2). At kilometre 19.4 (mile 12.1) from Dempster Corner, a pull-out to your left has a view of the Tintina Trench. About 250 metres (800 feet) wide at this point, the trench stretches along the Pelly River for part of its extent from around Watson Lake to the Eagle area of Alaska. Trenches like this one form where two of the giant plates that make up the earth's surface—such as an oceanic plate and a continental plate—meet and one gets forced down beneath the other. In this case, the south-western block is estimated to have shifted 450 to 1200 kilometres (280 to 750 miles) to the northwest along this fault over millions of years.

Tintina Trench.

This part of the drive is through forest, with a few glimpses of the mountains. Kilometre 85.4 (mile 53.1) brings you to the right-hand turn for Partridge Creek Farm, where you can buy vegetables in season.

You cross Moose Creek at kilometre 29.2 (mile 18.1) from the turn-off for Partridge Creek Farm. Moose Creek Lodge is to your left, just past the creek. In the yard you can see Murray the wooden moose, who is made of logs, Max the mosquito, who is made of burls, and a telephone up in a tree. If it rings, will you be the one to climb the ladder leaning against the tree to answer it? Part of the gift shop and restaurant section of the lodge used to be an old trapper's cabin.

Mosquito at Moose Creek Lodge.

Mayo, Keno City and Elsa

In 23 kilometres (14.3 miles) from the lodge you come over a hill and you can see the Stewart River to the right and the bridge over it ahead of you. At kilometre 23.8 (mile 14.8), a turn to the right would keep you on the highway and take you across the bridge to Stewart Crossing. To take a side trip to Mayo, Keno and Elsa, go straight ahead onto the Silver Trail (Highway 11).

Binet House in Mayo.

As you head toward Mayo, you are following the Stewart River. McIntyre Park Day Use Area is to your right at kilometre 50.3 (mile 31.2) from the junction. You cross the Mayo River and reach the right turn for Mayo, which bills itself as 'the Heart of the Yukon,' at kilometre 51.2 (mile 31.8).

The 75-hectare (185-acre) Mayo townsite was surveyed and established in 1903 to serve the mines of the area. At the confluence of the Mayo and Stewart rivers, the town was close to the Duncan Creek Road (see sidebar below). The flat banks of the Stewart River made access by steamboat easy. The town was named after Captain Alfred H. Mayo, who had taken shiploads of supplies up and down the Yukon River and its tributaries in the late 1800s.

The visitor reception centre is in an annex of the Binet House Interpretive Centre on the corner of Second Avenue and Centre Street. If you want to see historic buildings or their sites, pick up a walking-tour pamphlet here. The centre is also a good place to ask about road conditions if you plan to drive the Duncan Creek Road on your way to Keno City.

You can tour the Binet House, built in 1922, by yourself, but you need to ask the visitor centre staff to let you in. On the ground floor of the house, the displays, a

Duncan Creek Road

Gold was discovered on a creek in the area north of Mayo by Duncan Patterson in 1901 and the creek became known as 'Duncan Creek.' More claims were staked and a settlement, Duncan Landing, was established at the confluence of Duncan Creek and the Mayo River. Shortly afterward, the Duncan Creek Mining District was formed.

Although travel in the Yukon Territory was mainly by river, the miners built a number of trails to make it easier to bring in their equipment and supplies. Eventually, the territorial government constructed a wagon road beside Duncan Creek in 1904 and a winter road, called 'the Liberal Road' after the government then in Ottawa, was built. The wagon road meandered from Dawson City through the Klondike gold-mining regions to Duncan Creek and then southward to Minto. The journey over the bumpy road took several days in horse-drawn coaches, with travellers staying overnight in roadhouses.

In the 1920s, silver mines were opened on Keno Hill and near Elsa. The ore was taken from the mines to Mayo by wagon in summer; in winter, the wheels were removed from the wagons and runners attached. From Mayo, sternwheelers took the ore to Dawson or Whitehorse. However, the Duncan Creek Road was inefficient and a better road was needed. A new road was built from Mayo to Elsa and then extended to Keno, bypassing Duncan Creek. Tractors replaced the horses and then big trucks took over the hauling of the ore to Mayo and later, all the way to Skagway.

Duncan Creek Road is still as a scenic alternate route to Keno.

Keno City Mining Museum.

relief map of the area and black-and-white pictures show events from the town's history. When you go upstairs, it is like entering a turn-of-the-century hospital, complete with old equipment and displays.

Back on the Silver Trail, you begin a circle tour to Keno and Elsa. The road to Wareham Dam (also called 'the Mayo Hydro Dam') is 4.9 kilometres (3 miles) from the turn-off for Mayo. The equipment at this dam, built in 1950, supplies power to Mayo, Keno and Elsa. You cross a bridge over the Minto River at kilometre 13.5 (mile 8.4). Near here there was a small settlement that was flooded when the Wareham Dam created Wareham Lake.

Minto Lake Road is to your left at kilometre 17.5 (mile 10.9). It is a 19-kilometre (11.8-mile) drive, first on a secondary road and then on a narrow dirt road, to the lake, which is good for boating and fishing for grayling, pike and lake trout.

Just past Minto Lake Road, turn right onto Duncan Creek Road, which is part of the Silver Trail. This road is narrow, winding and bumpy and the speed limit is 50 kilometres per hour (30 miles per hour). Although the road does go through a burn area, it is a lovely drive. There are a number of small rest stops along the way—most consist of just a small pull-out and a garbage can and some of them mark the sites of vanished roadhouses from the early mining years. Two of these rest stops are Stones Farm, at kilometre 6.3 (mile 3.9), and Coles, at kilometre 17.6 (mile 10.9).

You come to a Y at kilometre 22.3 (mile 13.9). The right turn goes to Mayo Lake, which is 8.5 kilometres (5.3 miles) down the road, where you can try for jackfish, lake trout and grayling. Go left to continue to Keno.

A short distance past the Y, at kilometre 23.3 (mile 14.5), a rock with printing on it is to your right. The side road here leads to the Duncan Creek Gold Dusters, a company that offers guided tours. They start at 2 PM and include a view of placer operations, a chance to pan for gold and refreshments.

Van Cleeve's rest stop is to your left at 24.1 kilometres (15 miles) from the beginning of Duncan Creek Road. You climb slowly and, at kilometre 39.5 (mile 24.5), you reach Keno City and the end of the Silver Trail. The Keno City Mining Museum is in a two-storey wooden building that was built in the 1920s and was once a dancehall. Inside there are displays that explain the history of the gold and silver mining in the area. If you are interested in hiking, pick up the Keno City Trails pamphlet while you are here.

In 1919, silver was found on Sheep Mountain, later to be called 'Keno Hill.' Keno City started in the 1920s as the supply centre for the silver mines—some of their names were 'Shamrock,' 'Roulette' and 'Lucky Queen.' The settlement was named after a popular gambling game.

As you face the museum, a road to your left goes up to a parking lot on Keno Hill.

It is a steep, 10.8-kilometre (6.7-mile) climb to the top, with lots of switchbacks. A car, truck or even a motorhome will make it if it has enough power for going up and good brakes for coming down but, if you are pulling a trailer, you should leave it in town.

The top of Keno Hill is at an elevation of 1849 metres (6066 feet), amidst rock and tundra. You can walk over some large rocks to get to a signpost that is set near the edge of the hill. When you stand beside the signpost, you can see many mountaintops and look down into Faro Gulch. Arrows on the post are labelled with the names of various cities around the world and the distances to them (in miles) and point in the appropriate directions. Some of the cities are Heidelberg, Mexico City, Rio de Janeiro, Lagos and Cape Town.

The original signpost was erected during the International Geophysical Year (IGY), which took place during 1957–58. The IGY was organized by the International Council of Scientific Unions to encourage global research into oceanography, seismology, gravity, atmospheric phenomena and other areas of geophysics. During an IGY event in Canada, some members of the gathering came to the Yukon and were entertained by executives of the United Keno Hill Mine. The company put up the sign to honour the countries involved in the conference.

Moving the Signpost

The original signpost erected on Keno Hill was made of wood. It had to be replaced every few years, because of damage by the weather and by visitors taking the arrows as souvenirs. In the mid-1980s, the sign was taken down by the United Keno Hill Mine, which wanted to move it to a new pit-mine site. However, that mine closed before the sign could be erected and it was discarded.

The Silver Trail Association decided to replace the sign on Keno Hill. But they wanted a metal one that would weather better and be impossible to steal. On August 6, 1991, a concrete base was poured by Keno residents and the new steel post was set into place on the hill by a Transnorth Air helicopter as a favour to the people of Keno.

Cairn on top of Keno Hill.

Also at the summit of Keno Hill is a cairn dedicated to Alfred Kirk Schellinger, who staked the Keno mineral claim on this location on July 29, 1919. Two hiking trails begin from the parking lot: the 5-kilometre (3.1-mile) return Silver Basin Trail, which ends at a cairn and a viewpoint overlooking Silver Basin Gulch, and the 2-kilometre (1.2-mile) return Monument Hill Trail, which ends at two large rocks and the remains of an old cabin.

Return to Keno and head toward Elsa. You are on the main road that was built between Mayo and Keno to replace the Duncan Creek Road.

The turn-off for Hanson and McQuesten lakes is to your right at kilometre 8.4 (mile 5.2). These lakes are named after contemporaries of

View from Keno Hill.

Alfred Mayo who were also in the river transportation business. Hanson Lakes are about 8 kilometres (5 miles) down the side road and McQuesten Lake is about 24 kilometres (15 miles) down it. These lakes are great for canoeing.

The former site of Elsa is 13 kilometres (8.1 miles) from Keno. When you reach a Y in the road, take the right fork, as the left one goes to an active mining area that is closed to the public. As you go down this road, you reach a pull-out with an old sign at kilometre 15.2 (mile 9.4) from Keno. The sign tells about the silver claim staked by Charlie Brefalt in 1924 and named after his sister, Elsa. This discovery began the silver mining in the area and led to the building of the town of Elsa.

At this viewpoint a sign shows where the town of Elsa, with its three thousand inhabitants, once stood. All that you can see now is meadow. When the United Keno Hill Mine closed down in 1989, the houses were sold and moved out and the land was returned to its natural state. Just across the road from the pull-out is the Elsa School, no longer in use, its windows boarded up.

Some silver mining still goes on in the region, but the low price of silver has kept the industry from growing. However, if the economics of mining silver do improve and the mines do open here again, the mining company will set up a camp for the workers, rather than build another town.

As you continue along the road, you reach South McQuesten Road at kilometre 23.7 (mile 14.7) from Keno. This side road leads to Silver Centre Campground, which is 7.3 kilometres (4.5 miles) away, or, if you were to follow it 28.4 kilometres (17.6 miles) further, you would arrive at a bridge that spans the South McQuesten River, where you can camp and fish for grayling.

You are facing Mount Haldane as you drive away from Elsa and then the road swings to the left so that you are driving with the mountain to your right. At kilometre 33.7 (mile 20.9) from Keno, you reach Halfway (Midway) Lakes. Parking for the Mount Haldane Trail is 3.5 kilometres (2.2 miles) down the road to your right. The trail is 6.7 kilometres (4.2 miles) long and climbs about 1220 metres (4000 feet), using a series of switchbacks, to the summit. From the top you can see Mayo and the former site of Elsa. Plan on taking at least one-half day for this trip and carry lots of water.

About 42 kilometres (26 miles) from Keno City, the loop has brought you back to the Duncan Creek Road and you are heading toward the junction with the Klondike Highway just before Stewart Crossing.

Stewart Crossing to Whitehorse

Stewart Crossing and Pelly Crossing

Back on the Klondike Highway, you cross the Stewart River and enter the settlement of Stewart Crossing. A visitor reception centre is to your right, and the Stewart Crossing service station and a privately run RV park are to your left.

Seventy kilometres (43.5 miles) from Stewart Crossing you cross the Pelly River and enter the town of Pelly Crossing, billed as 'the Home of the Northern Tutchone.' The Pelly River, which empties into the Yukon River, has been used for centuries by the Northern Tutchone people. It was named after a Hudson's Bay Company governor, Sir John Pelly. The Pelly River formed part of the route from Edmonton, Alberta, to the Klondike that was charted by Inspector John Moodie of the North-West Mounted Police in 1897–98.

The Selkirk First Nation (Ts'eki' Huch'an), part of the Northern Tutchone Council and having about five hundred members, has set up a heritage centre, Big Jonathon House. It is located next to Selkirk Groceries and Selkirk Gas Bar.

Beside Big Jonathon House there is a long line of information panels. One tells of the Selkirk people's legend that Crow was the one who divided them into two clans, the

Native signs at Pelly Crossing.

Crows and the Wolves. Another shows the traditional land use of the Selkirk people—where they had their meat cache, their hide cache, their foot-trails, their fishing sites and their camps. Stop and read all the panels to gain an insight into the past and present lives of the Ts'eki' Huch'an.

As you leave the village, a small visitor reception centre is to your left.

A few minutes' drive south of Pelly Crossing you begin travelling through an area that got burned in 1995. Two fires, one on each side of the Yukon River, were started by lightning. They burned until the end of July, destroying about 131,500 hectares (325,000 acres) of forest.

Minto and Five Fingers Rapids

Turn right onto the gravel road at the turn-off for Minto, 33.4 kilometres (20.8 miles) from the visitor centre in Pelly Crossing (there is no sign). In 1.6 kilometres (1 mile) from the highway, you come to a left turn to go to the Yukon River and the old site of Minto.

Long before the non-Natives arrived, the Northern Tutchone camped here on the Yukon River to fish for dog salmon. From 1902 until the 1930s, Minto was the site of a roadhouse on the White Pass and Yukon Railway Company's winter mail route. In summer, the roadhouse supplied passing steamboats with wood. However, after airplanes took over the mail service in the 1930s and the road from Whitehorse to Dawson was completed in 1955, the steamboats were no longer needed on the river, and the roadhouse closed down. Today there is a government campsite here along the river, but remnants of old buildings in the woods still remain.

Old building at Minto.

Beginning around kilometre 23 (mile 14) from the Minto turn-off, from time to time you can see a thin layer of white volcanic ash in the bank to your left. This ash is from a volcanic eruption about 1200 years ago, though scientists are not sure from which mountain.

At kilometre 50.1 (mile 31.1), you reach the turn-off for the Five Finger Rapids Recreation Site. Drive in, park and walk to the platform, which overlooks the river. You can look down and see the erosion-resistant basaltic rocks in the river that make up the fingers. However, you can not see all five fingers from the platform—look at the map on the railing to see how one smaller rock is hidden by the largest one and that the channel closest to the river bank is hidden by trees. For a closer look, take the steep 1.5-kilometre (0.9-mile) interpretive trail to the river bank. The trail begins with a set of steps at the platform.

The stampeders heading for the Klondike ran these rapids with boats that they built

Yukon River at Minto.

themselves. At the time, the westernmost channel was considered the safest one to take.

On the way to the hamlet of Carmacks, there are occasional views of the Yukon River Valley to the right. As you near Carmacks, you can see Tantalus Butte ahead of you, where coal mining took place between 1906 and 1981.

At kilometre 21.2 (mile 13.2) from Five Finger Rapids you reach the junction with the Robert Campbell Highway (Highway 4), which goes toward Ross River, Faro and Watson Lake (see Chapter 10). Continue straight ahead for Carmacks.

Carmacks and Lake Laberge

You cross the Yukon River at kilometre 23.1 (mile 14.4) from the Campbell Highway and arrive in Carmacks less than 1 kilometre (0.6 miles) from the bridge. The Tutchone Centre shopping centre, a general store, a service station and a restaurant are situated along the high-way. Turn right onto Freegold Road at the service station to enter the hamlet itself. Continue down Freegold Road to reach River Drive, which runs alongside the Yukon River.

A 2-kilometre (1.2-mile) long boardwalk is on the bank of the river. It begins 0.4 kilometres (0.2 miles) to your right from the corner of Freegold Road and River Drive and runs beside the river to your left for 1.6 kilometres (1 mile) to a little park.

Boardwalk along Yukon River at Carmacks.

Go left and 0.5 kilometres (0.3 miles) past the park is one of the last remaining roadhouses on the old Dawson Trail (also known as 'the Yukon Stage Line' and 'the Overland Trail'). It has been restored as a heritage site but is not open to the public at this time. Beside the roadhouse there is a one-lane wooden bridge that crosses the Nordenskiold River. The Northern Tutchone once used the banks here, at the confluence of the Yukon and Nordenskiold rivers, as the site for a trading camp.

Carmacks is named after George Washington Carmack, who established the area's first trading post here in 1892. He found coal near Tantalus Butte in 1893, before going on to play his part in starting the Klondike Gold Rush a few years later (see 'The Beginning of the Klondike Gold Rush' on p. 154). Carmacks became a stopover on the road between Whitehorse and Dawson.

Montague House.

On your left, 1.7 kilometres (1.1 miles) from Carmacks, there is a roadside pull-out with a large mural entitled Moment at Tantalus Butte. It was painted in 1992, on the one-hundredth anniversary of George Carmack setting up his trading post. The mural shows the history of Carmacks, including a riverboat, George Carmack himself, Tantalus Butte and parts of Carmacks.

Whitehorse Trough Conglomerate.

After Carmacks you can see more of the line of volcanic ash that you saw earlier. At kilometre 13.2 (mile 8.2), look on your left for the Plume Agate Gem and Mineral Trail. You can follow the trail and find white plume agate deposits in a clearing at the 0.5-kilometre (0.3-mile) mark and geodes at 0.9 kilometres (0.6 miles) from the trailhead. Information panels tell you how to recognize these two kinds of stones.

At a pull-out 21 kilometres (13 miles) from the trail, you can see the remains of Montague House, built in 1899 as a stop on the trail to Dawson City. The roof is gone, but the log walls are in good shape. Trees are growing in the centre of the house—some are already tall enough to be seen from the outside. Look at the huge logs that were used to build it. Walk around the remains to see the old building behind them.

If you are interested in geology, pull over at the pull-out on the left at kilometre 44 (mile 27.3). Here you can see the Laberge Conglomerates. They are part of the Whitehorse Trough Conglomerates, a line of boulders that were eroded from volcanic mountains to the west and pushed by glaciers into a basin, the Whitehorse Trough. The line runs from Atlin, BC, to Whitehorse, Yukon. The spacing between adjacent boulders varies from metres to kilometres. As you continue southward, you can see more of these conglomerates beside the road.

If you want to camp on the shores of Lake Laberge, the setting for Robert Service's poem 'The Cremation of Sam McGee,' turn left at 74.2 kilometres (46.1 miles) from the pull-out for the conglomerates. The campground is 3 kilometres (1.8 miles) down the road. You might not want to go swimming, because the water is very cold.

Takhini Hot Springs pool.

Takhini Hot Springs and Whitehorse

Take the right turn for Takhini Hot Springs 26.9 kilometres (16.7 miles) from the road to Lake Laberge. Along this paved road you pass residences, businesses and bed-and-breakfast establishments. At kilometre 8.8 (mile 5.5), turn left onto Takhini River Road, and 0.5 kilometres (0.3 miles) from there you reach the parking lot for Takhini Hot Springs.

In the past, the hot springs were reached via the Takhini River and then, later, via the trail to Dawson. During the building of the Alaska Highway, the soldiers working on it had a greenhouse here in which they grew vegetables throughout winter.

The water comes out of the ground at a temperature of about 48° Celsius (118° Fahrenheit) and a rate of 390 litres (86 Imperial gallons or 103 US gallons) per minute. The water is directed into an artificial pool in which you can soak. There is a campground to stay at and there is also a coffee shop, if you are here for just a short visit.

At kilometre 5.9 (mile 3.7) from the turn-off for the hot springs you reach the junction of the Klondike Highway with the Alaska Highway (Highway 1), just northwest of Whitehorse. Turn left onto the Alaska Highway and in 11.6 kilometres (7.2 miles) you are at the traffic lights for Two Mile Hill Road in Whitehorse.

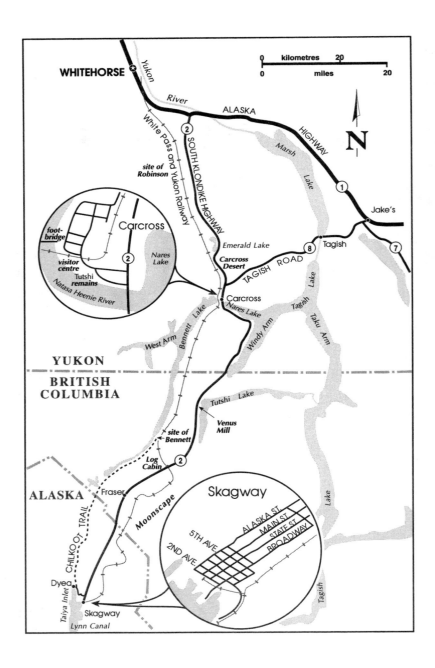

9
Whitehorse to
Skagway

Dawson City may have been the intended destination for the estimated one hundred thousand men, women and children who headed northward for the Klondike Gold Rush, but many of them got no further than somewhere between Skagway and Whitehorse. Many turned back when faced with the challenge of dealing with the hardships of the Chilkoot or White Pass trails, crossing Lake Bennett and then navigating the White Horse Rapids in Miles Canyon (see Chapter 1, p. 40), while other lost their lives in the effort.

This chapter will guide you to where the gold-rush stampeders were dropped off by boats at Skagway and Dyea. En route, you can see part of the White Pass Trail and, if you really want to walk in the footsteps of history, you can hike the Chilkoot Trail.

Robinson, Emerald Lake and the Carcross Desert

Heading southeast from Whitehorse, it is 21 kilometres (13 miles) from the traffic lights at Two Mile Hill Road to the junction with the South Klondike Highway (Highway 2), which goes through Carcross to Skagway. (From the junction with

Robert Service Way, the south entrance to Whitehorse, it is 15 kilometres [9.3 miles].) After you turn onto this highway, there are some businesses and shops before you head into a forest of tall pines, spruce and poplar.

To your right at kilometre 18.3 (mile 11.4), there is a pull-out with a picnic area. A path from the parking lot leads across the railway tracks to the Robinson Roadhouse and two outbuildings. The settlement of Robinson began as a siding on the White Pass and Yukon Railway in 1899. When gold

Robinson Roadhouse.

was discovered in the area in the early 1900s, a townsite was surveyed. A few businesses opened and Robinson's postmaster started one of the Yukon's first ranches nearby, but low gold yields caused the townsite to be abandoned in 1915.

At kilometre 40.8 (mile 25.4) a viewpoint to your right overlooks small, beautiful Emerald Lake. Its colour is the result of blue-green light rays reflecting off its bottom, which is made up of pieces of decomposed shell and clay, a material called 'marl.'

Watch to your left at kilometre 49.9 (mile 31) for the turn-off for Frontierland Heritage Park and Wildlife Gallery. As you turn down the side road to Frontierland, look to your right and above the fence to see Dall sheep standing or lying on a dirt mound. Continue to the parking lot and go into the building labelled 'Museum' to

pay for your visit. From the entrance into Frontierland you can follow a path that takes you past a monument to the caribou, a replica of a Native village, a lynx enclosure, a petting farm, a gold-panning area, a replica of a trapper's cabin and a replica of a fort, to name a few of the attractions.

As you drive along the highway beyond the turn-off for Frontierland, you

Frontierland.

pass sand dunes with trees and bushes growing on them and, in less than 1 kilometre (0.6 miles), you are at the Carcross Desert, said to be the smallest desert in the world. A pull-out is to your left.

What is now the Carcross Desert was once the bottom of a glacial lake. As the last of the glaciers melted, the level of the lake dropped until just the sandy bottom was left. Winds off Lake Bennett keep the sand moving and prevent most vegetation from taking root here.

Carcross and Conrad City

The junction with the road to Tagish (see Chapter 10) is 1.4 kilometres (0.9 miles) from the desert. At kilometre 2.3 (mile 1.4), turn right to enter the village of Carcross, whose name is short for 'Caribou Crossing.' The visitor reception centre is in the old train depot to your left as you come into town. In the yard of the centre there is a little black railway locomotive, the *Duchess*.

The *Duchess* and her counterpart, the *Duke*, were a matched set of engines that were built in 1878 and were used to pull coal cars for the Wellington Colliery Railway on Vancouver Island. In 1899 the White Pass and Yukon Railway bought the *Duchess* for operation on the Taku Tram.

The 3.2-kilometre (2-mile) long Taku Tram, originally (in 1898) a Canadian Pacific Navigation Company portage tramway powered by horses, ran from Graham Inlet on Tagish Lake to Atlin Lake, BC. Tours were run from Carcross to Atlin: tour participants would board a stern-wheeler to cross Tagish Lake and enter the passenger car being pulled by the *Duchess* for the trip to

Remains of *SS Tutshi* today in Carcross.

Atlin Lake, which they would also cross by stern-wheeler. The *Duchess* ran the return journey backward, because no turntable or loop was at either end.

Though the *Duchess* worked until 1919 (the tramway shut down in 1940), it was not until the 1950s that she was moved to Carcross for display.

Also in the visitor centre yard is the remains of the stern-wheeler *SS Tutshi*, which burned here in July 1990. You can still make out where the riverboat rested. The wooden parts burned, leaving the blackened front hull and the metal machinery that operated the vessel in the position in which it stood when the ship was intact.

The *Tutshi* was built in Carcross in 1917 and she ran passengers and freight from Carcross to various places on Tagish Lake throughout her 39 years of service. She was dry-docked in July of 1956. Restoration began in 1984 and was almost complete when she burned in what has been called 'a mysterious blaze.'

The last spike for the White Pass and Yukon Railway was driven in Carcross on July 29, 1900. Walk past the visitor centre to the railway bridge that crosses the Natasa Heenie River ('river of clear water' in the Tlingit language), a narrows between Bennett Lake and Nares Lake. This 125-metre (410-foot) long swing bridge was built with a 45-metre (150-foot) middle section that pivots on a central axis, thereby allowing boats to pass on either side. Once the railway was completed, however, water travel was reduced and the pivoting feature was seldom used.

General Store in Carcross.

It takes about 15 minutes to walk through the village of Carcross, though allow more time if you stop in at the shops and read all the interpretive signs. Watch for the three large gold pans with murals painted on them—they are on the corner across from the Caribou Hotel, which was built in 1898. Also, visit the Carcross Barracks, where you can buy souvenirs and see the small jail cell that held prisoners when a detachment of the North-West Mounted Police was stationed here.

If you want to see the graves of two of the three men who started the Klondike Gold Rush, go to the Carcross Native cemetery, which contains the graves of Tagish Charlie and Skookum Jim Mason and also of Kate Carmack, George Carmack's Native first wife (see sidebar, page 154). This cemetery is

Bove Island

In 1883 Frederick Schwatka, a lieutenant in the 3rd Cavalry of the US military, led a party of six men from Portland, Oregon, to Alaska. His mission was to do a survey of the Native peoples there, in case the US had to defend its new territory.

En route to Alaska, Schwatka's group were among the first non-Natives to use the Native route over the Chilkoot Pass and the first non-Natives to pass through the Carcross area in the Yukon Territory. Schwatka led his team along Lake Bennett (which he named) to Nares Lake. He named the island at its end for a Lieutenant Bove of the Italian Navy. He also named the long lake on the other side of the island for the Italian, even though the Tagish and Tlingit peoples, who had been here for centuries before the non-Natives arrived, already called it 'Tagish Lake.'

Bove Island.

The Canadian government became concerned that the US Army was renaming Canadian geographical features that already had names, Native or otherwise. To remedy the situation, it sent George Mercer Dawson, of the Geological Survey of Canada, to the Yukon Territory in 1887. Though Dawson changed the name of the lake back to 'Tagish,' he left Bove Island's name as it was.

not promoted as a tourist attraction, so ask at the visitor reception centre for directions. If you do go there, please respect the graves and anyone else who is visiting.

Back on the highway, you cross Nares Bridge. It spans the Natasa Heenie River as it flows from Bennett Lake, upstream to the right, into Nares Lake (which joins Tagish Lake) on the left.

The highway follows Nares Lake and then you come to a pull-out on your left at kilometre 10.5 (mile 6.5) from the turn-off

Remains of Venus ore storage bin and mill built in the 1960s.

for Carcross. A platform at the pull-out overlooks Bove Island, which is situated where Nares Lake (to your left) meets Tagish Lake (beyond Bove Island) and Tagish Lake's Windy Arm (to your right). Signs at the platform tell about the local Native peoples, the animals in the area, Bove Island and the lakes.

To your left at kilometre 16.5 (mile 10.3), you will see a tower that was part of the tramline of the first Venus Mine. At kilometre 18.9 (mile 11.7), you pass the concrete foundations from the second Venus Mine's ore storage bin and mill, which are to your left. This mill was built in the late 1960s, but by 1970 it was no longer in use, so it was taken down and sold. The foundations are now covered with graffiti. Although lots of raspberry bushes are beside the foundations, do not eat the berries because of their high arsenic content.

At kilometre 20.7 (mile 12.9), look uphill to see more of the tram towers against the sky. Look ahead to see the wooden structure built from the highway down to the lakeshore. A pull-out is to your left there. This building is the first Venus Mill, which preceded the one whose foundations you already passed.

Venus Mill built in 1908.

The mill had its origins when Colonel John Howard Conrad of Montana bought a large number of claims in the Windy Arm area in 1904 and began to mine the ore. (Two years earlier, Conrad had put up bonds to secure a gold claim just south of Carcross on Montana Mountain, which he named.)

A respectable town, Conrad City, grew on the edge of Windy Arm to service the mines. By 1906 it had three hundred residents, one laundry, one restaurant, three hotels, one drugstore, three other stores and one brothel.

John Conrad built the first Venus Mill on the lakeshore in 1908. A 6-kilometre (4-mile) long aerial tramway was constructed to bring the ore from the mines to the mill, where it was crushed and bagged to be sent by water to Carcross and from there onward to Skagway.

The White Pass Trail

When the Klondike Gold Rush got into full swing in 1898, the White Pass Trail was seen as an attractive alternate route to the Chilkoot Pass Trail. Although longer, it was not as steep, which meant that pack animals could theoretically traverse it. Goldseekers who could afford horses to haul their 900 kilograms (2000 pounds) of supplies usually chose the White Pass Trail over the Chilkoot, where everything would have to be carried by humans. However, the White Pass Trail was rough and narrow, with huge mudholes and dangerous drop-offs making it more treacherous than expected.

Three thousand horses were taken over the pass and most of them died, either from the hard work or from falls. Many of the horses were old and tired to begin with and some people claim that the exhausted and poorly fed animals committed suicide by deliberately walking over the edge. So great was the toll on horses that the route became known as 'the Dead Horse Trail.'

The trail fell quickly into disuse when the White Pass and Yukon Railway was completed in 1900.

In spite of John Conrad's ambitions, not enough gold came out of the mines and the mill closed after just two years. The buildings of Conrad City, once expected to become the capital of Yukon, were then hauled over the winter ice of Nares Lake to Carcross.

Look up the hill across the highway from the mill to see other buildings from more recent mining attempts.

At kilometre 25.3 (mile 15.7) from the Carcross turn-off, you enter BC and soon after that you have Tutshi Lake to your left. There are a number of pull-outs where you can enjoy the view of the mountains across the lake. To your left at kilometre 31.3 (mile 19.4), there is a newer Venus Mines Mill that closed in 1981.

Log Cabin, a 'Moonscape' and Customs

You follow a canyon for a short distance. At kilometre 61.7 (mile 38.3) from Carcross, cross the White Pass and Yukon Railway tracks and turn right into the large parking lot at the site where Log Cabin used to be. Log Cabin was the last stop before Bennett Lake on the White Pass Trail. It had hotels, restaurants and saloons. The North-West Mounted Police set up a post here to collect customs duties from the Klondike-bound stampeders. During the building of the White Pass and Yukon Railway, Log Cabin became a construction camp and, once the railroad was completed, Log Cabin disappeared.

If you plan to hike the Chilkoot Trail, this lot is one place where you can park your vehicle. An information panel here gives you a trail report and advises you of restricted activities within Klondike Gold Rush National Historic Park. (See the sidebar, 'Arranging to Hike the Chilkoot Trail,' on p. 195.)

Just past the Log Cabin turn-off you reach the beginning of the Tormented Valley or 'Moonscape' on your left. The highway and the adjacent White Pass and Yukon Railway tracks follow the edge of the valley for a long way, and there are lots of pull-outs. The first one is at kilometre 0.9 (mile 0.6) from Log Cabin.

At kilometre 6.9 (mile 4.3,) a pull-out to the left has interpretive signs about Fraser (the border crossing), the Moonscape and the building of the White Pass and Yukon Railway.

Shortly after the previous pull-out, you reach Canada Customs, which is open 24 hours per day in summer. A station for the White Pass and Yukon Railway is nearby. Although customs buildings are usually right next to the border, in this case both Canadian and US customs posts are about a 10-minute drive away from the border in opposite directions.

You are climbing and still driving through the Moonscape when you reach the Canada–US boundary (where there is a time-zone change) at kilometre 12.5 (mile 7.8) from the Canadian customs post. At kilometre 13.1 (mile 8.1) you reach White Pass Summit, with an elevation of 1003 metres (3292 feet).

From the summit you begin descending, with deep gorges appearing alternately on both sides of the highway. Pull-outs allow you to pull over to look down into these chasms. On your right at kilometre 18.1 (mile 11.2) is Moore Falls and then you cross the Captain William Moore Bridge, which spans a 33-metre (110-foot) wide gorge. (See the write-up on 'Skagway and Dyea' on p. 190 for information about Moore.) Beginning at about kilometre 19 (mile 11.8), look to your left across a canyon to see the railway tracks hugging the mountainside.

To see Deadhorse Gulch—so named because it was once littered with the carcasses of horses that died there while on the White Pass Trail to the Klondike—stop at the pull-out on the left at kilometre 21.3 (mile 13.2). The entrance to the gulch is to the left, below the railway tracks on the other side of the gorge.

At kilometre 23.6 (mile 14.7) there is a pull-out to your left from which to view Pitchfork Falls. This waterfall creates a number of cascades and routes as it flows down the mountainside. It then passes under the railway tracks and drops down into the gorge.

The Tormented Valley

The best time to visit the Tormented Valley is during a mist or fog, when the trees take on a spooky, unearthly look and you seem to have been transported to another planet. This look gives the area its nickname of 'Moonscape.'

The landscape of the Tormented Valley consists of ponds set between huge rocks on which stunted fir trees and sparse grasses attempt to grow. It is the transition area between the lush trees of the lower regions and the alpine vegetation of the higher levels.

Because the soil on the rocks is so sparse, tree growth during summer is slow, so those small, misshapen firs (also called 'mopheads') are actually decades old. In the winter their lower branches are protected by snow but the higher ones are left exposed to the cold winds.

Moonscape.

The vegetation and soil of the Moonscape are very fragile, so if you do walk on it, stay on paths wherever possible and walk in single file. When you come to an area with no path, spread out and walk gently. Where you can, walk along lakeshores or on bare rock with no vegetation.

The height and density of the trees increase as you descend toward tidewater. At kilometre 25.2 (mile 15.7) from the Canada Customs post, you reach the US Customs building. Watch for views of the railway trestles across the gorge. In 6.8 kilometres (4.2 miles) from the US Customs post there is a turn-off to the right for the townsite of Dyea. Continue toward Skagway.

Skagway and Dyea

You cross the Skagway River before entering the city of Skagway, which is at the river's mouth where it enters the Lynn Canal.

Although there is general agreement that 'Skagway' came from a Native word, there have been many spellings and attributed meanings. The second most popular spelling is 'Skaguay' but 'Skagua,' 'Schkague,' 'Schkawai' and 'Shkagway' have been used and the supposed meaning varies from 'home of the north wind,' to 'end of salt water,' 'spirit of the cruel wind,' and 'rough water.'

Early in 1887, Captain William Moore, guided by Skookum Jim Mason, helped to survey the White Pass route into the Yukon for the Canadian government. In fall of that year, Moore and his son, Bernard (Ben), claimed 65 hectares (160 acres) and built a cabin, a sawmill and a wharf at the mouth of the Skagway River. They believed that there would eventually be a gold rush in the Yukon and that a port city would be needed at the beginning of the new trail into it.

However, the Moores' foresight did not help them as much as they had hoped. When gold was discovered in the Klondike, and the Moores' cabin was still the only building at the mouth of the Skagway, the first eager prospectors who arrived in 1897 ignored the Moores' property claim. Frank Reid and a group of surveyors surveyed a town-site and over one thousand lots were sold, many on the Moores' homestead. The Moores did not receive any

The Shoot-out

Frank Reid came to Skagway from Oregon where, after taking part in fights with the Natives, he had worked as a schoolteacher and had been acquitted of a murder. He became Skagway's engineer and surveyed the town lots.

Jefferson Randolph 'Soapy' Smith came to Skagway (via the wild silver-mining camp of Creede) from Denver, Colorado, where he had been the head of the city's criminal underworld. There was no law enforcement in Skagway at that time, and he immediately set up his own network of secret police upon arriving in 1898. He ran a two-hundred-plus person operation that dealt in theft, fraud, armed robbery, gambling, prostitution and sometimes murder in the lawless town.

Finally, on July 8, 1898, the more law-abiding citizens held a meeting in Sylvester Hall to determine how to get rid of the criminals in Skagway. When more people showed up than the hall could hold, the meeting was moved to Juneau Wharf. A guard of four men was set up at the entrance to the wharf, one of them being Frank Reid. Soapy Smith arrived with his gang. The meeting between Smith and Reid resulted in them shooting each other.

Smith died immediately, but Reid lingered for 12 days before he, too, died, celebrated as a hero for ridding Skagway of Soapy Smith.

compensation for the loss of their property and they were even forced to move their cabin, because it now sat in the middle of a newly surveyed street.

By August of 1897 Skagway was a tent city of four thousand people and by October it had become a town of 20,000 and wood-frame buildings had replaced the tents. It continued to grow until 1899, when gold was discovered in Nome and most of its residents moved on. Nevertheless, Skagway was incorporated as the first city in Alaska on June 28, 1900.

Skagway, like Dawson City, is a place where you will want to spend at least two days soaking up the gold-rush atmosphere. At the end of the gold rush, many of the shops were moved to front on Broadway to be near the White Pass and Yukon Railway tracks. Because fire has never ravaged Skagway, many of the buildings are the original ones. Most of the shops in Skagway today are still on Broadway, with a few on the side streets.

Former red light district house in Skagway.

The visitor reception centre is on 5th Avenue just off Broadway. For information about the Chilkoot Pass Trail, stop in at the Klondike Gold Rush National Historic Park's visitor centre at the corner of Broadway and 2nd Avenue.

You can take a streetcar tour of the city or you can park and walk the boardwalks in front of the restaurants, stores, museum, historic buildings and interpretive centres. Although the outsides of the buildings look authentic, inside you will find modern-day souvenirs, clothing and food. (Note that some of the shops in Skagway open only on the days when a cruise ship is expected.)

As a 1997 centennial project, the city commissioned an artist to create the Skagway Statue. Located in a small park near where the railway tracks cross Broadway, it features a prospector looking toward the pass and a Native packer leading him along the trail.

As you leave Skagway heading back up the highway, watch for the sign for Gold Rush Cemetery Road. Turn right onto that road, which takes you between the railway yard and the river. You cross the tracks and then follow the road to the left. In 0.9 kilometres (0.6 miles) from the turn-off, you arrive at a small parking area to your right. From the parking lot, take the path through the trees until you come to 'the largest nugget in the world' at the gravesite of Martin Itjen.

Itjen founded Alaska's first visitor sightseeing operation in Skagway in 1923. He built streetcars to take tourists to the historic sites of the city. According to stories, Itjen claims to have panned this 'nugget' from the Skagway River in 1898. He is said to have carried it to the cemetery and chained it to a tree so that it would not be stolen.

Follow the path to the east of the nugget to come out at the road. Turn right, and in a few steps you reach a set of stairs. Climb them. At the top to the right is the grave of the notorious Soapy Smith. It has a small white marker and a rail fence around it. To the left from the stairs is the large monument that marks Frank Reid's grave. Some

A grave in the Skagway Gold Rush Cemetery.

of the other people who were buried in this cemetery died just after getting to Skagway in 1897 and 1898. A few markers are new, replacing the old and dilapidated ones, though others are the original ones and can still be read—some just have 'Unknown' on them.

Follow the path past Reid's grave to reach Reid Falls. It is about a five-minute hike to a viewpoint from which you can see the lower part of the falls. Go a little higher and you can see more of it. Adventurous people can climb, at their own risk, even further up the wet rocks for the best view.

Return to the highway, drive to Dyea (pronounced as 'die ee,' or 'die ee ah') Road and turn right onto it. Drive carefully because, although this road is very scenic, it is narrow and winding and has drop-offs along it. At kilometre 2.1 (mile 1.3), a pull-out to the left overlooks the town of Skagway, the cruise ships in the harbour and Taiya Inlet. The pavement ends at kilometre 2.8 (mile 1.7). Then the road becomes especially winding as you follow it around Long Bay.

At kilometre 10.8 (mile 6.7), you reach a turn-off to the left for the Dyea campground. Park your vehicle here if you intend to hike the Chilkoot Trail from this end, because hikers are not allowed to park at the trailhead. (See the sidebar 'Arranging to Hike the Chilkoot Trail' on p. 195) Continue past the turn-off for the Chilkoot trailhead and the old site of Dyea.

You enter the Dyea Unit of the Klondike Gold Rush National Historic Park at kilometre 11.4 (mile 7.1). The Chilkoot trailhead is to the right. Cross the Taiya River and at kilometre 11.7 (mile 7.3) you reach a Y in road. Take the left fork and head for the Dyea Historic Site and the Chilkoot Slide Cemetery.

At 12.2 kilometres (7.6 miles) is the site of Trail Street in what was uptown Dyea. It was a muddy, wagon-lined street with hotels, restaurants and saloons along it. This strip was the last bit of civilization that a stampeder saw before embarking on the Chilkoot Pass Trail.

In 12.8 kilometres (8 miles) from the beginning of Dyea Road you reach a T-intersection. Go right, toward the Chilkoot Slide Cemetery parking area. From the parking area, a short path leads to the cemetery itself. The avalanche that killed the people buried here occurred along the Chilkoot Pass Trail on April 3, 1898, between Sheep Camp and the Scales. Gold-rush stampeders in the area stopped their trek for four days to rescue the survivors and recover the dead.

Skagway and cruise ships in the harbour from viewpoint on Dyea Road.

The cemetery contains only 49 headboards, although an estimated 70 people were killed in the avalanche. The date of death on all of these headboards is April 3, 1898, except for one that belongs to someone who survived until April 4. However, avalanches were not the only disasters awaiting the stampeders on the trail: flooding, disease and cold weather also took their toll.

Return to the T-intersection and continue straight ahead to the Dyea Historic Site. In 0.6 kilometres (0.4 miles) from the T, look to your left for the fallen-down Pullen Barn, all that remains of the farming that took place here for a short time in the early 1900s.

Just past the barn you reach the end of the road at a pool of water. If it is late June or early July, the field before you will be full of purple irises. There are information panels about the area and pictures of prospectors each pushing their mountains of goods up the river in scows, of men standing beside their mounds of supplies in Dyea, and of the cemetery and the dock.

From here a path leads through the trees to the old townsite of Dyea on Taiya Inlet.

The Chilkoot Pass Trail

The Chilkoot Pass Trail was considered to be the 'poor-man's route' to the Klondike. It ran from Dyea to Bennett Lake, following an old Native path. Most of the people who started for the Klondike were cheechakos, a Native word for 'greenhorn' or 'novice.' It was only after a person had spent a winter in the North that he or she became a 'sourdough.' Because of the isolation and long, cold winters, the North-West Mounted Police decreed that each gold-rush stampeder had to have at least 900 kilograms (2000 pounds) of equipment and supplies before they would allow him or her to enter the Yukon Territory.

Each stampeder taking the Chilkoot Trail had to haul those supplies up and over the Chilkoot Pass summit. Some were able to hire Natives to help, but many had to do it themselves. They would carry as much as they could on each trip up the 'Golden Stairs' (steps cut into the solid snow of the pass, said to be so named because of the tolls charged by the men who had carved them), then slide back down to their cache and begin again. Most folks made some 40 trips to move all of their goods. Once a miner got onto the steps, he did not dare get off until the top, because if fatigue forced a person to step out of line, he seldom managed to make it back in.

By the spring of 1898, three trams had been built to help haul loads up to Chilkoot Pass, for a price. Meanwhile, the people who had already made it over the pass during winter and had camped at Bennett Lake had cut down the trees around the lake to make boats. Once the ice broke, over 7100 craft set sail down Bennett Lake, beginning the 900-kilometre (560-mile) journey down the Yukon River to Dawson City. Records show that a total of about 30,000 people travelled from Bennett Lake to Dawson City in 1898.

Once they made it past the rapids at Miles Canyon, the worst was over. However, by the time the gold-seekers arrived at their destination, especially those who arrived at Dawson later in the year, they found that all of the worthwhile claims had been staked by prospectors who had arrived earlier.

Like the White Pass Trail, the Chilkoot Pass Trail was abandoned in 1900 when the White Pass and Yukon Railway was completed.

It was not until 1969 that the 53-kilometre (33-mile) long Chilkoot Trail was selected as a Canadian component for the joint US and Canadian Klondike Gold Rush International Historic Park. Because of the many historic sites and artifacts along it, this trail is now sometimes referred to as 'the Longest Museum in the World.'

Hiking The Chilkoot Pass Trail Today

Some people who have hiked the Chilkoot Trail and climbed the Chilkoot Pass have loved it, while others have stated that it was the worst trail that they had ever been on. Although park staff do recommend that you be an experienced hiker, even inexperienced—but determined and suitably equipped—hikers have succeeded, and

Taiya River beside the Chilkoot Trail.

they have ranged from children accompanying their parents to octogenarians. You will have to decide for yourself if it's for you.

The trail starts out with the Taiya River on your left. You will be continually climbing and descending beside it until you reach Sheep Camp. And, until Sheep Camp, you will be walking through a rainforest with tall trees that create nice cool shade on hot days. You will climb over tree roots, stumps and rocks. In places there is a drop-off, so make sure that your pack is secure and does not wobble. You will walk on boardwalks and cross a number of metal, split-log and plank bridges. If you are here in June or early July, there are two places where you will want to put on your sandals to keep your hiking boots dry. At the first of these spots, there is some water over the path and at the other you need to negotiate a mud bog.

For about 1.5 kilometres (about 1 mile), you hike through private land—watch for the signs. While on the private land, you pass the remains of an old vehicle and an old building. For a short distance, the trail is as wide as a single-lane road.

Soon after leaving the private land, you reach Finnegan's Point, the site of the first campground on the trail. It is 8 kilometres (5 miles) from the beginning. The point was named after Pat Finnegan and his two sons who set up a ferry service here in 1897. Later, they built a road through the damp, boggy areas to replace the ferry and charged a toll. They operated the road only in the summer, because the prospectors pulled their goods on sleds along the frozen river ice in winter. This point was also used as a cache where the stampeders left their bundles of supplies while they went back to Dyea for more.

The campground has a shelter where you can dry out your clothes if it is raining and cook your meals. To avoid attracting bears and other animals to the campsite, proper food hygiene is essential. Pour your used dishwater down the screened greywater disposal pipe and scrape any food particles off the screen and into your garbage. Make sure that you hoist your food and garbage up the bear pole, out of

Arranging to Hike the Chilkoot Trail

To preserve both the fragile tundra and the cultural features of the trail, and to enhance the visitor experience, the Canadian government has limited the number of people permitted to cross the border into Canada via the Chilkoot Trail to 50 per day.

You can begin registering for the hike in February by contacting Parks Canada at 1-800-661-0486. You will be charged a reservation fee and be told where you can pick up and pay for the backcountry permits that you will need before starting the trail. Parks will also send you an information package with a map. There are 10 campsites along the trail, so when you book your time, you will have to decide how far you wish to walk each day, taking into account the slow climb up to the pass.

Here are some of the options for getting to the trailhead and getting back to your vehicle after you have completed your trek:

- Park at the Dyea campground and walk to the trailhead. At the far end of your trek, take the charter boat across Bennett Lake to Carcross. From there you can catch the highway bus to Skagway and take a shuttle-bus back to the Dyea campground.

- Park at the Dyea campground, do your hike, and then follow the railway tracks out to Log Cabin, about 12 kilometres (7.5 miles). Then take a shuttle-bus back to Dyea. (Note, however, that hiking the tracks is not recommended by the railway company.)

- Park at Log Cabin and ride a shuttle-bus to the Dyea campground. Then, when you hike out to Log Cabin, your vehicle will be waiting for you.

- Park in Skagway and take the shuttle-bus to the Dyea trailhead. Arrange your hike so that you arrive at Bennett Lake in time to catch a scheduled White Pass and Yukon Railway trip to Skagway.

- It's easiest if you have two vehicles to work with. Leave one at Log Cabin and use the other one to bring everybody to the trailhead at Dyea. After the hike, drive back to Dyea for the other vehicle.

Part of the Chilkoot Trail.

- Hike the trail all or part way and retrace your steps to your starting point.

You will need to make reservations for any of the above buses, trains or boats. Phone Chilkoot Water Charters at 1-403-821-3209 for the trip across Bennett Lake to Carcross. (The charter operators can also tell you the highway bus schedule.) Phone Frontier Excursions at 1-907-983-2512 for shuttle-bus services between Skagway, Log Cabin and the Dyea campground. Phone 1-800-343-7373 for the train schedule. (For any service that crosses the border, be sure to check the time zone for the departure and arrival times. Also, carry proof of citizenship for customs and immigration checks.)

Helpful Hiking Hints

No matter what time of year you hike the Chilkoot Trail, you can expect snow, rain, wind, sun, mist and cloud. When travelling over snow bridges, undo the belt on your pack so that if you fall through you can get out of your pack easily.

When walking in snow, do not step close to any boulders or outcroppings that stick out, or you may fall into a hole. When the sun heats a rock, the heat radiating from the rock melts the snow beneath the top layer, leaving an overhang near the boulder. This overhang can collapse if you step on it. Stop near a boulder to listen for the water gurgling around it. If your group is walking through an avalanche area, spread out.

Bring sandals to wear around camp and also to put on when crossing wet areas or streams, to keep your boots dry. Carry a rope to hang your food and garbage out of reach of bears. Carry an extra set of clothing in case you get wet or cold. Avoid wearing jeans, because they can chafe your legs, can prevent freedom of movement and are hard to dry when wet.

Bears like to use the trail, too. If you meet one, walk slowly backward away from it into the forest until it is no longer interested in you (but keep track of where the trail is!) and wait for it to pass.

reach of hungry bruins. Never keep any food with you in your tent.

There is a spot along the Taiya River here where you can relax, take off your boots and soak your feet, if you wish.

Canyon City Campsite is nearly 5 kilometres (3 miles) from Finnegan's Point. The log shelter here has a verandah with a table on it where you can eat outside on pleasant days.

To reach the actual site of Canyon City, continue along the trail for 0.8 kilometres (0.5 miles) past the camp until you reach a sign with the distances to various places along the trail.

Follow the path to the left, cross over the wooden bridge and then the suspension bridge. You soon reach a sign that marks Canyon City Historical Site. You are now walking where Canyon City stood over one hundred years ago. Past an old, rusted cook stove you come to a huge, rusted boiler with 'Union Iron Works SF 1886' stamped on it. This 50-horsepower steam boiler was used to operate an aerial tramway between here and the Chilkoot Pass. It cost 16.5 cents per kilogram (7.5 cents per pound) to send goods over this tram. That worked out to about $150 for the minimum outfit and not everyone could afford it.

Back on the main trail, you reach Pleasant Camp 4.5 kilometres (2.7 miles) from Canyon City. The climb out of the canyon between the two camps was thought by some stampeders to be the worst part of the trail.

A little ways past the camp you cross a suspension bridge over a series of cascades. Another 2 kilometres (1.2 miles) brings you to Sheep Camp, which is beside the Taiya River. At this camp, the last stop before the Chilkoot Pass, every day at 7 PM Alaska time a ranger gives a talk about the conditions at the pass. In addition, the ranger will remind you to leave no later than 7 AM the next day, to drink 2 litres (2 quarts) of water on the trail (get it from the river and filter/purify it), and to expect to take about 10 hours to reach Happy Camp, the next campsite.

When you leave Sheep Camp, the ground is level for the first while. At one point you come across a building that looks almost like a train station. Then, after you begin climbing, there is an old log building with glass windows, a little patio and cooking utensils hanging on the wall. Although you are mostly on a path as you climb, sometimes you need to clamber over boulders. After about 1.6 kilometres (1 mile), you start to come out of the forest into the alpine meadows.

When crossing the boulders, watch for the cairns (piles of rocks) on them that mark the trail, or you may get lost.

Up until mid-July, and beginning again in September, you could be walking on snow as you approach the pass. It is a 6.8-kilometre (4.2-mile) climb from Sheep Camp to the Scales. The Scales were so named because it was where the prospectors who had hired professional Native packers had to reweigh their goods. The packers wanted more money, up to $2.20 per kilogram ($1 per pound) to carry the supplies up and over the pass. Consequently, many items were left behind and some can still be seen today.

From the Scales you can see the Chilkoot Pass across the valley. You cross alpine tundra to reach the base of the pass. Further along the valley from the Chilkoot Pass is Peterson Pass, a longer but easier Chilkoot alternative that was used by some Klondikers.

Above the Scales, Klondikers who travelled the trail in winter climbed the Golden Stairs, which were cut into the ice and snow up to the pass. Those who came in summer, when the snow had melted, had to traverse the huge boulders and loose rock left by a slide. Today this part of the trail is much as it was then.

The climb is steep and you must lean forward to prevent the weight of your pack from pulling you over backward. Some people go slowly, working their way from solid rock to solid rock, while others hike through the loose rock as they would climb stairs.

Watch for mountain goats, either across the valley or beside the slide. Also look for rufous hummingbirds, which are attracted to red clothing, flitting about. If you are not afraid of heights, stop and look down to see how far you have come.

Just before the top you reach a plateau. On the plateau, look up to your right to see a cairn that marks the border between Alaska and BC.

When you reach the summit, you have climbed 823 metres (2700 feet) above Sheep Camp. A shelter and an outhouse are located here. Stay only long enough to warm up and eat, because it is still a 6.4-kilometre (4-mile) hike to Happy Camp and storms can come up suddenly at the top.

As you hike down the Canadian side of the summit, you have the most magnificent view of Crater Lake, alpine tundra and the surrounding

Toilet at the Chilkoot Pass Summit.

mountains. The wind blows almost constantly here. There are a lot of streams to cross—some have rocks to hop across on, while at others you just have to look for the shallowest spot. Again, depending on the time of year, you could be walking on snow in places. Watch for the short, colourful flowers—in purple, white, red, yellow and pink—and the grasses of the alpine tundra. Do not walk on the tundra, because it is not easy for the flowers and grass to grow here.

At Stone Crib there is a pile of rocks that anchored the cables for an aerial tramway on this side of the summit. There is also a large sawmill blade that someone decided he did not need anymore.

If it was cloudy on the Alaskan side of the summit, look back from this side, as you are walking, to see the grey cloud hanging over the summit—it looks like it is stuck there. Although it usually does not get any closer to you, mist sometimes rolls this way from the summit.

Happy Camp is on a river between Crater Lake and Long Lake, both of which are beautiful. The food cache here is inside a section of the shelter.

For a short distance after Happy Camp, you are walking on loose gravel. When you reach a sign pointing toward Deep Lake, turn in that direction. You will climb and soon be up above Long Lake. In the gold-rush days, there were ferries on Crater, Long and Deep lakes for those who could afford the price.

You hike up and down the hills and then suddenly you come over a rise and see a lovely lake, a bridge over a river, trees, and a camp in the centre of the mountains.

Across that bridge, you reach Deep Lake Camp. A wagon road ran from here to Lindeman City. You can see some old sleigh runners at the camp.

When you leave Deep Lake Camp, as you walk beside the lakeshore, watch for a metal boat frame. After you leave the lakeshore, the trail follows Deep Lake Gorge.

The further you go, the more trees there are. It is very beautiful and peaceful as you walk among the tall pine trees. You reach Lake Lindeman Camp nearly 5 kilome-

Looking down on ice on Crater Lake from the Chilkoot Pass Summit.

tres (3 miles) from Deep Lake Camp. There are two campgrounds, one close to the lake and one further away. You might want to take the one further away, because the wind coming off the lake can be strong and cool.

The Klondikers set up a tent city here and some of them built boats during winter for sailing across Lake Lindeman. At the other end, they portaged around the rapids between Lindeman and Bennett lakes. Others carried their supplies along Lindeman Lake and built their boats at Bennett Lake.

So that future visitors can have the same quality of experience as you did, please do not disturb the historic sites at Lindeman Lake. It is worth a visit to the tent museum near the river. As you are leaving Lindeman Camp, alongside the trail there is a small roof-covered panel with a drawer. Inside the drawer there is a book for you to record details about your party and its destination. In case of an emergency, this logbook helps the wardens to keep track of who has passed through here.

Watch for the rufous hummingbirds again along this part of the trail. If you are wearing red, one might come and hover over you and then dart off to sit in a tree. Keep your camera handy, because these birds move quickly.

One Ton of Supplies

Because of concerns about greenhorns starving or freezing to death during the long, bitterly cold winters in the North, the North-West Mounted Police required each Klondiker entering the Yukon Territory to have one year's worth of equipment and provisions. Although the various accounts differ as to the items required and their quantities, a complete outfit added up to about 900 kilograms (2000 pounds).

Here is a list of a typical Klondiker's inventory (without quantities):

Clothing: flannel overshirts, pants, a sweater, stockings, wool socks, underwear, overalls, mitts, leather gloves, coats, a vest, a mackinaw, moccasins, rubber boots, high walking boots and a stiff-brimmed cowboy hat.

Sleeping Supplies: a sleeping bag, wool blankets, a waterproof blanket, a rubber sheet and a tent.

Food: beans or split peas, flour, bacon, rolled oats, butter, rice, sugar, cornmeal, condensed milk, coffee, tea, salt, pepper, baking powder, baking soda, yeast cakes, mustard, vinegar, beef extract, ground ginger, hard tack, Jamaica ginger, citric acid, evaporated peaches, apricots, apples, onions and potatoes.

Cooking Utensils: a coffee pot, a pie plate (as a dinner plate), cutlery (including a large spoon), a frying pan, a cup, a saucepan, a pail and a sheet-iron stove.

Toiletries: a wash basin, soap, towels, a toothbrush, a medicine chest, handkerchiefs, a mirror and a comb.

Panning Equipment: a pick and an extra handle, a shovel and a gold pan.

Building Equipment: an axe and an extra handle, an axe stone, nails, pitch, a chisel, a tape measure, a rope, a single block pulley, rivets, saws, a plane, files and a hatchet.

Miscellaneous: canvas sacks, matches, buttons, needles, thread, pack straps, a knife, a compass, candles, candlewick, a dunnage bag and mosquito netting.

If you like the haunting call of the loon, plan to stay at Bare Loon Camp, about 5 kilometres (3 miles) beyond Lindeman Lake Camp. Shortly after Bare Loon Camp, a cut-off leads to the tracks of the White Pass and Yukon Railway. Many hikers go only this far on the trail and hike along the tracks to Log Cabin. Although this short-cut is a popular way of getting off the trail, the railway company warns that you should not walk on or beside the tracks. If you do decide to walk to Log Cabin, find out the schedule of the train and, even if there is no train scheduled, watch for unscheduled speeders carrying maintenance crews.

Bennett Lake campground is 6.4 kilometres (4 miles) from Bare Loon Camp. Here the two long, tired columns of Klondikers—those from Chilkoot Pass and those from White Pass—met in late 1897 and early 1898 and spent the winter. They established an instant tent town. In spring the stampeders built boats for the sail across the lake and down the Yukon. The town of Bennett grew after the railway from Skagway reached it in 1899. It had warehouses, shipping offices and steamer docks.

St. Andrews Presbyterian Church, built in 1898 by volunteer workers, is the only gold-rush building still standing in Bennett. If you are tired of hiking, you can get onto a train at the station here.

Once you have gotten back to your vehicle, drive back up the South Klondike Highway to Carcross to continue with Chapter 10.

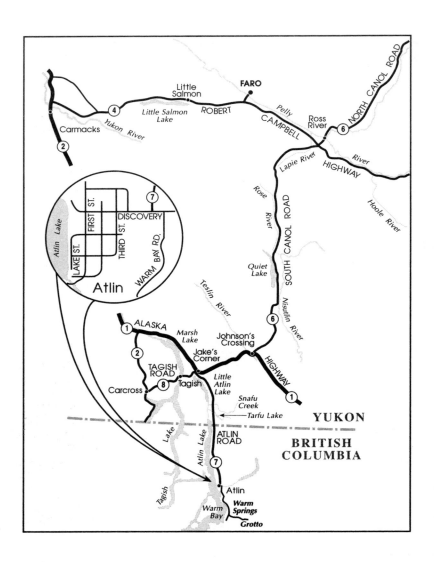

10
Carcross to Ross River to Watson Lake

While following this chapter, you will travel beside the largest natural lake in British Columbia; drive on a road built for a pipeline that was in use for less than two years; and visit a modern town established to house the workers of a lead, zinc and silver mine. Most of what you will see on this trip is Mother Nature's scenery.

Carcross to Atlin

Carcross, Tagish and Atlin Road

From Carcross, take the Tagish Road (Highway 8), which goes toward Tagish. The Tagish Store and Cafe is to your left at kilometre 32 (mile 19.9). The Tagish Recreation Site is at kilometre 32.9 (mile 20.4) and then you reach the Tagish Bridge and the Tagish River, which connects Tagish Lake with Marsh Lake.

The Tagish Bridge is a very popular place for fishing. A walkway is along the north side of the bridge. You can fish for northern pike, arctic grayling or whitefish and, if you are here in late June or July, you might want to try for the lake trout, which are said to be the finest in Yukon. At the end of the bridge there is a marina that sells fishing supplies. The road becomes gravel after the bridge.

Atlin Museum.

At kilometre 52.5 (mile 32.6) from the junction, you reach the road southward to Atlin (Highway 7). Turn right onto it (you would end up at the Alaska Highway if you went straight ahead). The road to Atlin is also gravel. At kilometre 2.8 (mile 1.7) from the turn-off, you round a curve and can see Little Atlin Lake ahead. A boat launch is on the lakeshore at kilometre 3.7 (mile 2.3).

Kilometre 24.9 (mile 15.5) brings you to Snafu Creek and the road to Snafu Lake Campground is to your left at kilometre 26.3 (mile 16.3). The road to Atlin was constructed by the US Army and 'Snafu' is an army term that is short for 'Situation Normal, All Fouled Up.'

As you head southward you can occasionally see Mount Minto in front of you. The road to Tarfu Lake Campground is to your left at kilometre 32.7 (mile 20.3). Tarfu Lake is stocked with rainbow trout. Its name comes from another army term, which is short for 'Things Are Really Fouled Up.'

At kilometre 41.4 (mile 25.7) you cross the Yukon–BC border. You can occasionally catch sight of Atlin Lake through the trees to your right. Finally, at kilometre 44.4 (mile 27.6), the lake is directly to your right, with Mount Minto across it. At 789 square kilometres (305 square miles), Atlin Lake is the largest natural lake in BC. The highway follows the lake from here to the town of Atlin, giving you good views of it and the Coast Mountains on the other side.

The gravel changes to pavement at kilometre 64.4 (mile 40). Then, at kilometre 80.1 (mile 49.8), Davie Hall Lake is to your right. Although it is a good area for birding, you have to park on the roadside because there is no parking area.

At kilometre 93.3 (mile 58) you reach the junction with Discovery Avenue. The road to your left goes to the old site of Discovery, Surprise Lake, Warm Bay and the airport. Turn right to go into Atlin, which bills itself as 'the Switzerland of the North.'

Atlin

Atlin's visitor reception centre and the Atlin Historical Museum are in a 1902 schoolhouse on Third Street. Classes were held in this building until 1968.

Some old machinery is in the museum yard. Take a look at the two steam shovels. They were bought in Detroit and brought to the area in the mid-1930s to work at a claim to the southeast on Spruce Creek. Some people believe that either one or both of these steam shovels worked on the Panama Canal in the early 1900s.

Steam shovel at Atlin Historical Museum.

Drive down to Lake Street, which runs along the shore of Atlin Lake, and look at the two boats sitting on the beach. The MV *Tarahne*, built in 1917, was the first propeller-driven, gas-powered boat in the North. The ship was lengthened from 23.8 metres (78 feet) to 36.3 metres (119 feet) in 1928 to haul more cargo and passengers and then removed from service in 1936. The *Tarahne* has now been restored—ask about tours at the visitor centre.

Beside the *Tarahne* is a small boat, the Atlinto. Built in 1914, it hauled freight and supplies, towed log booms and was used as a tour boat until it was beached in the late 1950s.

The older buildings in the town have signs on them that give some of their history. For example, the Moose Hall was constructed in nearby Discovery in 1905 as the settlement's Arctic Brotherhood Hall. Later it was split into two and moved to Atlin, where it was reassembled and became the Moose Lodge and Community Hall. Today, its windows are boarded up.

St. Martin's Anglican Episcopalian Church sits at the corner of Third Street and Trainor Avenue. The first service to be held in this church was on Easter Sunday in 1900, and it was performed by the Reverend F.L. Stephenson.

The Globe Theatre, on Pearl Avenue at Second Street, was built in 1917 by Edwin Pillman, who wanted to lift everyone's spirits after the second fire in two years had raged through Atlin. In those days, motion pictures were run through hand-cranked projectors. When it was almost time for a picture to start, a young boy would be sent to run through the streets ringing a bell to alert the residents. Besides the moving pictures, live theatre, boxing matches, Christmas concerts and band performances were also held here.

When Edwin Pillman retired and moved south in the 1940s, the theatre was closed and it slowly fell into disrepair. In 1977 the movie *Never Cry Wolf* was filmed in Atlin, and the Globe was fixed up enough to be used in some scenes. It was not until 1995 that the Atlin Historical Society, which eventually came to own the Globe, was able to begin restoration. It was completed in 1998, in time for Atlin's gold-rush centennial.

Head eastward on Discovery Avenue past the junction at Atlin Road by an additional 0.4 kilometres (0.2 miles) and then turn right onto Warm Bay Road. This road bends to follow Atlin Lake and, at kilometre 11.4 (mile 7.1), there is a pull-out to your right at a viewpoint for Llewellyn Glacier, which is across the lake and at the end of an arm. The glacier looks big enough with the naked eye but binoculars will show just how large it really is.

Atlin Gold

Gold was discovered in Pine Creek on July 27, 1898, by a German immigrant named Fritz Miller and a Nova Scotian named Kenny McLaren. When word of the strike reached the outside, miners who had been on their way to Dawson City had second thoughts about going to the Klondike where, they had heard, there was no more good ground left to claim.

Three thousand of these miners headed instead to Pine Creek and proceeded to stake claims on it and other creeks in the area. Soon the towns of Atlin and Pine City, later renamed 'Discovery,' were established. Discovery, 7 kilometres (4.3 miles) east of Atlin, grew to be a tent city of 10,000 people.

In 1904, the British American Dredging Company and the British Columbia Dredging Company had dredges working in the area. Both companies moved their dredges out in 1908. Even when the gold rush ended, many miners stayed on and continued to make a living. By 1960, though, the population of Discovery had dwindled to just two.

When you reach a Y in the road, take the right fork. Warm Bay Forest Service Recreation Site, with a small pebble beach, is to your right at kilometre 22.4 (mile 13.9).

Turn left at kilometre 23.2 (mile 14.4) to visit Warm Springs. The small natural pool, set in a large meadow, has a pebble bottom. Clear water bubbles out of the ground to fill the approximately 0.5-metre (1.6–foot) deep pool and then overflows at one end. You can just lie back and relax in this warm water, which has no sulphur smell. There are no picnic tables and there is no camping area, but there is a garbage container.

At kilometre 2.7 (mile 1.7) from the springs, you reach Grotto Forest Service Recreation Site. (If you brought a holiday trailer, leave it here, because the turn-around place up ahead is quite small.) Just past the recreation site you cross Grotto Creek. Look to your left to see the cave that gives the site its name. It is set back in the trees and you can see the underground creek flow out from under a rock, covered by tree roots, into a very small clearing surrounded by trees. There is just room enough to walk under the trees and sit beside the cave. It is a 'must' stop.

Turn around and head back to Tagish Road, because the road is not maintained beyond this point.

Jake's Corner to Watson Lake

Jake's Corner and the South Canol Road

Back at the junction with the road to Tagish, turn right and in 1.7 kilometres (1.1 miles) you reach the Alaska Highway at Jake's Corner. Turn right onto the Alaska Highway and drive the 46.5 kilometres (28.9 miles) to Johnson's Crossing.

One kilometre (0.6 miles) past Johnson's Crossing, turn left onto the South Canol Road (Highway 6). Make sure that you gas up first, though, because there are no services until the village of Ross River, some 230 kilometres (143 miles) hence. Also, check your brakes before beginning this road—you will encounter some steep hills.

Plan for a long, slow drive on a narrow, winding road with a speed limit of 60 kilometres per hour (about 35 miles per hour). Although there are no human-made tourist attractions along this route, the nature-made sights are lovely and the time will pass quickly.

As you head northward, you cross creeks and rivers and see mountains and valleys. Spruce trees are interspersed with pine. If you travel this road early in the morning or on an overcast day with mist, you will be rewarded with haunting scenery. Although there are some side roads along the way, they lead to private land or gravel pits.

While driving this highway, watch for moose walking down the road in the early morning or evening—perhaps you will see one at kilometre 22.3 (mile 13.9) as you cross Moose Creek.

In places it is as if you are driving down a scenic country lane. There is not much traffic on this road, so feel free to stop, get out of your vehicle and take a deep breath of the warm-summer-day-in-the-country smell.

Use care and keep to your side of the road when you see signs, such as the one at kilometre 48.8 (mile 30.3), that warn of 'blind hills.' At kilometre 76.7 (mile 47.7) you reach the Quiet Lake Campground, which offers a boat launch and a picnic area. You briefly leave the approximately 28-kilometre (17-mile) long lake as the road climbs and descends and then, at kilometre 87.8 (mile 54.6), you cross Lake Creek and are down beside Quiet Lake again. Quiet Lake Recreation Site is to the left at kilometre 98.3 (mile 61.1). Just after the recreation site is the Quiet Lake Maintenance Shop, which maintains this part of the road. Beside the highway in front of the facility stand an old pull grader and an old truck that date from when the Canol Road was built.

You cross the Rose River six times between kilometre 105 (mile 65.2) and kilometre 155.1 (mile 96.4).

The Canol Project

After the Japanese bombing of Pearl Harbor on December 7, 1941, the US military became concerned about the security of its operations in Alaska. Construction on the Canol (Canada Oil) Project was begun in the spring of 1942. Intending to secure a steady supply of oil for the airfields in Alaska, one that was protected from Japanese warships (and to fuel equipment being used to build the Alaska Highway), the military constructed a pipeline south from an oilfield that had been in production since the 1920s at Norman Wells, NWT. Besides the pipeline, a refinery was built in Whitehorse, 10 pumping stations were set up, airstrips were constructed, telephone lines were run and the Canol Road was laid to help transport the workers, equipment and supplies into place.

The project's cost, originally predicted at $30 million, rose to over $134 million.

The feared Japanese attack did not materialize and the war ended, so the project was shut down in 1945, less that a year after the pipeline was completed. Incidentally, a few years later the refinery was sold to Imperial Oil, disassembled and shipped to Edmonton, Alberta.

Lapie Canyon on
South Canol Road.

At kilometre 172.7 (mile 107.3) you cross the Lapie River for the first time and then climb above it to drive along its canyon. You descend to the river again at kilometre 190 (mile 118.1), only to climb again after crossing Fox Creek. The road narrows, with a rock wall to your left and a drop-off into the canyon to your right. You descend into and climb out of the canyon before you cross the Lapie River again at kilometre 212.8 (mile 132.2). You then follow the canyon for 2 kilometres (1.2 miles) more.

At kilometre 220.2 (mile 136.8) you reach the Robert Campbell Highway (Highway 4), named for an explorer who became the first Hudson's Bay Company trader in the area. Turn left here to continue on to Faro, Ross River and the North Canol Highway. If you would rather go directly to Watson Lake, turn right instead (see 'Robert Campbell Highway to Watson Lake' on p. 209).

Almost immediately after turning onto the Campbell Highway you reach the old road to Ross River, which is about 9 kilometres (5.6 miles) away; it is very scenic but steep. Continue along the highway and, at kilometre 8 (mile 5) on your right, you reach the northbound turn-off for the continuation of the Canol Road; Ross River is 10 kilometres (6.2 miles) along it. Continue straight instead to visit Faro first. At kilometre 9.4 (mile 5.8) you cross the Lapie River. Look to the right to see its gorgeous canyon.

At kilometre 60.6 (mile 37.6), turn right to go to Faro. You cross the Pelly River in 8 kilometres (5 miles). Then turn right into Faro, just 1 kilometre (0.6 miles) past the bridge.

Faro

The visitor reception centre is in the green-roofed log building to your right as you come into town. The building is also an interpretive centre that contains pictures and displays of the history of the area, including the building of the Canol Road and other war efforts in the Yukon, and the local lead, zinc, and silver mine. Also be sure to take a look at the mammoth tusk.

Faro is above the Tintina Trench (see p. 172), through which the Pelly River flows here. This mining town was established in 1969 to house the employees of the Cyprus Anvil Mining Corporation. During its construction, the town was destroyed by fire and had to be rebuilt. It has twice survived the closing of the largest open-pit lead, zinc and silver mine in the world. Check at the visitor centre to see if the mine is open and if tours are available.

If you want to take a short hike to see a waterfall, take the road into John Connelly Park, which is across the road from the visitor centre. The 1.3-kilometre (0.8-mile) VanGorder Creek Trail to the falls begins just 0.3 kilometres (0.2 miles) into the park at a turn-around, where you can park if you drove in. Bring insect repellent and a hat, if the day is sunny. The woodchip path crosses two roads before getting into the woods (for guidance, watch for the hiker sign on a post).

After climbing, you descend to cross VanGorder Creek on a footbridge and begin climbing up the other side. Soon you reach a platform that overlooks the falls. Although the falls are not very spectacular, the hike through the trees is quiet and relaxing.

Return to the Robert Campbell Highway. Turn left to return to the Canol Road and continue on to Ross River. (Although this book does not cover the westernmost part of it, the Campbell Highway continues past Faro

Falls at Faro.

to Carmacks and the Klondike Highway [Highway 2]. It is mainly paved with some gravel areas around Little Salmon.)

Ross River

As you return along the Campbell Highway in the direction of Ross River, turn onto the first road for Ross River that you come to, at kilometre 60.6 (mile 37.7) from the turn-off for Faro.

You reach the welcome sign for Ross River 9.6 kilometres (6 miles) from the Campbell Highway. Beside it is an old Ford pickup truck left from the building of the Canol Road. The community of Ross River began as a trading post on the far bank of the Pelly River, where the Ross River flows into it. When the Canol Road was completed in the early 1940s, it linked Ross River with the outside. The village, which consists mainly of people belonging to the Ross River Dena Council of the Kaska Nation, was moved to its present site on this side of the Pelly River in 1964.

As you drive into the village, look to your left to see the old pull grader in front of the Ross River Maintenance Camp. Continue on this road to the Pelly River and the barge that will take you across. The barge operates from 8 AM to noon and from 1 PM to 5 PM. There is also a footbridge over the river.

Before you head out, especially if the weather has been wet, check with the barge operator or another local resident about the condition of the North Canol Road, which begins north of the Pelly River.

The North Canol Road

The North Canol Road has some steep hills and is narrow in places. The speed limit is 60 kilometres per hour (about 35 miles per hour), and there are bad spots where you have to go even slower. Sections of the road can get slippery and people have had to wait for them to dry before returning to Ross River. Some of the local people recommend that you go only as far as Sheldon Lake, but they do say that the occasional visitor has gone as far as Macmillan Pass.

Ross River flowing into the Pelly River.

One kilometre (0.6 miles) from the river crossing, a right turn into the forest leads to the old townsite of Ross River (and, just beyond, there is another turn-off into the area). It is now a wide, open field with one lone log building standing in the middle. From here you can see where the Ross River flows into the Pelly.

The North Canol Road follows the Ross River for the next 9 kilometres (5.6 miles), although trees sometimes block your view of it. The scenery at the beginning is not as pretty as on the South Canol, but keep going—it does improve.

The road climbs and descends and winds its way beside lakes and valleys and through the forest. Watch for the signs that warn of more blind hills and notice the burn areas—the policy governing forest fires here is that if the trees are not marketable, no one bothers fighting the fire.

At kilometre 112.5 (mile 69.9), an industrial garbage dump is situated in a burn area to your left. Among the items in the dump is the nose section of a Scottish Aviation Twin Pioneer airplane that crashed in the area. This transport plane, of which just 3 of the 87 that were built in 1955 are known to still be flightworthy, is considered by many to be one of the safest planes made. However, nothing is known about the circumstances surrounding the crash of this one.

Between crossing Twin Creek No. 1, at kilometre 114.4 (mile 71.1), and Twin Creek No. 2, you pass Twin Creek Maintenance Camp, which is on your left. Around kilometre 121 (mile 75) you can see large Mount Sheldon ahead.

At kilometre 127.1 (mile 79), you round a curve and Sheldon Lake comes into view. There is a side road that leads to the lake at kilometre 128.7 (mile 80).

When you reach kilometre 151.3 (mile 94), look to your left to see a row of old machinery and vehicles that were used in the construction of the Canol Road and were then left here when the project was abandoned. To your right is an old skid shack where some of the construction workers lived. Just past the row of vehicles, look to your left again to see a slight slope with concrete foundations on it. Climb the hill to see all that remains of a depot where construction vehicles were repaired.

At kilometre 152.7 (mile 94.9), another row of abandoned vehicles is to your left. Although these vehicles are almost overgrown by trees, you can still make out some lettering on the doors. In an hour or so you reach more abandoned vehicles, this time on the right, at kilometre 207 (mile 128.6). Then the road climbs to Macmillan Pass, elevation 1366 metres (4482 feet), and the border between the Yukon and the NWT, which you reach at kilometre 231 (mile 143.5). Although you might be able to drive a little further, it is not recommended. From here to Norman Wells, the Canol Road has become a 370-kilometre (230-mile) heritage trail, which most hikers (and a few courageous cyclists) begin at the far end.

The mountain scenery is much better on the return trip to the Campbell Highway. If possible, time your return for the evening, when the setting sun gives the mountains a coppery gold colour.

Robert Campbell Highway
to Watson Lake

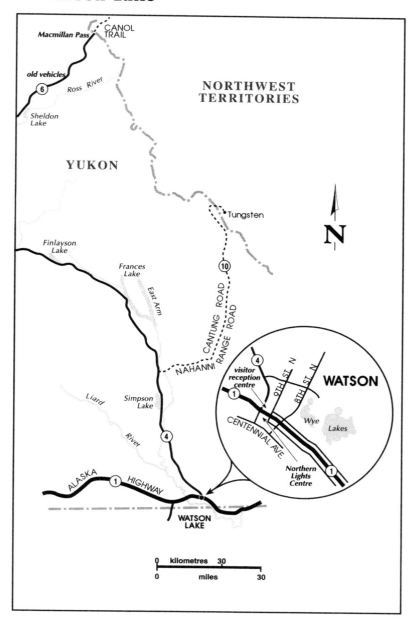

Restoring the Finlayson Caribou Herd

In 1982 the size of the Finlayson Caribou herd was about two thousand animals and it was declining. The Yukon government and the area's First Nations decided to work together to restore the herd to a more acceptable size.

The survival of the animals is affected by diseases, parasites, weather, food supply, hunters and predators. Although only hunters and predators could be controlled, the hunting of caribou was still drastically reduced; 454 wolves were 'removed' (killed) between 1983 and 1989.

By 1990 the caribou herd had increased to five thousand and moose numbers had doubled. Hunting continued to be limited but the wolf population was left to recover, which it had by 1992.

Today hunting of the Finlayson herd continues to be curtailed and the numbers of caribou, moose and wolf are still being carefully watched.

The Robert Campbell Highway between the Canol Road and Watson Lake, where it meets the Alaska Highway, is mainly gravel. Like the other roads in this chapter, it is has its ups and downs, its narrowness, and its lovely scenery.

Coffee Lake, which is to the right at kilometre 3.6 (mile 2.2) from the junction with the South Canol Road, is stocked with trout. You can also see a tall ridge of the Campbell Range on your right.

Just before you cross the Hoole River at kilometre 52 (mile 32.3), you can turn off for the parking area at the confluence of the Hoole and Pelly rivers, where you can try your hand at panning for gold. Do not expect to have much luck, however. You can also see the confluence of the rivers from the bridge.

A turn-off to the left leads to Finlayson Lake, 72 kilometres (44.7 miles) from the Hoole River crossing. You can picnic, camp and boat here, but the fishing is no good because, it is said, Native net-fishing activity took out most or all of the fish over a decade ago.

Finlayson Lake, which is 16 kilometres (10 miles) long, was named by Robert Campbell for Duncan Finlayson, who was a member of the Hudson's Bay Company's board of directors. Although the lake's waters flow to the Beaufort Sea via the Liard and Mackenzie rivers, it is next to the Continental Divide, so the rivers to the north and west of the lake, and some to the south, deliver their water via the Yukon River to the Bering Sea instead.

The Finlayson Caribou herd spends its winter in the lowlands of the area around the lake. In summer, the herd heads for the higher elevations of the St. Cyr and Logan mountain ranges to the west, south and east of here.

There is a left turn for Frances Lake Campground 61 kilometres (37.9 miles) from Finlayson Lake. Here you can picnic, camp or boat. In 1840 Robert Campbell named this lake in honour of Lady Frances Simpson, the wife of the governor of the Hudson's Bay Company, Sir George Simpson. The company built its first fort in the Yukon at the southern end of Frances Lake in 1842. It was abandoned nine years later.

Viewpoint at Finlayson Lake.

At 63.6 kilometres (39.5 miles) from the Frances Lake turn-off, the Cantung (Canada Tungsten) Road goes left to the townsite of Tungsten (in the NWT) and the Canada Tungsten Mining Corporation Mine, which began operation in the early 1960s and shut down in 1986. Although some maps show this road, also known as 'the Nahanni Range Road' (Highway 10), as an active highway, there is a barricade at the beginning of it, along with a sign that states that the road is closed because of washouts and no maintenance. This 200-kilometre (124-mile) road serves as a hiking trail, and there are no plans to reopen it to traffic because, with the mine closed, there is no economic reason to do so.

It is 98.3 kilometres (61.1 miles) from the Cantung Road to Watson Lake. At Watson Lake take one last look at your sign in the 'the Sign Post Forest' (see p. 33) before heading home (if you live to the south) via the Alaska Highway and Dawson Creek or via the Cassiar Highway, the Yellowhead Highway and Prince George. (Chapter 11, as noted in Chapter 1, covers the side trip from Haines Junction, Yukon, to Haines, Alaska.)

'M & J' sign my husband and I put up at Watson Lake signposts in 1987.

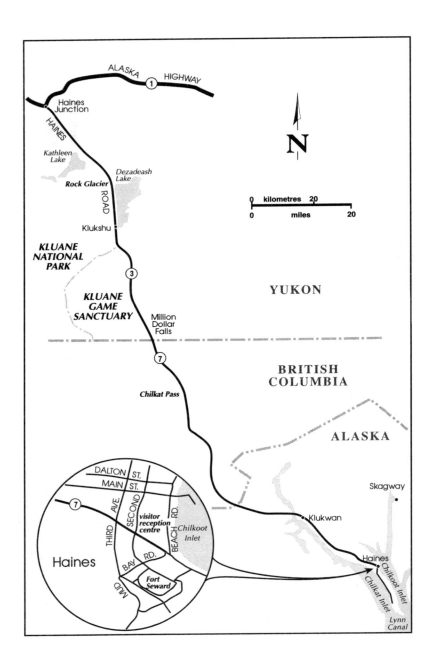

ALASKA HIGHWAY

1

Haines
Junction

HAINES

Kathleen
Lake

Dezadeash
Lake

Rock Glacier

ROAD

Klukshu

*KLUANE
NATIONAL
PARK*

3

*KLUANE
GAME
SANCTUARY*

Million
Dollar
Falls

7

Chilkat Pass

YUKON

**BRITISH
COLUMBIA**

ALASKA

Skagway

Klukwan

Haines

Chilkoot Inlet

Chilkat Inlet

Lynn
Canal

N

kilometres 20

miles 20

DALTON ST.

MAIN ST.

7

SECOND

AVE

THIRD

*visitor
reception
centre*

BEACH RD.

*Chilkoot
Inlet*

Haines

BAY RD.

MUD

*Fort
Seward*

11
Haines Junction to Haines

You will be travelling with Kluane National Park and Preserve to your right as you drive south from Haines Junction, Yukon, on the Haines Road, which is also known as 'the Haines Cut-off' and 'the Haines Highway' (Highway 3 in the Yukon, Highway 7 in Alaska). There is only one road into the park, and one campground, but there are a number of hiking trails that enter the park.

As you leave Kluane National Park and Preserve behind, you will enter BC and the Tatshenshini–Alsek Wilderness Provincial Park will be to your right (but there are no access roads). Once you cross the Canada–US border, you will enter Alaska. Further toward Haines, this chapter takes you through the Alaska Chilkat Bald Eagle Preserve.

Watch for grizzlies along this highway. Time your travelling to take into account that the US customs port at Dalton Cache is open only from 8 AM until midnight Alaska time.

Haines Junction to Haines

Kathleen Lake and the Rock Glacier

Kathleen Lake.

As you leave behind the Alaska Highway and Haines Junction (see p. 48), you cross the Dezadeash River. At kilometre 6.5 (mile 4) from the river, the trailhead for the Auriol Hiking Trail is to the right. This trail is the first of many into the park from the Haines Road.

Beginning at about kilometre 12 (mile 7.5) you can see the beautiful deep bluish-green of Kathleen Lake surrounded by mountains. You cross the Kathleen River at kilometre 24.7 (mile 15.3). The race of rainbow trout in the Kathleen River is the only native one in the Yukon—other rainbows in the Yukon have been brought in from elsewhere. To protect them, fishing on the entire length of the river downstream of Kluane National Park is strictly catch-and-release with barbless hooks. These rules also apply to Lower Kathleen, Rainbow and Crescent lakes and to all of their tributary systems. (Check a current copy of the Yukon fishing regulations for updates.)

You pass Kathleen Lake Lodge, where they have a restaurant, a service station and cabins, on the left and then you reach the right turn for Kathleen Lake at 1.6 kilometres (1 mile) from the Kathleen River.

A campground and the lake are just a short distance down this side road. You can camp, picnic, swim, boat and hike along the lakeshore or fish for kokanee salmon here. Kokanee are actually sockeye salmon that, because of a blockage in the river in

Kluane National Park

Kluane National Park, established in 1972, is Canada's highest mountain park. Icefields cover half of its area and at one point the ice is reported to be 1.6 kilometres (1 mile) thick. Mount Logan, Canada's highest peak, at 5959 metres (19,550 feet) according to Natural Resources Canada, is within the park.

Kluane is a true wilderness park, with just one road into it and only basic camping facilities, although hiking and mountain-climbing are popular within its boundaries. Kluane National Park is the Canadian part of a United Nations Educational, Scientific and Cultural Organization (UNESCO) World Heritage Site that also includes Alaska's Wrangell–St. Elias National Park.

The park supports thousands of animals, from snowshoe hares to grizzly bears. In fact, it has the largest protected population of grizzly bears in the world. Over 150 species of birds have been seen here, with 106 species nesting in the park. There are also about two hundred different types of alpine plants.

Incidentally, Kluane means 'place of many fish' in the South Tutchone language.

which they spawn, have been cut off from the saltwater part of their natural migration and have adapted to living entirely in fresh water. This situation happened here in the 1700s, when the advancing Lowell Glacier forced the sockeye to migrate to Kathleen Lake to spawn. The new generations adapted and have remained in the lake.

Rock Glacier.

The Rock Glacier pull-out is to your right, 17.4 kilometres (10.8 miles) from the Kathleen Lake turn-off. A rock glacier is formed when the bedrock of the mountainside is broken into pieces by the constant freezing and thawing of water over thousands of years. These large pieces slowly accumulate. The ice and meltwater allow them to slide down the mountain, creating an advancing glacier of rock that eventually stabilizes after the last of the ice melts.

Before starting on the interpretive trail, make sure that you are wearing good, sturdy shoes. The trail through the trees to the base of the rock glacier begins with boardwalk but parts of it are woodchip path. You can follow the trail as it continues onto the rock glacier—just remember that the rocks can be slippery and that they may slide under your feet as you descend. From the rock glacier you have a great view of Dezadeash Lake, which is across the highway, and the mountains behind it. Back at the parking lot, look up to see where the rock glacier starts, almost as high as the mountaintops.

Klukshu and the Million Dollar Falls

In 19.4 kilometres (12.1 miles) from the Rock Glacier pull-out, there is a left turn for the Tutchone village of Klukshu, which is less than 1 kilometre (0.6 miles) off the highway. Although it is traditionally a fishing village, the fishing has been restricted because of reduced salmon stocks. Amongst the old log houses are a gift shop and a museum that is open from time to time only. There are large display panels in the village with write-ups about the residents' fishing lifestyle. Pictures show, for instance, how fish traps were set up in the river to catch the fish.

You cross Klukshu Creek in 1.2 kilometres (0.7 miles) from the turn-off for the village and at kilometre 24.1 (mile 15) you cross Takhanne River. Just after crossing this river, turn onto the road to your right to go to the Million Dollar Falls and campground, which are 1.4 kilometres (0.9 miles) down the road. The campground is at the site of a construction camp that was set up during the building of the Haines Road in 1944.

Check the posted map to find the short trail to the falls. It leads from the parking lot to a fence along the canyon and there you go to your right. You can hear the

Drying Fish

The Southern Tutchone peoples of Klukshu have a long tradition of drying fish. Both men and women would catch the fish in traps or gaff them from the river bank. After they had been caught and killed, the fish would be left in the water for a number of days so that the flesh would harden a bit. When the fish were ready, the women would cut and clean them.

Drying racks were then set inside a small, square fenced-in area and the fish draped over them. A fire would be lit under the racks. A pole roof with brush on it was placed over the fish to protect them from the sun and rain.

The fire was kept burning under the fish as they dried to keep the flies away. The fish were turned every day. Depending on the weather, they could have taken up to 10 days to dry.

Fish-drying site.

falls before you reach the stairs that lead down to the viewpoint. Because of a curve in the canyon, you can not see the full height of the waterfall, which is 60 metres (197 feet) high.

Although there is much disagreement about how the waterfall got its name, there are at least four theories: it cost $1 million to build the road this far; $1 million worth of equipment is buried here; the construction camp cost $1 million to set up; and a plane with $1 million in payroll crashed near here. (If the last theory is the correct one, is the money still there?)

The BC Border and the Alaska Chilkat Bald Eagle Preserve

A sign welcomes you to British Columbia at kilometre 13.6 (mile 8.5) from the falls, and you begin driving beside Tatshenshini–Alsek Wilderness Provincial Park. You cross the Nadahini River at kilometre 50.5 (mile 31.4) and begin to climb slowly. In summer, look here for flowers amid the sparse tufts of grass. The height of the bushes and trees decreases as you go higher. Kilometre 57.4 (mile 35.7) brings you to the Haines Road (or Chilkat) Summit. The elevation here is 1070 metres (3510 feet).

You descend from the summit and at kilometre 12.7 (mile 7.9) from it there is a pull-out for you to check your brakes. As you descend, the trees become taller. At kilometre 15.2 (mile 9.4), as you cross Seltat Creek, look down and to your right to see the canyon.

Go through the Canadian Customs port at kilometre 30.6 (mile 19) and US Customs (the Dalton Cache Station) at kilometre 31.4 (mile 19.5). Jack Dalton built a trading post on the border here as part of his approximately 490-kilometre (305-mile) toll road, which largely followed established Native routes between tidewater and Fort Selkirk on the Yukon River. He opened it in the 1890s, before the

Klondike Gold Rush, and originally charged $1 for a man with a pack and $2.50 for each head of livestock. Later on, though it never became popular with Klondikers, those miners who took it had to pay $150 for travelling on his road. It fell into disuse after the completion of the White Pass and Yukon Railway.

The highway becomes steep and winding, with some curves posted at 50 kilometres per hour (30 miles per hour). At kilometre 46.4 (mile 28.8), you enter the Alaska Chilkat Bald Eagle Preserve. This 19,425-hectare (48,000-acre) preserve was created in June of 1982 to protect the world's largest population of bald eagles. Parts of the Tsirku, Klehini and Chilkat rivers are within

The Haines Road

The 257-kilometre (160-mile) Haines Road was built in 1943 as a haul road to connect Fort Seward, Alaska (now part of Haines), with the newly built pioneer Alaska Highway. It was to be used as an extra supply and backup route in case the White Pass and Yukon Railway from Skagway was blocked. In addition, it was to serve as an evacuation route to the coast should Alaska be attacked by the Japanese.

The road followed the trade routes of the Chilkat people and the Dalton Trail (or Toll Road). It was built quickly, at a cost of $13 million, and then ignored when fighting with the Japanese in the Aleutians ended. In 1945, when it was decided to reopen the road for use by the general public, washouts, slides and collapsed bridges had to be dealt with first.

It was not until 1963 that winter travel was allowed on the road. Survival shelters were built and tall poles were set up to show where the edge was during high snowfall. Drivers along the road had to stop at each of five checkpoints. The staff at each checkpoint would radio ahead to the next one that someone was scheduled to arrive. If the driver had not arrived by a certain time, a search party was organized. The checkpoints were closed in 1974.

Much of the highway was rerouted and paved between 1978 and 1990.

the preserve and so fishing for salmon in these rivers is controlled to make sure that there are enough for the eagles.

As you come out of the forest, the Klehini River is to your right. The Porcupine Road, which crosses the Klehini River and goes to the former gold-rush site of Porcupine, is to the right at kilometre 54.1 (mile 33.6). At kilometre 58.1 (mile 36.1), you cross the Chilkat River.

The turn-off for Klukwan Indian Village is at kilometre 61.7 (mile 38.3).

Klukwan Village and Haines

Klukwan Village is 0.4 kilometres (0.2 miles) off the highway. There are a lot of old buildings on stilts here. Some of them are still occupied but some have been left to the elements—most of the people here now live in mobile homes. This riverbank village is quite picturesque. No matter whether the residents look out their front doors or their back doors, they see mountains.

As you head toward Haines from Klukwan Village, the Chilkat River Flats are to your right. There are some pull-outs along this winding, narrow stretch of highway where you can stop and observe the bald eagles or pull over to let faster traffic pass.

Bears

There are three species of bear in Alaska: the brown bear (also commonly known as the grizzly), the black bear and the polar bear. The black bear, which can also come in a cinnamon colour, is more common and smaller than the brown bear, except in Denali National Park (and elsewhere in the Alaska Range), where the two-toned Toklat grizzly is about the size of a black bear. The Kodiak bear is a large subspecies of grizzly. The best way to tell the difference between grizzlies and black bears is that a grizzly has a hump at the back of its neck and a black bear does not. The polar bear, found only along the northern coast, is easily distinguished by its white fur.

It is best to avoid bears of any kind. If you see one while you are driving, do not get out of your vehicle; if you want to take pictures, do so through the window. When you go camping, keep your food in scentproof containers and tie them up in a tree higher than a bear standing on its hind legs can reach. Cook away from your campsite. Wash away any smell of food left on your body and avoid using scented soaps and shampoos, especially if you are sleeping in a tent.

It is safest to stay away from the bear's food sources, such as berry patches and salmon streams. However, if you are going to intrude into bear territory, whether you are hiking, picking berries or fishing, always make enough noise so that any bears in the area will hear you while you are still far away. If you do so, the bears can leave the area and you will not surprise them at close range. Jingle your keys, talk and laugh, carry a 'bear bell' or put some small stones in a juice or pop can and shake it to alert any bears to your presence. When a bear is surprised, angered or threatened, it can become very dangerous. If you see a bear cub, move away from it. Mother bears are very protective and will attack if they think that their cubs are in danger.

The largest pull-out is at kilometre 3.9 (mile 2.4). Although you may see a few eagles in spring and summer, the best time is from late October to January, when thousands of them come to feed on the chum salmon in the ice-free lower Chilkat River.

Every year in early November the Alaskan Bald Eagle Festival is held to celebrate the arrival of the eagles in the valley. Among the many activities are an art exhibit, presentations featuring actual live eagles and Native dancing. The highlight of the festival is the releasing of eagles that had been found injured and were then nursed back to health over the year.

The road hugs the mountainside on the left and the river on the right. You leave the Alaska Chilkat Bald Eagle Preserve at kilometre 19.7 (mile 12.2) from the village and you reach the city limits of Haines at kilometre 32.5 (mile 20.2).

As you come into the main section of Haines, you reach a Y where the Haines Road/Highway goes to the right. Go left, instead, onto Main Street. Follow it to Second Avenue and turn right. The visitor reception centre is on Second Avenue near Willard Street. If you want to learn more about bald eagles, continue on Second Avenue to the Haines Highway. On the far left corner is the American Bald Eagle Foundation's Natural History Museum.

To see Fort Seward, continue on Second Avenue; after it curves left you arrive at the fort.

Fort William H. Seward, named after the secretary of state who oversaw the purchase of Alaska, was established in the early 1900s, with soldiers arriving to take up residence in 1904. The purpose of Fort Seward was to help bring order to the gold-rush stampeders and to support the position of the US in boundary issues with Canada. During the early 1920s, all the other military posts in Alaska were closed and Fort Seward was renamed 'the Chilkoot

One of the homes at Fort Seward in Haines.

Barracks.' The Chilkoot Barracks remained the only army post until the Second World War. After the war, in 1946, the Chilkoot Barracks was closed. In 1947 it was sold to a group of veterans who wanted to set up a business cooperative. This idea failed but most of the families stayed and formed the community of Port Chilkoot.

The stately old homes that used to be officers' homes or bachelor officers' quarters are spaced around a 3.6-hectare (9-acre) parade square. Most of them are now private residences. Walk along the sidewalk in front of the homes and read the information panels. The parade grounds were used for training exercises and, when they were not in official use, they were used for golf and skiing. Although the flagpole still seems high now, at one time it stood 33.5 metres (110 feet) tall, twice its current height.

In 1970 Port Chilkoot and the Main Street area joined under the name 'Haines.' This name came from a mission that had been established here at the invitation of the Chilkat people in the early 1880s. Originally known as 'the Willard Mission,' in 1884 it had been renamed after the chair of the fund-raising committee that made its construction possible, Mrs. Francina Electra Haines of the Presbyterian Board of Home Missions.

To see the Davidson Glacier, get onto Mud Bay Road and then follow the signs for Chilkat State Park, which take you beside Chilkat Inlet. Straight ahead is a viewpoint where the road curves left (if you get to a campground, you have gone too far). From the viewpoint you can see the Davidson Glacier across the inlet. Use your binoculars. In the 1800s this glacier extended about 3 kilometres (2 miles) into Lynn Canal.

Haines Road Summit.

Drive back up the Haines Road to Haines Junction to return to the Alaska Highway and continue from where you left off (see Chapter 1).

Index

LONE
PINE

Look for these other Lone Pine titles:

Plants of the Western Boreal Forest
ISBN 1-55105-058-7
$24.95 Cdn • $19.95 US

Plants of Northern British Columbia
Revised and expanded edition
ISBN 1-55105-108-7
$26.95 Cdn • $19.95 US

Canadian Rockies Access Guide
ISBN 1-55105-176-1
$19.95 US • $16.95 US

Canadian Orders
1-800-661-9017 Phone
1-800-424-7173 Fax

US Orders
1-800-518-3541 Phone
1-800-548-1169 Fax

Visit our website at <www.lonepinepublishing.com>